Anna Xavier Murphy, RSCJ
(1793-1836) MISSIONARY TO LOUISIANA

Mary Blish, RSCJ
and
Carolyn Osiek, RSCJ

Society of the Sacred Heart
St. Louis, Missouri

Anna Xavier Murphy, RSCJ (1793-1836)
Missionary to Louisiana
© 2021 Mary Blish, RSCJ and Carolyn Osiek, RSCJ
All rights reserved.

No part of this book may be used or reproduced by any means, graphic, electronic, or mechanical, including photocopying, recording, taping or by any information storage retrieval system without the written permission of the authors, except in the case of brief quotations embodied in critical articles and reviews.

ISBN: 978-1-7364924-0-6
Book Design: Peggy Nehmen
Photos: Society of the Sacred Heart Archives

Printed in the United States of America.

Published by:

Society of the Sacred Heart™
United States – Canada

4120 Forest Park Ave.
St. Louis, Missouri 63108
rscj.org

CONTENTS

Introduction 1
Abbreviations 5
Biography 7
Journals and Letters
    Introduction 67
    Chronological List 69
    Journals 73
    Letters 101
Appendices
    Appendix 1: Anna Murphy's Irish Background 299
    Appendix 2: Ship's Log 302
    Appendix 3: Building Details 304
    Appendix 4: Notes on Reverend Mother Xavier Murphy, given by Miss Rebecca Terrel, alumna of Grand Coteau 307
    Appendix 5: Last Will and Testament of Anna Xavier Murphy, September 26, 1835 310
Index of Biographical Notes 315

INTRODUCTION

This biography of Anna Xavier Murphy, RSCJ, missionary of the Society of the Sacred Heart in Louisiana, was the inspiration of Mary Blish, RSCJ, who began to collect materials and did the original draft in the first decade of the twenty-first century. Her death in 2017 put an end to these efforts. The completion comes now in time for the bicentennial celebration of the place that both Mary and Xavier so dearly loved, the Academy of the Sacred Heart in Grand Coteau.

Mary Blish was born in Chicago, Illinois, on May 17, 1928, and educated by the Dominican Sisters before attending Maryville College in Saint Louis. She entered the Society of the Sacred Heart in 1950, and received the M.A. from Manhattanville College in 1955 and the Ph.D. from Saint Louis University in 1967. All three degrees were in English Literature. She taught in several academies, then at Maryville College, where she was president from 1960 to 1964. Her happiest years were as Professor of American Literature at the University of the Sacred Heart in Tokyo from 1977 to 1996.

The research materials that she gathered included documents not only from the provincial archives of the Society of the Sacred Heart in the United States, but also from the Society's general archives in Rome, the archives of the Archdiocese of Saint Louis, and several archival sources in Louisiana. She was not able to complete the work before diminishment forced her to abandon it. Following her death in 2017, Carolyn Osiek, RSCJ, took up the project. Sister Blish had already done the greater part of drafting the biography and editing the letters, though most translations and transcriptions were incomplete and in need of editing. However,

Mary Blish, RSCJ, 1928-2017

the structure of the narrative is hers, with development and considerable expansion at some key points.

The biography is here presented first, followed by a collection of three journals and sixty-nine letters, the majority written by Xavier herself. Xavier's French letters to recipients in Paris—spontaneous and not too grammatically correct—were quickly edited into good French for circulation to communities. In some cases, these edited versions are all that survives. In other cases, however, the original has survived. Both these edited versions in notebooks and the originals that have survived are here translated. Her letters to all others are in English, here transcribed as closely as possible to the originals. When Xavier writes in her own language, her enthusiasm and winsome style are apparent, as are the differences in wording, style, and punctuation from contemporary English.

Life at Grand Coteau during these years was a life of struggle with oppressive heat, diseases, and overwhelming labor. During the years that Xavier Murphy lived at Grand Coteau, 1822 to 1836, at least seven of the community died, including Xavier; average age at death was thirty-two. It is difficult today as we read their writings to understand how they could have continued, given what they were facing daily. Only an invincible faith could have kept them going.

Special thanks go to the Archives of the Archdiocese of Saint Louis and to Emory Webre for the Rosati correspondence, and to Federica Palumbo at the General Archives of the Society of the Sacred Heart in Rome for her patient and efficient responses to many requests.

Several translation conventions should be pointed out. In some cases, "subjects" is translated as "religious," which is the meaning. French usage of the time did not distinguish the ordinary male title Mr. from Father for priests, nor Monseigneur (Msgr.) for bishops, nor Madame (Mme) for a woman religious. When it is known that a reference is to a priest, the title Father has been substituted for M., Bishop for Msgr., and Sister or Mother for Mme.

ABBREVIATIONS

A.M.D.G.: *Ad majorem Dei gloriam.* To the greater glory of God. Jesuit motto often used by Xavier in her letters.

B-D Corr.: *Saint Madeleine Sophie Barat-Saint Philippine Duchesne, Correspondence.* Edited Jeanne de Charry, RSCJ. Original publication in French, 1988-2000. English translation Barbara Hogg, RSCJ, Joan Sweetman, RSCJ, April O'Leary, RSCJ, and Mary Coke, RSCJ. 4 vols. Society of the Sacred Heart, 1988-1999. All references are to the English edition.

Baudier: Roger Baudier, *The Catholic Church in Louisiana.* New Orleans: Louisiana Library Association, 1939.

Callan PD: Louise Callan, RSCJ, *Philippine Duchesne: Frontier Missionary of the Sacred Heart, 1769-1852.* Westminster, Maryland: Newman Press, 1957.

Callan SSHNA: Louise Callan, RSCJ, *The Society of the Sacred Heart in North America.* New York: Longmans Green, 1937.

GASSH: General Archives, Society of the Sacred Heart, Rome.

HJ: House journal, 1821-1841. Convent of the Sacred Heart, Grand Coteau, Louisiana. French original. Translation by Katherine Townsend, RSCJ, 1976-1978. All references are to the English translation.

MSB: Saint Madeleine Sophie Barat, RSCJ, superior general of the Society of the Sacred Heart, residing in France.

Paisant: Chantal Paisant, ed. *Les années pionnières, 1818-1823 : Lettres et Journaux des premières missionnaires du Sacré-Cœur aux États-Unis.* Paris : Éditions du Cerf, 2001.

PD-MSB: Correspondence between Philippine Duchesne, RSCJ and Madeleine Sophie Barat, RSCJ. See B-D Corr.

Rosati Collection: Bishop Joseph Rosati, C.M. papers. RG01B. Correspondence Women Religious; Sacred Heart Sisters; Murphy, Mother Xavier. Archdiocesan Archives, St. Louis, Missouri.

USCA: Archives of the United States-Canada Province, Society of the Sacred Heart, Saint Louis, Missouri.

PDCGO: *Philippine Duchesne: Pioneer on the American Frontier (1769-1852). Complete Works.* 2 vols. Edited Marie-France Carreel, RSCJ, Frances Gimber, RSCJ, and Carolyn Osiek, RSCJ. Original publication Brepols, 2017. English translation Society of the Sacred Heart, 2019. All references are to the English edition.

XM: Anna Xavier Murphy, RSCJ.

BIOGRAPHY

Xavier Murphy, RSCJ, Pioneer Educator in Louisiana

The facade of the Academy of the Sacred Heart in Grand Coteau, Louisiana, with its long galleries overlooking the formal garden that stretches to the road, stands as the signature of a remarkable Religious of the Sacred Heart, Anna Xavier Murphy, who was superior of the Academy from 1825 to her death in September 1836.

More impressive is the effect she had on the students of those years. One of them, Rebecca Terrel, wrote many years later:

I am now elderly, I have known the world well, but never have I known, nor do I hope to see another Mother Murphy. Such a combination of gifts, of talents, of virtues is found in very few whom God wishes to serve him to do great things for his glory. Her judgment was sound, just and straight: those in difficult positions came to consult her, she often was able by her wise counsels to reestablish union and peace in families, settling the difficulties that had divided them. The young found in her a support for their weakness; older persons put all their confidence in her.[1]

Origins

Anna Murphy was born in Ireland July 26, 1793, "a near relative of the bishop of [Cork]."[2] If this identification as niece of the bishop of

---

1 Rebecca Terrel, born 1817 in Rapides Parish, entered the school July 14, 1829, with her sister, Henrietta, two years older. Ms. GASSH. M. Blish translation.
2 B-D Corr. II-II, p. 48, n.1. Dubourg to PD, New Orleans, 2.22.1822. Bishop John Murphy, eldest of five brothers, was ordained in 1796 and was bishop of Cork from 1815 to his death in 1847. http://corkandross.org/priests/most-rev-john-murphy/

Cork is correct,[3] she was a member of the Murphy family that prospered in the leather tanning industry and as traders and merchants. Their influence spread as far away as the Americas and the Far East, which may have influenced Anna's eventual interest in the missions in North America. She was educated by the Ursulines in Cork.[4] In keeping with the practice of many elite Irish families of the time, she then spent time in France. How she encountered the Society of the Sacred Heart is not known, but she entered at the motherhouse and novitiate, rue des Postes.

Referring to her, Madeleine Sophie Barat wrote to Philippine Duchesne[5] April 11, 1820,

> The postulant who is writing to you, dear Philippine, seems to be an excellent subject. She chooses our Order in view of America. But as she has not yet taken the habit, we have decided that she will pay her own passage to America and complete her noviceship with you; for if you find her unsuitable you are absolutely free to accept or refuse her.[6]

The next day:

> I let you know that a novice who speaks English wants to go to you at her own cost. We are teaching her French as far as we can. She is thirty-plus years old [actually 27] and comes from Ireland. The Irish character resembles ours to a remarkable degree.[7]

---

3   PD to MSB September 25, 1823. B–D Corr. II-II, L.175. PDCGO L 218. "Her bishop in Ireland" thinks she could be a superior.
4   The Ursuline school in Cork has two extant account books for that period showing Miss Murphy of Waterford as enrolled in the terms beginning October 1805 and October 1807.
5   Madeleine Sophie Barat, RSCJ (1779-1865), founder and superior general of the Society of the Sacred Heart; Rose Philippine Duchesne, RSCJ (1769-1852), pioneer missionary in 1818 from France to the New World.
6   MSB to PD, April 11, 1820; PD-MSB Corr. II-I L. 124. This seems to have been the original idea, but in fact, Anna Murphy made her first vows in Paris on November 6, 1822, just before departure.
7   MSB to PD, April 12, 1820; B-D Corr. II-I, L.125; March 24, 1821, B-D Corr.

According to the noviceship journal of Paris, Anna Murphy received the habit and became a novice on May 5, 1820,

> with a lively desire to go as soon as possible to exercise her zeal in foreign lands, not believing that she had done enough in already leaving Ireland her native land. She wished to uproot herself to go to a land far from her own to partake in the fatigues and dangers of the fortunate sisters in Louisiana. On that occasion Father Varin took as his text the words God addressed to Abraham: 'Forget your kindred and your father's house and go to a place that I will show you; and I myself will be your recompense.'[8]

Mother Duchesne may not yet have received Anna's letter five months later, but she responded to Mother Barat's letter with a note of caution on October 30:

> We have a special need for the Irish religious. But if she knows only Irish, that is not English. We have many Irish in this country whom the Americans, who speak English, cannot understand.[9]

A few months later, Philippine had received Anna's letter, no longer extant, and acknowledged it in her response to Mother Barat on February 18 of the next year:

> As for the Irish woman, I was delighted with her letter, and as regards English, she will be very useful. But I think we must give her a true picture of our position here: inconvenience everywhere, above all for lodging, not even knowing where to put our work, our writing,

---

II-I, L.134; as shown below, in 1821 Madeleine Sophie Barat herself was mistress of novices and thus knew Anna Murphy well.

8   Ps 45:10. Paris. Noviceship Journal. GASSH. M. Blish translation. Elsewhere May 5 is given as her date of entrance, but Madeleine Sophie already calls her a postulant on April 11.

9   PD to MSB, October 30, 1820; BD Corr. II-I, L.131; PDCGO L.160.

no table to oneself, food often unattractive with not much variety, rigorous cold and overwhelming heat, and no spring. God alone and the desire for his glory: there is nothing else.[10]

The time of Anna's novitiate was unusual because the third General Council of the fledgling Society of the Sacred Heart was held in Paris from August to October 1820, so she had an opportunity to know the early leaders of the congregation: the assistants general Josephine Bigeu, Catherine de Charbonnel, Henriette Grosier, and secretary general Henriette Ducis. The Council agreed that more space was needed, and in September the Hôtel Biron on the rue de Varenne was acquired. This historic property (now the Rodin Museum) gave space for the Academy and also the novitiate, and it was Anna Murphy's home from mid-November until her departure for America a year later, by which time she had adopted Xavier as her personal religious name.[11] During this winter the mistress of novices, Josephine Bigeu, was ill, and the novices (about thirty in number) were under the direction of Madeleine Sophie Barat herself. This unique situation gave Xavier her feeling of intimacy with the foundress, as will be seen in her letters to the mother general from Louisiana.

The novices' retreat in February 1821 was given that year by Nicholas Tuite MacCarthy, SJ, a noted preacher of the time.[12] On days when he had other obligations, Joseph Varin, SJ, filled in.[13] After one of Father Varin's talks, a novice threw herself at the feet

---

10 PD to MSB February 18, 1821; BD Corr. II-I L.133; PDCGO L.163.
11 In these early years of the Society, adoption of a Jesuit name was common. There were many Xaviers, Regises, and Aloysias, especially. The custom ceased after 1826.
12 Nicolas Tuite de MacCarthy, S.J., also known in France as Abbé de Lévignac (1769 Dublin-1833 France) went to France with his parents at the age of four, part of the Irish elite resident there. Ordained in 1814, he soon became a renowned preacher. He was Anna's novitiate spiritual director, her "pole star."
13 Joseph Desiré Varin d'Ainvelle, SJ (1769-1850), was associated with the Society of the Sacred Heart from its earliest days in Paris and had given the retreat for the members of the General Council of 1820.

of the priest and quietly asked if he would permit her to go to Louisiana. The priest repeated her request aloud, and the novice then made the same request to Mother Barat. "Then Sister Anna, the Irish novice who for a long time had hoped to embark for that interesting mission, also knelt to ask again for assurance that, as she had often requested," she would be sent.[14]

Father MacCarthy also presided at Xavier Murphy's ceremony of first vows, November 6, 1821, held before she had completed two years of noviceship by a special exemption in view of her immanent departure for Louisiana and her total dedication to the Society. In his discourse for the ceremony, Father MacCarthy spoke of the exterior and the interior of a religious, saying that the black clothing, the ring and cross function to make one respectable; but the exterior sign is useless if the interior is not striking in the eyes of God so that all the glory of the daughter of the King comes from within."[15] Xavier's letters from Louisiana often send regards to Father MacCarthy, or to her "pole star," as she referred to him.

To America

Two days later she left the motherhouse with Lucile Mathevon; it was a wrenching departure: "Dear Sister Anna was almost ill, so great was her sensibility caused by this separation in the midst of the tears and sobs of all the community. These two heroines of religion left to the edification of all who envied them."[16]

Anna Xavier Murphy and Lucile Mathevon, the second group to be sent to the American mission, set sail from Pauillac, port of Bordeaux, on the ship *Hector* out of Philadelphia. On Thursday,

---

14 Journal of the Noviceship of Paris, February 1821. GASSH.
15 Journal of the Noviceship of Paris, November 6, 1821. GASSH.
16 Journal of the Noviceship of Paris, November 8, 1821. GASSH. Lucile Mathevon, RSCJ (1793-1876) entered the novitiate at Sainte-Marie d'En-Haut in Grenoble in 1813 while Philippine was living there, and made her final profession there in 1818. She went from arrival in New Orleans directly to Missouri, where she reopened Saint Charles in 1828 and was superior of the Potawatomi mission at Sugar Creek, where she remained nearly all the time until her death.

December 6, 1821, at four o'clock in the afternoon, they departed from the port. By early the next day, the ship had cleared the channel and entered open sea. For the first nineteen days of the voyage, they had contrary winds, yet remarkably, all passengers seemed happy. Both religious were listed as "Madam" but identified as "Ursuline nuns" on the passenger list of the ship.[17] There were seventeen listed passengers, four of them minor children. Two others had only first names and were listed as "servant." They were possibly enslaved persons of other passengers. The captain was a Protestant with outstanding qualities that the sisters admired. They spent a considerable time in conversation with him and learned much about the country to which they were going. Xavier also befriended another Protestant man with whom she had long conversations about faith that could only be characterized as spiritual direction; according to her account, by the end of the journey he was on the point of wanting to become Catholic. There was no priest on board, but they were taken under the wing of a Mr. Nagliss,[18] a respectable Irishman and friend of Anna's family, who was going to New Orleans. The two religious, according to their own accounts, were treated like royalty on the ship, seated at the captain's table, and given great respect. Descriptions of the journey by both of them give wonderful insights into the two different characters. Lucile Mathevon seems to have worried habitually and often been sick; the voyage was dreadful for her. Xavier was rarely seasick and called it "a delightful trip."[19]

Their route took them north of the Canary Islands, between Saint-Domingue (Haiti) and eastern Cuba, around the south side of Cuba to Cape Saint Anthony on the west side, where on January

---

17 See Appendix 2 and the accounts of the crossing. This ship should not be confused with two earlier ships of the same name operating in Nova Scotia and Boston.
18 The ship's passenger list does not have any entry for Mr. Nagliss, apparently because he had chartered the ship to transport his cargo. See Appendix 2.
19 See their shipboard journals for details.

25, they encountered Spanish pirates, who might have brought disaster to them had not a favorable wind arisen to enable them to escape. The two religious attributed their escape to the intercession of Aloysia Jouve, Philippine Duchesne's saintly niece, for whose intercession they had prayed for deliverance.

By February 1 the ship was at the mouth of the Mississippi River, where the contrary current was too strong for a sailing vessel, so the passengers disembarked and boarded by launch a steamboat coming from Cuba and bound for New Orleans. Xavier compared the interior of the steamboat to the Hotel de Biron, the Society's new school in Paris, with regard to elegance of mirrors and gold trim. Again, they were seated in places of honor, and Xavier was amazed at the decorum and respectful behavior of all the Americans on board, who refrained from any disrespectful speech in the presence of the sisters.

After landing in New Orleans, Lucile wrote to Madeleine Sophie:

> We are in very good health. America is our element. I am enchanted by the Americans and I cannot pass over in silence that though we remained in the steamboat for twenty-four hours with more than fifty persons, we did not hear a single swearword. I admired their silence; if they spoke it was very quietly, with propriety, with refinement. They are amused with a nothing; they gave us much polite attention. When we entered the room, all rose, someone brought us a stool, another oranges, pineapples, etc. We had the first places at table everywhere. On the steamboat, they said the grace aloud; all were standing with their hats off. It was the captain who led the grace, but in the Protestant version; we said it as

Catholics. I regretted that these good men, so perfect in their religion, were not Catholics.[20]

With the Ursulines in New Orleans

When they landed the next day in New Orleans, Xavier's friend Mr. Nagliss took charge of escorting them to the Ursuline convent. Later that day, February 2, 1822, Lucile Mathevon wrote to Madeleine Sophie about her companion as follows:

> I must cease speaking in order to tell you about dear Sister Xavier. I can only rejoice to have had her as companion; she knew how to gain the heart of the Americans and if we have been respected, loved, and cherished by them, I attribute it to her. We were always very united, we did nothing without consulting one another and we acted always for the greater good. When we were in danger and I was afraid, I said: "Lord, save us for this Francis Xavier that I have with me; I am good only to be thrown into the sea, but this one can make you known and loved, she has the spirit that is necessary for the Americans." She has a good spirit, good judgment; I have discovered in her many virtues that she hid in Paris, but when she was launched, she has let them appear, and I have no doubt that Mother Eugenie and Mother Duchesne will one day praise her to you. The bishop is her confessor and he is very happy with her.[21]

As did many missionary nuns in the nineteenth century, they stayed with the hospitable Ursulines, who had been in New Orleans since 1727, to recover from the ocean journey, fifty-five days at sea in winter for this pair. They soon learned that Josephine

---

20 Lucile Mathevon, journal entry for February 2, 1822.
21 Lucile Mathevon to Madeleine Sophie Barat, New Orleans, February 7, 1822. Paisant L. 119, pp. 455-56.

Meneyroux had been staying there and had just left the evening before for Grand Coteau.[22]

At first Xavier was astonished and bemused at the dark cloisters of the Ursulines and the parlors with their grilles, but very soon she and her companion were won by the evangelical charity of the sisters. Apparently the Ursulines were pleased with their visitors as well, for Xavier was told that she fit in so well that she would make a good Ursuline. Within the next week, the Ursulines not only assisted them materially but also inserted them into their community life. The RSCJ assisted at Office and helped as replacement teachers for those in the community who were ill.[23] They were soon present at the election of the next superior, presided over by Bishop Dubourg.[24] They were also greatly attracted by the spirit of the Sunday evening worshipping community, largely composed of people of color. The chapel was an island of fervor in the midst of a city that they otherwise considered a "veritable Sodom!"[25] Xavier recovered quickly from the voyage and reported that she was in excellent health, with great energy and appetite.

Only a few days after their arrival, Xavier wrote:
> I had scarcely arrived when I had the happiness to learn that the bishop was in the house; we were soon presented to him. I had never seen anyone with whom

---

[22] Rosalie (Josephine) Meneyroux entered in Grenoble in 1814 and made first vows in Paris in 1820. In spite of her poor health, Louis Barat encouraged her to sail to America, apparently without permission or even knowledge of his sister. Josephine stayed with the Ursulines in New Orleans from her arrival December 24, 1821 to February 1, when she went to Grand Coteau. She had had a terrible voyage and was in miserable health (Lucile Mathevon to Madeleine Sophie, February 8, 1822; Paisant L. 120, p. 458.) She returned to France in May and left the Society.

[23] Lucile Mathevon to Madeleine Sophie, February 8, 1822; Paisant L. 120, p. 458. Elsewhere Xavier reported that they were sixteen in the community and half were elderly or ill.

[24] Louis William Valentine Dubourg (1766-1833) was the Bishop who brought the first Religious of the Sacred Heart to the United States in 1818, settling Philippine Duchesne and her four companions in St. Charles, Missouri. At this point, he was bishop of the entire Louisiana Territory. He returned to France in 1826 to become bishop of Montauban, then was named archbishop of Besançon, but died soon after.

[25] Lucile Mathevon, journal entry, February 3, 1822.

I was so quickly able to think aloud; he filled me with such confidence that I imagined myself speaking with my "pole Star." I asked him to hear my confession and he consented and the following morning he came early; he told me that he would be always available to us, anytime I wished to see him. If I remain here some time, I will ask to make a retreat, in spite of the memorable retreat of last year which I think of often. On his first visit, he told us our destination, which, in keeping with the Sacred Heart, is to be separated after having such a long voyage together. It is natural that I feel that a little for Mother Lucile who is full of attention and kindness. I gave her more trouble than all the others during the trip; nevertheless, she never complained and never seemed unhappy.[26]

Their weeks in New Orleans were eventful for the Ursulines. A new superior was elected on February 10, 1822, and the next month the death of the former superior, Mother Saint-Michel Gensoul, was "that of a saint."[27] She had been superior when Philippine Duchesne and her companions stayed with the Ursulines in 1818. (Of that visit, Philippine had lamented that they would not be the first to bring devotion to the Sacred Heart to the United States: "I saw a book printed in this city full of prayers to the Sacred Heart. There is also a beautiful picture painted in Rome."[28])

---

26 Journal of the crossing, Xavier Murphy. New Orleans, February 6, 1822. Paisant, p. 452.
27 Teresa Wolf, OSU, *The Ursulines in New Orleans and Our Lady of Prompt Succor*. Ed. Henry C. Semple, SJ. N.Y.: Kenedy, 1925, p. 85. Unfortunately there is no Ursuline house journal for this period, as in the years around 1822 the Ursuline community was half Spanish and half French. Bishop Dubourg required that the annals be written in Spanish, but the annalist of the community was French, so she simply wrote that nothing significant happened in those years! Telephone conversation M. Blish with Joan Marie Aycock, OSU, archivist, April 30, 2007.
28 Philippine Duchesne to Eugenie de Gramont, New Orleans, First Friday of June, 1818. PDCGO L. 99.

To Grand Coteau

After spending about six weeks in New Orleans, the two new missionaries parted on March 12. Lucile Mathevon went to join Philippine Duchesne and her small community in Florissant near Saint Louis, taking with her the only copy of the 1820 provisional Constitutions they had brought from Paris, with the rulings and decrees of the recent general council of the young Society of the Sacred Heart. Xavier Murphy left for Grand Coteau, Louisiana, after making her retreat under the direction of Bishop Dubourg. She reached her destination on March 30, accompanied by Carmelite Landry, a coadjutrix postulant with the Ursulines who transferred to the Sacred Heart with the permission of her superior and that of the bishop.[29]

The previous summer Eugenie Audé, one of Philippine Duchesne's four companions in the first missionary band in 1818, had traveled to Grand Coteau, Louisiana. With her was Mary Layton, the first American to join these religious.[30] This was in response to Mrs. Charles Smith's offer to the bishop of land and a building to establish a school for girls. They arrived August 25,

---

29 Carmelite Landry, RSCJ (1792-1852), born in LaFourche, Louisiana, had entered the Ursulines as a coadjutrix sister, but transferred to the Society on April 30, 1822, at Grand Coteau, the first native of Louisiana to enter the Society. A few months later, Philippine Duchesne at her visit made Carmelite a choir religious. She was professed at Grand Coteau in 1825 and remained there the rest of her life in various offices. Prior to the Second Vatican Council, the Religious of the Sacred Heart and some other orders comprised two groups: the choir religious who taught in the schools and the coadjutrix sisters who looked after the domestic needs of the convent.

30 Eugenie Audé, RSCJ (1795-1842), one of the first group with Philippine Duchesne, was born of an elite family of Savoy, and entered the Society at Grenoble in 1815. She made her final profession on February 8, 1818, hours before the departure of the group from Paris. After founding the house at Grand Coteau, she was foundress at St. Michael in 1825. Named assistant general for America in 1834, she returned to France and became superior of the Trinità dei Monti in Rome, where she died. Mary Layton, RSCJ (1802-1876), born in Kentucky, entered the Society as a coadjutrix sister in Florissant in 1820 and was still a novice when she left for Louisiana with Eugenie Audé. She was the first to enter the Society in America and remain. After Grand Coteau, she returned to St. Louis, then in 1845 went to the Potawatomi mission in Kansas, where she remained for the rest of her life.

Original house of Mrs. Smith, first Sacred Heart convent, 1821

1821, staying first with Mrs. Smith, a widow. On the 28th the two took possession of the two-story wooden building, 55 feet long with a gallery the length of the building, and one-story out-buildings for kitchen, infirmary, and laundry. They received the first five pupils in October of that year, one of them Mrs. Smith's niece, Mary Sentee.[31]

When Xavier Murphy arrived the following March, she brought with her a letter from Mother Barat to Eugenie Audé with this description of the new member of her community: she "will help you with the boarders, as she knows English very well and is well educated, but she might not follow the Society's plan of studies in her teaching, so you must guide her. She did not know enough French to learn about it."[32] One of responsibilities that she assumed was the keeping of the house journal, begun in French,

---

31 See Cunningham, Ruth, RSCJ, *The Untold Story: Eugénie Audé, RSCJ*. Society of the Sacred Heart, United States Province, 1986, for the story of the foundress of the Academy in Grand Coteau.

32 Madeleine Sophie Barat to Eugenie Audé, September 13, 1821. In 1822 there was no copy of the Plan of Studies in the American convents.

but from June 6, 1822, it is written in English by Xavier. At first, it parallels, but is not identical with, the journal she was keeping to send to the motherhouse. That ceased after July 1823, but her faithful recording of the house journal continued until August 31, 1827, when Louise Dorival took it up in French.

The parish church in Grand Coteau had been established in 1819 as directed by Mrs. Smith's late husband, Charles Smith, who had come from Maryland in 1805 and was buried in the church of Grand Coteau. Its first pastor, Hercule Brassac, remained until 1822. But the proximity of the Academy to the church did not guarantee access to Mass. In February 1822, the then pastor, Auguste Jeanjean,[33] left for Europe. Thanks to the good will over the years of Father Flavius H. Rossi,[34] of Saint Landry Church in Opelousas, the nuns had Mass occasionally; otherwise they were frequently deprived even of Sunday Mass as the successive pastors of the church in Grand Coteau often were away, a situation that continued until the year after Xavier Murphy's death. For instance, the house journal notes, from May 1834 to September 19 of that year, Mass seldom, including "three long months" without spiritual aid. So the extant letters to the motherhouse, as well as entries in the house journal, frequently mention the deprivation of spiritual aid; however, they also mention in detail the visits of various priests and especially the bishops of the period who attempted to fill in for the acute shortage of priests on the frontier. As will be seen, Xavier Murphy not only welcomed these members of the clergy and built a cottage in 1832 for their convenience when in the neighborhood, but also was instrumental in assuring the solution of this pressing need.

---

33 Auguste Jeanjean (1795-1841) came from France with Bishop Dubourg in 1817. Ordained by Bishop Flaget in Bardstown, he went later to St. Louis then to Louisiana. Named to succeed Leo De Neckere as bishop of New Orleans in 1833, he refused the appointment but was vicar general of the diocese until his death.
34 Flavius Rossi, secular priest, had been recruited by Bishop Dubourg in Europe. He was in Opelousas as pastor at least 1817 to 1819.

Cottage built for visiting priests, 1832

The journal Xavier kept of the events of April and May 1822 is not extant, but in her letter of May 17, 1822, to Madeleine Sophie, she explains that Bishop Dubourg had come to the convent a few days earlier. After a visit he decided that she was ready for final profession; thus Xavier Murphy was the first Religious of the Sacred Heart to be finally professed in the new world. She pronounced her vows in English on May 14. In the same letter she explains that in spite of her joy in her missionary vocation, she felt no taste for things spiritual and had lost her usual facility for prayer. She had made a promise "in all things to act against nature" and to act only according to the spirit of faith. She discussed these things with the bishop, who assured her that she was indeed doing what God asked of her. Exactly one month later, the novice Mary Layton, who had come from Missouri with Eugenie Audé, made her first vows at Grand Coteau.

First Visit of Philippine Duchesne

A signal event five months after Xavier reached Grand Coteau was the arrival of Philippine Duchesne on August 7, 1822, for her first visit south, bringing a copy of the Constitutions of the nascent Society, as well as the rulings and decrees of the general council. With her were two additions to the community, Emily Saint-Cyr who had just made her vows, and Mary Mullanphy, a coadjutrix novice.[35] Mother Duchesne found several in the community ill, but

---

35 Emily Saint-Cyr (1806-1883), born in St, Louis, was Philippine's student and novice at Florissant. She went with her to Grand Coteau the day after making first vows on July 16, 1822. Later she lived in several other houses, and was superior at

was so impressed by Carmelite Landry that she recommended that her status be changed to that of choir religious. Mother Duchesne passed her fifty-third birthday there on August 29 in prayer all day, only telling the community at the evening recreation, too late for them to celebrate. She left Grand Coteau for New Orleans on September 2 and later wrote to Mother Barat in Paris, "I was delighted with the children's progress. The bishop and the parents are all equally surprised. They are seventeen in number and soon will be twenty."[36] In her turn, Xavier Murphy was so consoled by this first opportunity to meet the pioneer missionary that she wrote to Mother Barat: "Mother Duchesne to whom I disclosed my thoughts eased my fears. She understood me in English and never have I spoken with greater facility, and never felt greater peace and consolation than when she gave me her decision. She is a woman totally after my own heart." In the same letter: "... in prayer I found myself in a state of apathy. However when it was finished I found myself full of vigor to carry out my duties and more courageous to do everything against nature." She adds, "I have written in English and our dear Mother Duchesne translated my letter and will send it to you."[37]

In March 1823 she gave some details about her life:
Perhaps Mother Duchesne told you all the roles she gave me, and I am not able to fulfill them. My principal work is with the children, who give me the greatest satisfaction; even in times when I was weakened by fever, when I entered the class I felt a strength that sustained me, and that grace I attribute to the merits of the vows. All my attraction is for religious instruction; we have several Americans who give me occasion to give myself to that

---

Saint Charles when Philippine arrived in retirement in 1842. Mary Mullanphy did not remain in the Society.
36 PD-MSB, September 8, 1822. B-D Corr. II-II L. 160; PDCGO L. 196.
37 Xavier Murphy to Madeleine Sophie Barat, August 27, 1822. That letter, however, is not in the handwriting or style of Philippine Duchesne.

occupation dear to my heart. I also have black men and women with the little boys.[38]

The mention of a fever is repeated in many subsequent letters, not only hers but those of others about her. In spite of her previously robust energy and assurance of robust health upon arrival in February 1822 after the Atlantic voyage, she seems soon after to have been attacked by malaria or some other tropical fever. A few months later, on October 9, Eugenie wrote to Madeleine Sophie that "Sister Xavier has fever less often, and is regaining her strength." But it was to be with her for the rest of her short life. Three years later, Carmelite Landry wrote to Madeleine Sophie on April 12, 1826, that the increasing number of students

> gives much work to our dear mother who is constantly weak. It is only her zeal that can sustain her. I am very afraid that the heat will tire her too much. If the Heart of Jesus did not sustain her, she could not stand it.

There are more frequent mentions especially from 1829 on. On August 27 of that year, her assistant, Louise Dorival[39] wrote to Madeleine Sophie: "I have been in great worry. Last week, Mother Xavier had three attacks of fever. She felt so weak that she asked me to have the confessor come. Fortunately, here she is well, but I am always in fear of a relapse." This condition would continue until finally, six years later, it weakened her to a point that she could not overcome it.

---

38   According to the 1830 census for Grand Coteau, there were 15 free colored adults and 22 enslaved adults in a population of 296, of whom 80 were under 10 years old.
39   Louise Dorival was born in Paris in 1795 and had tried two other religious congregations before entering the Society of the Sacred Heart in 1823. She was the first missionary from France in the Society to die in the New World in 1832, and the first to be interred in the convent cemetery.

Life with Eugenie

Xavier's first years in Louisiana included many new things: the culture, the climate, and new ways of living. One of the new things she had to accustom herself to was slavery. Mrs. Smith, the foundress of the school, had loaned to the religious at the beginning some of her enslaved people to help them get started. The exact number is not known. In 1822, Mary Ann Hardey arrived in the school. Hers was one of many wealthy Maryland families who had emigrated to Louisiana, land rich and cash poor. Instead of cash payment for her costs at the school, an enslaved woman was sent from the family to help with the manual work at the school. She remained in the possession of the Hardey family, and we do not know her name.

Xavier had arrived in February 1822. By April 1823, she was involved with religious education of the black residents of the house and perhaps the town. It is clear from her account that she loved this ministry.

> **April 6th** (1823) Low Sunday. My black men and women[40] made their First Communion. But one of my little boys was old enough – they all came after church to thank and tell me how happy, happy they felt – this you will easily conceive was mutual on both sides. I brought them into our little chapel to renew their baptismal vows. I hope by Pentecost to have another band and to have them all ready to present *notre digne évêque* at his visit to make them perfect Christians.

A few months later, in July 1823, the first enslaved person was purchased by Mother Audé for the convent: Frank Hawkins, age 22 according to the document of sale, though he was probably

---

40 Who were "my black men and women" in April 1823? We do not know of anyone as yet belonging to the convent. Possibly they were the enslaved of Mrs. Smith and the Hardeys, and possibly, too, free persons of color in the town. See note 38 above.

older. In later years, Frank and Mother Murphy were to have a special relationship.

There were both difficulties and successes in the early years. Already in August 1822, Xavier wrote to Madeleine Sophie that there was friction between her and Eugenie, and that their characters were completely opposite. A letter from Mother Duchesne to Mother Barat on January 16, 1823, indicates that Eugenie and Xavier did not always see eye-to-eye. As Mother Duchesne put it, "The two heads do not fit in the same bonnet."[41] That May, Mother Duchesne wrote to Paris, "[Xavier] is much loved by the children and the parents who insist upon English."[42] In September Mother Duchesne remarked on

> Mother Xavier's extraordinary state of health, which I suspect is caused by habitual nervous tension, and seeing that she is not able to get along with Mother Eugenie, maybe even less now. I have had the thought that she might be one of those people who need both mental and physical activity for their well-being, like Mother Bigeu; she might be suitable for the direction of the foundation the bishop is proposing. He admires her very much, for her virtue as well as her English…. We certainly could give a few religious to assist Mother Xavier. Her bishop in Ireland judged her suitable to be a superior, and Mother Eugenie believes her to be ready to direct a house."[43]

Her correspondence with Philippine about the matter continued, for in May 1824, Xavier wrote to Madeleine Sophie that Philippine had offered her a change of house, which would have meant Missouri, "for the reason that you know." Xavier, however,

---

41   PD to MSB, January 16, 1823. B-D Corr. II-II L. 166. PDCGO L. 205.
42   PD to MSB, May 20, 1823. B-D Corr. II-II L. 168; PDCGO L. 212.
43   PD to MSB, September 25, 1823. B-D Corr. II-II L. 175. PDCGO L. 218.

continued to decline the offer "even though my heart says yes," for fear of hurting the school, and that "God is asking this sacrifice of me in order to eliminate my too strong sensibility and my attachment to nature and independence."[44]

Apparently whatever the difficulty between Xavier and Eugenie, it did not prejudice Eugenie's opinion, for she recommended Xavier as her replacement when, at the end of October 1825, Eugenie left to make the foundation at Saint Michael, present-day Convent, Louisiana.

Among Xavier's new experiences in these years was her first Louisiana storm (a hurricane?), and she apparently managed the day school, described in a journal entry, July 19, 1822, sent to Mother Barat:

> I believe I have not described our extern school. It is about the size of the novices' infirmary [in Paris]; the chimney occupies one side – on the other is the door, which also serves as a window (as it is the only means by which light is given). Of course we have an hospitable appearance as the door is always open – in fine the whole is made of mud which the rats nearly destroy *malgré* the industry *de nos enfants* who each day fill up the holes made during the night – in this chamber I feel more real content than if I were an inhabitant of the Tuileries. A few days ago one of the externs brought a large bale of worsted – and presenting it without preface said, "M. Xavier, my cousin says will you knit her some socks – I laughingly told the girl that even if I had the time I do not know how to knit socks."[45]

Another indication of the poverty experienced in these first years is the entry for December 19, 1822, in the journal she kept: "No

---

44 Xavier Hamilton to Madeleine Sophie Barat, May 4, 1824.
45 Journal Xavier Murphy June-July 1822, entry for July 19, 1822. Paisant, p. 499.

bread for breakfast but the strong nourishment of doing the will of God and of promoting his glory gives here a *'je ne sais quoi'* to all our privations."

Xavier had a special attraction for little boys as the following journal entry of April 6, 1823, shows:

> Some time ago a little brother of one of our children came with his mamma to see his sister. Mother Eugenie was in the parlor, and seeing this little fellow tormenting his sister, she asked him what he desired. "To see Mother Xavier for she will teach me my Catechism," but said his sister, this is Mother Eugenie won't she do – "Oh, no, Mother Eugenie is very good for girls but Mother Xavier for the boys." So Mother Eugenie came to call me saying there is a little boy who absolutely says he must see you.

A New Foundation and a New Superior

By late 1823, a new foundation closer to New Orleans was envisioned, at Saint Michael. Eugenie wrote to Madeleine Sophie on October 9 that she had been notified by Bishop Dubourg of the donation of land for the new establishment on the Mississippi, sixty miles from New Orleans, in a good and healthy climate. By January 1825, the subscription had raised 35,000 francs, and by the end of February, 39,700 francs, or $7,460. Eugenie was named to begin the foundation, after first traveling to Saint Ferdinand in Missouri to confer with Philippine Duchesne and gather some religious destined for the new establishment. On February 27, she was in New Orleans about to embark on the steamboat *General Brown* to Saint Louis. By that time, she had seen the plans for the house located on two arpents of land in front and forty arpents deep.[46]

She arrived in Florissant on March 21, 1825, bringing some gifts of cash from friends and provisions from the New Orleans Ursulines. She was able to spend considerable time there, including

---

46 The arpent was a commonly used French colonial measure roughly equivalent to an acre.

Holy Week and Easter. When she headed south on May 12 on the steamboat *Magnet*, she took with her to Grand Coteau Mathilde (Xavier) Hamilton, Judith (Ignace) Labruyère, Marguerite (Aloysia) Tison;[47] and though not documented, it is highly likely that with those from Missouri went Liza Nebbitt, an African American enslaved child who had been given to Philippine years earlier by Bishop Dubourg.[48]

By the time Eugenie left Grand Coteau for the foundation of Saint Michael in October 1825, Xavier had been named superior at Grand Coteau. With Eugenie went at least six and probably seven people. Xavier Hamilton was newly professed, could teach in both English and French, and would be her assistant. Judith Ignace Labruyère had made her first vows as a coadjutrix sister in Florissant the year before, and Mary Mullanphy, destined to be the cook, had made her vows at Grand Coteau just before departure. There were three novices from Grand Coteau: Philippine Jourdain, Sophie McGown, and Mary Aloysia Hardey,[49] an early pupil at Grand Coteau who had received the habit the previous

---

47 B-D Corr. II.II L. 197; PDCGO L. 253. Mathilde Xavier Hamilton (1802-1827), born in Ste. Genevieve, Mo., with her sister Eulalie (Regis) was one of the first vocations from the boarding school in Florissant. She made first vows in 1823 and final vows in 1825 in order to accompany Eugenie Audé to the foundation of St. Michael, where she died suddenly two years later. Judith (Ignace) Labruyère (1801-1831) also came from Ste. Genevieve, entered the Society in Florissant in 1824, went to St. Michael in 1825, and made her final profession at the time of Philippine's second visit south in 1830. She died there the following year. Marguerite Aloysia Tison, born in 1800, entered the Society in Florissant in 1822, came to Grand Coteau in 1825, and left the Society from there in 1826.

48 Liza (Eliza) Nebbit (Nesbit) was probably born in Kentucky, then lived in Missouri before being sent south to St. Michael. In later years, she married at least twice and had several children, but returned to live her last years at the convent, where she had a special place in the chapel and was known for her nursing care. When she died in 1889, she was buried in the convent cemetery and commemorated with a biographical entry in the *Annual Letters*.

49 Most of them were short-lived: Xavier Hamilton died there in 1827; Ignace Labruyère in 1831; Philippine Jourdain in 1835, and Sophie McGown in 1836. Mary Mullanphy left the Society in 1831. Aloysia Hardey (1809-1886), however, succeeded Eugenie Audé as superior in 1833 and went on to oversee many foundations in the Eastern States, the foundations in Canada and Cuba, and then to become the first American assistant general at the motherhouse in Paris. See M. L. Martinez, ed. *Southward Ho!* St. Louis: RSCJ U.S. Province, 2003, pp. 37-60.

day.[50] Though Liza Nebbitt's name is not recorded, it would seem that she also accompanied them.

Back at Grand Coteau, Xavier Murphy was now superior of a very diverse group. Carmelite Landry, a year older at 34, was the only native of Louisiana among them. Emily Saint-Cyr, a pupil of Florissant and the first choir religious to make her vows in the Society in America, brought to Grand Coteau by Mother Duchesne in 1822, was 20. Mary Layton, age 23, was born in Kentucky and lived at the Barrens in Missouri before she became the first American to enter the Society of the Sacred Heart; as a novice, she had been Eugenie Aude's only companion for the foundation at Grand Coteau. Mary Ann Summers, an orphan who entered the Society at Florissant, was 19.[51] Marguerite Manteau, one of Mother Duchesne's original companions on the voyage from France, was the oldest in the group at 45. She and Mary Ann Summers had been sent from Florissant to augment the community in summer 1823. So, an Irish woman was leader of a community of six, including a native of Louisiana, an American with French ancestry, a French woman, and two young Americans from Missouri. Of these, Xavier Murphy, Carmelite Landry, Emily Saint-Cyr, and Marguerite Manteau remained together at Grand Coteau until Xavier's death in 1836. Carmelite Landry was a most dependable helper, especially for money matters, and Marguerite Manteau gave religious example into saintly old age and probable senility.[52]

---

50   Information on participants in the group from letter of E. Audé to MSB, October 21, 1825 from Grand Coteau, GASSH; quoted in translation in Garvey, *Mary Aloysia Hardey*, p. 36; Callan, SSHNA, p. 159, quoting Garvey.
51   Born in Baltimore in 1804, Mary Ann Summers moved with her family to Missouri, then was orphaned. After entering the Society at Florissant as a coadjutrix sister, she became a choir religious at first vows in 1823. She was then sent to Grand Coteau, where she died suddenly in 1826 following a mysterious illness of only two hours.
52   The description of her by community members is always caring, and Philippine Duchesne's journal remark about her death in 1845, was that she died *dans l'enfance*, that is, senility.

There is ample evidence in Xavier's letters to Madeleine Sophie that the mother general wrote to her often, but only one letter has survived. The only extant letter from Mother Barat to Xavier Murphy, written in early February 1826 and received in August, was a response to a letter from Xavier written after becoming superior the previous October. The time lapse is an indication of the difficulty of exchanging letters at that time. Mother Barat wrote on February 6 to console the new superior:

> I received your letter, my very dear daughter, which M. Fournier[53] brought us with great care. It tells me of the approaching departure of Mother Eugenie and her companions and of your resignation and courageous acceptance of the cross laid on you. In spite of its weight, I have no doubt that the Heart of Jesus, for whom you accept it, will help you carry it and even soften it by the unction of his grace; no matter how it comes, always have confidence. God cannot abandon a soul who throws herself into his arms with love. Do what you can on your part, and leave the rest to God, who will not leave you.
>
> The one thing necessary, dear daughter, is to remain in peace. Draw near to Jesus Christ by frequent prayer especially in the problems and difficulties over external affairs for which you are in need of counsel. Turn too to Mothers Eugenie and Duchesne for advice as needed....
>
> Yesterday I gave news about you at general recreation; each one expressed in her eyes affection and veneration for you—Mother de Marbeuf[54] especially. What a sacrifice the Lord demands in taking you so far

---

53 Antoine Fournier, husband of Bishop Dubourg's sister Victoire.
54 As a novice Xavier formed a friendship with a fellow novice, Catherine de Marbeuf, widow of the former Governor of Corsica, who at the age of 55 entered the Society about the same time as Xavier. Although the correspondence is not extant, it seems that she was able to aid the community in Grand Coteau, and Xavier refers to her frequently in her letters to Paris.

away from us; that I cannot get used to, and to console myself I often say that I am going to visit you before I leave this long and sad exile of life. So far no one has heard me, and everyone seems to be against it; but if this desire is according to the will of God, he will change their hearts or give me a possible way to carry out the project that would be so enjoyable....

Don't worry over your faults; self-love will disappear or at least weaken at the sight of your misery and the important duties that you have to fulfill. Forgetfulness of self will be the result, and our God will be truly glorified by his little servant.... So be full of confidence in him who can do all things with a humble and supple instrument, conscious only of her own weakness and nothingness....

Receive, dear daughter, the assurance of the devotion, tenderness, and affection with which I am all yours *in Corde Jesu.*

Barat

The counsel to trust was lived fully by Xavier in the years ahead. That spring, on March 17, Xavier experienced

great affliction in the premature death of Mary Ann Summers, the youngest member of the community, an excellent subject and the only one here able to help me. She was taken in the space of a few hours without any help of our holy religion; judge, dear Mother, the sadness of my situation.[55]

Alas, she was to see the deaths of five more in her community, including two sent from France, before her own untimely death.[56]

---

55 Xavier Murphy to Madeleine Sophie Barat, October 19, 1826.
56 Letter of May 27, 1826. The cemetery behind the Academy received five of these, but Mary Ann Summers, the first to die, suddenly at the age of 21 in 1826, was

Good news about Xavier's success flowed north. On August 12, 1826, Philippine wrote to Mother Deshayes in Paris:
> Mother Xavier, your former novice, is fulfilling her office of superior perfectly at Opelousas and is loved by the 18 children who make up the boarding school and by her daughters as well, two of whom have been a burden: one, a novice, a [torn word] her departure; the other, an aspirant, who died suddenly [Mary Ann Summers].[57]

Expansion and Success

In 1827 letters from Mother Duchesne in Saint Louis to Madeleine Sophie about Grand Coteau said: "It seems that Mother Xavier steers her ship quite well and that she has a wonderful reputation in the area"; and "She is working wonders where she is. Protestant families, who could not bear to hear even the word Catholic without vexation and anger, are now saying: 'We like Mother Xavier's religion.'" After some criticism of Eugenie's coolness from Saint Michael toward the Missouri houses, "Mother Xavier Murphy, on the contrary, shares everything and helps us here as much as she can." Concerning the Indian girls and orphans in Saint Louis, "Fortunately we can clothe them through gifts from the boarding-school in Opelousas; the pupils there weep when their garments are not accepted for the poor. That house is blessed, under the guidance of Mother Xavier Murphy who, by her zeal along with her rare talent of speaking and writing English, charms the Protestant parents, of whom several have consented to let their children become Catholics."[58]

---

    buried in the parish cemetery, as was Frances Roche, novice, 1830, age 17. Louise Dorival was first to be buried in the convent cemetery in 1832, age 37; then Adele Toysonnier in February 1835, age 41; Ann Redmond, a novice, October 8, 1835; and Agnes Regina Cloney October 11, 1835, age 31. In the next year, it would be Xavier herself, followed in a few days by her faithful nurse, Rose Elder.

57 Philippine to G. Deshayes, August 12, 1826; PDCGO L. 274.
58 PD-MSB, May 13, August 18, October 7, 1827; PDCGO L. 288, 294, 299.

Bishop Rosati,[59] after visiting Saint Michael, paid a visit to Grand Coteau, and wrote to Philippine Duchesne on his way to Natchitoches on March 12, 1828, about his stay there. He had stayed eight days that passed very quickly. He had confessions and instruction to both community and boarding school in both French and English. He baptized three students with parental permission, and administered Confirmation to fifteen, among them several converts. Nothing but devotion, order, and happiness reigned at Grand Coteau.

Sometime in 1828 a group in Opelousas and Rapides proposed moving the Academy from Grand Coteau to Opelousas, the seat of Saint Landry (civil) Parish. Xavier Murphy of course sent this information to Philippine Duchesne and to Paris; her letters to Mother Duchesne are not extant, but she also wrote at the end of May to her trusted friend, Bishop Rosati, in words that show her religious spirit in this situation that directly affected her responsibilities:

> It appears that the inhabitants of Rapides & Opelousas wish conjointly to erect a handsome brick establishment for us at Opelousas, to which place the unanimous preference is given on account of its healthy situation. Now, Father, in the event of our acceptance of this proffered generosity, I foresee many many difficulties privations & sacrifices to make – but if by our *dévouement* the glory of God may be promoted and Religion extended, why in such case self must be forgotten or annihilated. I shall await your judicious decision with anxiety – in the meanwhile we are earnestly recommending the affair to the Father of lights and

---

59 Joseph Rosati, CM, was appointed coadjutor to the Bishop of New Orleans in 1823 and visited Grand Coteau in that capacity, beginning the friendship between Xavier and himself, which is reflected in their correspondence. In 1826 the administration of both St. Louis and New Orleans was confided to him; this arrangement lasted until the consecration of Leo R. De Neckere, CM, as bishop of New Orleans in 1830.

counsel – pray. Father, unite with your community that the will of God – alone – may be done. I have written Mère Duchesne on the subject. I see no probability of the Question being quickly decided <u>here</u> – but in the event of an application to me in the matter, I wish to be furnished with the <u>decision</u> and <u>answer</u> of My <u>Superiors</u>.

Apparently there was communication between Mother Duchesne and the bishop as well as with Mrs. Smith, whose generous donation of property and building at Grand Coteau had made founding the Academy possible seven years earlier. From Saint Louis, Philippine Duchesne was writing to Madeleine Sophie concerning this, and even thinking of going there:

> I was very taken up with the idea that I should also go down, since Mother Xavier was urging me strongly to do so because of the pressure she was under from the inhabitants of the town of Opelousas to transfer the school there....[60]

By November, it seems that the instigators of the plan were no longer actively pursuing it, and on the seventh, Xavier wrote again to Bishop Rosati that all she knew about the matter

> ...induces me to conclude that the wisest and most beneficial plan to be adopted is to renounce the enterprise, for I doubt much if the good resulting from the change would ever counterbalance the sacrifices – exposure & ostensibility [*sic*] we would incur by such an undertaking. Fortunately, we are still free to act on every side of the question, for having had your Lordship's permission for the change when waited upon by the Judge to sign the agreement, and after I received it seeing no urgent necessity to proclaim it, consequently

---

60 PD-MSB, July 24, 1828. B-D Corr. II-III L.241; PDCGO L.321.

leaves everything as yet entirely at our disposition. In addition to the above reasons, it appears that the parents and friends of the establishment unanimously prefer our present situation, arguing that the general good health and great progress *de nos élèves* are the best testimonies of the eligibility of the locale (which to all strangers appears delicious).

Indeed, dear father, I do think that sweet Providence has visibly presided over the affair, permitting and directing the whole for his greater glory & the ultimate good of the institution. The more I reflect on the subject the more I see its acceptance incompatible with our present situation. Admit only with respect to subjects [religious] where find them? and such an engagement with the public would make a sufficient number of <u>well formed</u> subjects indispensable – as to leaving this house exist (in the event of the change) it would be entirely useless. . . . . I wrote last summer to Mrs. Smith enclosing the paragraph on the Gazette[61] respecting the change[;] to this letter she has not replied. . . . . *Enfin bon père,* to conclude this subject
I must tell you that during the entire process of the cause I endeavoured to keep my mind entirely free. Whatever may be the event & the refusal and permission of my Superiors were both equally agreeable to my feelings . . . .[62]

In later November, Philippine in Saint Louis had not yet received the news of this turn of thinking about the move, for she wrote to Mother Barat:

I have to tell you that, with regard to Opelousas, the change of house is still undecided. Mother Xavier,

---

61 Probably the *Opelousas Gazette,* of which there are no known extant copies prior to 1841; e-mail from Jean Kiesel, University of Louisiana at Lafayette, July 31, 2007.
62 Rosati Collection, November 7, 1828.

under the pretext that she cannot express herself well in French,[63] begs me to ask you for two religious, for whom she will pay traveling expenses and trousseau. The essential for them would be knowledge of the French language and, if possible, piano and drawing; note that the two artists need not have great strength.[64]

This spirit of trusting in the ways of the Lord as manifested by events and the decisions of her superiors marked all the activities of Xavier's short life in Louisiana. In February 1829, she wrote to Madeleine Sophie her gratitude for the superior's approval of the possible move to Opelousas and added: "It seems that the obstacles on the side of Mrs. Smith joined to the disapproval of our Bishop have finished the business for the present." In the same letter, she wrote that all debts of her house were paid and $600 remained, while she had already sent $150 to Saint Louis where the convents were in need. This arrangement became a pattern in the years following: payments foreseen and generous sums sent to Mother Duchesne.

Somewhere before 1829, the convent acquired another enslaved person, an elderly woman named Melite. On July 20, 1829, the house journal records the acquisition of Martin "a good old negro, husband of Melite," who was about sixty according to the legal document. Martin was baptized on August 15, then immediately celebrated a church marriage to her.[65]

Meanwhile, Frank Hawkins was known to have a wife and two children left in Maryland when he was taken to Louisiana with the estate of Theodore Mudd. She was also brought to Louisiana about 1825. When this was known to Xavier Murphy, she took action. In December 1829, Xavier was represented in Opelousas by Dr.

---

63 This in spite of her multiple intimate letters to Mother Barat in French!
64 PD-MSB November 28, 1828. B-D Corr. II-III L. 246. PDCGO L. 329.
65 Martin died in 1835, but Melite lived until 1859, reportedly dying at age 111; however, this would make her about 80 in 1829, which is unlikely.

Littell to purchase from one Robert Barry "a Negress Zenia" (Jenny in the house journal) and her two little boys, Frank and Ben, for the sum of $1,200 in order to reunite the family with Frank, who had come to the property in 1823.[66] They arrived on December 8. The house journal records for that day:

> Jenny, wife of Frank, our negro, and her two children, Francis and Ben, have finally come to live here, full of gratitude to Mother Xavier, who brought them in order to alleviate their lot.

Frank Hawkins and Jenny Eaglin had three more children at Grand Coteau: John Henry born 1832, James born 1834,[67] and Marie Ann Xavier born in 1840, after Xavier Murphy's death. The bond of loyalty between Frank and Mother Murphy held beyond her death. When Frank was dying on February 9, 1842, six years after Xavier's death, the house journal records that "It was like a feast day for him, thinking that he was going to see again Mother Xavier Murphy, for whom he had always had a respect mingled with veneration." Jenny's brother David Eaglin would later come to the convent as well, from the property of Joseph Gardiner, on January 19, 1833. On January 21, David was married to Julitte (or Julie).[68] By 1834, new housing was needed for the three families of Frank and Jenny, Martin and Melite, and David and Julie. The house journal for

---

66 St. Landry Parish records: file 302, notary book C, p. 386, December 4, 1829, and HJ December 8, 1829. In her October 19, 1826, letter to Paris she mentions buying with the agreement of Mother Duchesne a Negro woman and her two small children. The 1830 census shows Madam S. Xavier (Convent) as having 2 adult males (Frank and Martin), 2 adult females all 36 or older (Jenny and Melite?), and 2 males under 10 years old. But legal documentation indicates a prior purchase of another woman, Philis, on July 10, 1826, with her son Charles age 3 and a girl age 6 months. Ages were always an estimation.

67 The parish register indicates his baptism on October 12, 1834, his sponsors Martin and Melite.

68 Original documents USCA IV E Box 13; sacramental records, St. Charles Borromeo Parish, Grand Coteau. In the marriage record, Julie is also an enslaved person of the Religious of the Sacred Heart. No previous information is extant about her. Later, in December 1834, the HJ mentions their wedding at church on the day of David's arrival.

Housing built for three enslaved families, 1834

December 15, 1834, records that, among other expansions, "we are building a place for our three families of negroes." This building still stands today. Descendants of these families formed the labor force at Grand Coteau late into the second half of the century.

The Leader

Madeleine Sophie Barat had been disappointed that the Society's first Louisiana foundation was not in New Orleans, as she felt that it was better to be in urban areas. By 1829, correspondence between her and Philippine Duchesne shows that she was thinking about New York and that Xavier Murphy might be the superior. In December Philippine wrote: "... she will immediately win a fine reputation, because the Catholic population is Irish, as are nearly all the priests, and people of this nation join up warmly with their compatriots"[69]; by September 1830, Madeleine Sophie wrote "I am still determined, if we make a foundation in New York, to take Mother Murphy. She is someone who needs scope, and in addition she will be well liked, I am sure. This is the kind of person needed to make a success [of a foundation]"[70]; but Philippine responded two months later: "... it is impossible at the moment to take away

---

69   PD-MSB December 11, 1829. B-D Corr. II-III L. 259; PDCGO L. 348.
70   PD-MSB September 25, 1830. B-D Corr. II-III, L. 268.

Mother Murphy just when the parents are providing her with half the money for the building, solely out of regard for her. They would consider her departure as a betrayal and the house would come to nothing."[71] Apparently Xavier was aware of this discussion, as Philippine wrote to Paris in December 1829 that Xavier thinks that "If she had a good English mistress, she herself would be free for New York."[72]

The school at Grand Coteau was much appreciated by both parents and pupils. The Register of Students in the Archives shows that new pupils entered mainly in October but also in May, and at other times when there were extenuating circumstances. Most remained between two and four years, but some for as long as six years. Catholic families sent their daughters to be prepared for their First Communion, and many of these ceremonies are noted in the house journal. In 1835 there were fifty-six new students added to thirty-four remaining from the prior year (and some of these would have stayed at school during the several week vacation in September). In the mid-1830s the fee for a boarder was $140.

It is difficult to know to what degree the students in these years were French colonial Creoles and how many were English-speaking Americans. There seems to have been a gradual transition from the former to the latter, though some of the perspective may have been that of the writer. In 1826, Xavier writes to Madeleine Sophie Barat that all their students are Creole, thus placing a burden on her whose French left something to be desired. Three years later, she contrasts "our Americans" to Eugenie's Creoles at Saint Michael. The same year, Louise Dorival, a French woman, writes that there has been a rapid transition to English among the students. Just after the second visit of Philippine Duchesne late in 1829, Xavier

---

71 November 25, 1830, B-D Corr. II-III, L. 270. PDCGO L. 374.
72 PD-MSB December 11, 1829. B-D Corr. II-III L. 259, PDCGO L. 348. As things worked out, the foundation was not made in New York until 1841. A major figure would be Aloysia Hardey, a pupil at Grand Coteau when Xavier Murphy arrived in 1822, and by this time an important person in the community at St. Michael.

puzzles why Philippine insisted on English spoken in the house, though the custom was to speak French.[73]

In a letter to Paris in August 1831, Philippine Duchesne reported that Xavier's "reputation is now at its peak, and the last state inspector to visit her school said that among the various notable towns he has visited, there was not one school that impressed him more than Grand Coteau; and it was a Protestant who said this."[74] However, the education was not entirely satisfactory to the religious. As late as 1830 Mother Duchesne discovered that the Society's Plan of Studies was not known in the Louisiana houses, only the list of subjects special to each class. The Plan was first drawn up in 1805, with revisions in 1810, 1820, and 1826,[75] so this was a great lack in the formation of class mistresses. A letter to Paris in the same year as the inspector's favorable report said: "Without seeing for yourself, it is difficult to understand the burden caused by the need to teach in two languages with equal perfection. This doubles all the classes, and necessitates doubling all the teachers."[76]

Xavier also noted that the highest class taught really was the third [from the top, according to the system of the time], so that those who left the school had not really "graduated." According to the French curriculum, there would be two more advanced levels.

> The fashionable idea now is that if a child pass a year in my class, she is finished. Unfortunately I have but five who say they are to graduate at the close of our year. They have been in the house four & five years and followed up all our plan. The grown girls who enter from other Institutions can only follow our fourth or third class. Consequently, the mistresses are overcharged, and if I take a few to place in mine, they would

---

73 Letters of October 19, 1826; March 3, 1829; August 14, 1829; January 20, 1830.
74 PhD to MSB, August 1, 1831, PDGCO L. 391.
75 Margaret Williams. *The Society of the Sacred Heart: History of a Spirit 1800-1975.* London: Darton, Longman & Todd, 1978, pp. 70-71.
76 Louise Dorival to Madeleine Sophie, November 12, 1831.

consider themselves also qualified to graduate at the close of the term. And with all this infatuation my class is only a second & they study but common literature, not a book of botany, philosophy, or such nonsense. All of which the parents now desire to be discontinued, seeing the little essential good their children derived from such pretended knowledge.[77]

The Builder

Madeleine Sophie Barat wrote to Philippine Duchesne from Paris in December 1827, when the question of building in Saint Louis was imminent, "If you can prudently enlarge somewhat, do have a general plan, well thought-out, and follow it in such a way that the parts added on keep to this plan, so as not to make the first outlay useless, as has happened in the majority of our houses."[78] Whether or not Philippine communicated this to Grand Coteau is not known, but it is evident that Xavier Murphy's building projects followed a definite plan resulting in the iconic central building of the Academy, completed only in 1872 under Mother Victoria Martinez, with the wing on the east balancing the 1850 chapel addition on the west.[79]

In spring of 1829, after the possible move to Opelousas was laid to rest, Xavier wrote to Bishop Rosati, "No more question of changing our local[e] but I have another plan in view." The first step of this plan was underway in 1830 after a contract was signed June 12; at some distance to the east of the original wooden building, a two-story brick building was erected. She gave some details

---

77 Xavier Murphy to Eugenie Audé, November 25, 1834. Eugenie was now in France.
78 MSB-PhD Corr. II-III, 1827 L. 232. Ironically, Mother Barat's immediate reference was Helene Dutour, then with Philippine at the City House in St. Louis, who wanted to build there on a grand scale. The next year, she would take charge of the house at LaFourche and do exactly that there, running the house into unmanageable debt.
79 Callan SSHNA p. 548. Aloysia Hardey, as visitatrix sent from the Motherhouse in Paris, approved the decision "to complete the convent building according to the original plan drawn by Mother Xavier Murphy." This east wing was for parlors, classrooms and accommodations for sodalists and retreatants.

New building with chapel on left, planned by Xavier but only built in 1850

in a letter to Bishop Rosati, "To God alone be glory, our building progresses; it will form a handsome addition of 50 feet in length and 53 in width including the gallery on the south to correspond with the present [wooden building]. Payments have been already made and the two next to be called for are ready."[80] This building, now to the left of center of the main academy building, is distinguished by a brick pattern known as Flemish bond, with the stretchers and headers of the bricks alternating across the rows, and splayed lintels framing the tops of the windows.

To continue the account of the building projects: in 1832 an infirmary and a separate linen room were built, and the original building was completely renovated. That November Xavier wrote to Bishop Rosati saying "We have just commenced a plain frame house at the end of the garden for a summer residence for our

---

80 X. Murphy to Rosati, December 30, 1830. Rosati Collection.

bishop. It is called the cottage of Grand Coteau." Although Bishop De Neckere died before he could avail himself of this refuge, the many priests who visited the Academy enjoyed its hospitality, especially in the first weeks of January 1836 when Bishop Rosati, Fathers Auguste Jeanjean, soon to be named administrator of the Diocese of New Orleans; Blaise Raho, CM; and John Timon, CM, later first bishop of Buffalo, gathered there.

Two contracts were signed on May 30, 1834. The first was for a brick kitchen to the rear: one story 88 feet long by 19.5 feet wide with a six-foot gallery. (This building burned in 1922; its replacement in the same style as the original still stands.) The second contract was for a brick extension to the 1830 structure: 78 feet 6 inches long by 45 feet deep with a gallery the same dimensions as in 1830 and connected to that building on the east. The windows were to be of the same workmanship, and there was to be a front door to add beauty. Also four dormers were to be added to the 1830 building and four front dormers with circular heads and pilasters for the new building as well as four rear dormers with square heads. The roof, with gable ends (not hipped as generally preferred by the French), was to be good red or yellow cypress shingles. The entire complex was to be finished with plaster of lime and sharp sand or marble dust to show a uniform front. Perhaps because the plaster would hide the difference, this addition used a different brick pattern, five rows of bricks with the stretchers showing, then one row with the headers showing. In the back to the side, quarters for the enslaved families were to be brick on the first floor with a second floor of wood in the center.[81] On October 27, 1834, she explained this to Bishop Rosati as follows:

> I have recently contracted for the completion of our Academy for what do you think—for $14,000—don't you think I have courage. I hold the plan to be fully executed. It may well be called a splendid building. After

---

81 *The Louisiana Architect* (February 1969) p. 6. Details of these building projects in Appendix 3.

this we shall commence a Church. That we are in great need of. This was the work I wished to undertake but at the solicitations of parents I ceded for the Academy, not having room for more than about eighty which number is full.

The following year in August there was a contract for a fish pond (125 feet by 36 feet wide by 5 feet deep), and the formal gardens between the buildings and the road were begun. At about this time Mother Xavier ordered the bricks needed for a chapel and the addition that would connect it to the main structure. By May 1836 she could write to Bishop Rosati that Father Jeanjean in New Orleans was reviewing the plans for the chapel and that the bricks were ready to burn. Indeed, "the season is so favorable that I have contracted for the same quantum for the corresponding wing."[82]

During these years of building Mother Xavier's zeal was not confined to the Academy but also reached out to the church in Louisiana. On February 19, 1830, she wrote to Rosati about a proposal to build a church in Rapides and also commented on the presence of Methodists in Natchez, although parents in that area continued to bring their daughters to Grand Coteau. By December she wrote that the Methodist schools in Natchez, Opelousas, and Lafayette were closed. She refers to the lack of English-speaking priests to meet the great need in the area, and in spring 1832, laments the presence of a Presbyterian clergyman in Rapides. In fall of that year Bishop De Neckere spent six weeks in the area, giving lectures to the religious, classes for the children, and talks in various towns. Her November letter told Rosati that in general he diffused consolation, peace and fervor, impressing all with his devoted zeal and enlightened piety. The

---

82 X. Murphy to Rosati, May 25, 1836. Rosati Collection. The corresponding wing refers to the present wing at the east end of the main building balancing the chapel at the west but not built for several decades. This is the last letter from Xavier Murphy in the Rosati Collection.

> people of Opelousas venerate his name and boast of his profound erudition. They are speaking and in fact commenced a subscription for a Catholic church at Alexandria – all our children of that parish persevere in our faith and diffuse a favorable idea of our holy Religion. So much so that the inhabitants recently refused cooperation with a Presbyterian minister for the erection of a temple, saying that they preferred the Religion of Grand Coteau, as they term it . . . .

Two years later she wrote to Rosati that "the Religion of Grand Coteau, as they term ours, is preferred for our youth in spite of the hostile animosity of the Presbyterians against us. They declare that this Institution is the destruction of the youth of the Country and that it is dangerous to see such influence and money between the hands of women – in short that it is the ruin of the [civil] parish . . . ."

March 14, 1835, she wrote to Bishop Rosati that the winter had been severe, "the cattle expiring by hundreds, no meat to be found, provisions of all kinds rare and exorbitantly dear, such is our present situation." Nevertheless, there is good news regarding the glory of God:

> We have at least succeeded in having all arranged for the speedy erection of a Church in Alexandria. The contract passed for $3,500; the present subscription only amounts to $2,800, but the inhabitants frequently assured me could they see the work commenced the money would be found. They propose blessing it on the 3rd of next December, feast of Saint Francis Xavier to whom it is to be dedicated, A.M.G.D. Another quarter now claims our attention. New Iberia, [civil] Parish Saint Mary, I have promised the people there a Church

& at this moment they could raise $5,000, had they anyone to encourage or come forward to decide.[83]

Thus, Mother Xavier's building projects reached far beyond the convent and Academy at Grand Coteau.
However, this zeal was gradually consuming her strength. It is from her letters to Paris, especially those to Madeleine Sophie that are extant, that we can learn her inner orientation and personal struggle. As early as May 17, 1822, following the joy of her final profession, she had written,

> My dear mother, since I have been here I have experienced a great combat between the inferior and superior parts of my soul,[84] a distaste for everything, not all my usual facility for prayer. In a word, [I am] deprived of any space for consolation on the part of the Creator and creatures, but the sweet certitude of doing the will of God enhances all my privations. I try in all things to act according to the promises I have made to my dear *pole star,* "to do everything against nature," and to act only according to the spirit of faith.

Later letters show that she kept this promise in spite of the difficulties she faced; on October 19, 1829, she wrote, "I think, but you know, dear mother, I am so accustomed to doing all against nature since my time in this country that at present I scarcely feel the struggle; my character is entirely subdued." But her physical strength reacted to her burdens: "I close this letter with great difficulty; my hand trembles because of the fever that I experience continually.[85]

---

83 There was a two-year gap between the death of Bishop Leo De Neckere and the consecration of Antoine Blanc as fourth Bishop of New Orleans in November 1835.

84 This comment reflects the classical tradition of spiritual theology in which she was instructed. The "appetites" (desires for other than God) pull the soul down, while reason pulls the soul up toward pure spirit.

85 In five letters to Madeleine Sophie between February 1829 and June 1830 she

I don't have any taste for prayer; *naked faith* is my only support. God gives me a great attraction for poverty...."

After her appointment as superior in 1825 she wrote, "I know nothing about government, money, expenses, etc. but above all about direction. Finally, dear mother, I fear not having the spirit of our dear Society, so pray that the Heart of Jesus will give me the graces that I need." As to government, money, etc. she clearly did very well. But she was always concerned about helping those in her community with their spiritual life, as many were French-speaking. As late as 1830 there was no copy of the Constitutions or of the Plan of Studies in Louisiana, so her concern about transmitting the spirit of the Society was not out of place; that year she wrote, "for our rules and usages French is much better and I fear making any innovation in our practices."[86]

In her first years as superior she wrote that the children returned for the new year with "a pleasure which surprised and consoled me." However, the children were Creole, so she had to speak her poor French with the parents, but over the years English came to prevail. In 1826 she had three classes each day, plus writing and handiwork, and was responsible for all the studies, along with preparation for First Communion, and in addition, all the business of the house. At the end of this letter, she laments that "I find myself often without time for the prayer of rule." But she saw to it that the others in the community "have enough time for all the exercises prescribed by the rule." She did receive Communion every day, and here she found "the strength and light" she needed. It is likely that this spiritual situation continued through most of the rest of her life.[87]

---

mentions her health: "Almost continual fever weakens me very much" (August 15, 1829). She probably had contracted malaria in her early months in Louisiana.
86 Xavier Murphy to Madeleine Sophie Barat, January 20, 1830.
87 Xavier Murphy to Madeleine Sophie Barat, October 19, 1826. Yet there were long periods of time in which they did not even have Sunday Mass. This suggests that they had Communion services with the reserved sacrament.

Increasing Complexities

In 1825 Bishop Dubourg had offered the Daughters of the Cross (known today as the Sisters of Loretto) the opportunity of opening a school in Assumption Parish on Bayou LaFourche. This order was founded in Kentucky in 1812 by a Belgian missionary, Father Charles Nerinckx. Three sisters arrived in Louisiana that November, all very young and with minimal religious formation. Vocations developed but none of the foundresses knew French, the language of the area, so they could not teach, and it proved impossible for them to train the novices. Bishop Rosati saw that the establishment could do much good and was against closing it. He proposed that the Society of the Sacred Heart take over this house and that the three sisters enter the Society, and Mother Barat gave permission.[88] Carmelite Landry was considered as superior, but Bishop Rosati judged that she would not be able to give the proper presentation of learning and that, moreover, she could not be spared from Grand Coteau without doing harm there.

Helene Dutour, recently arrived from France, led the efforts of the Religious of the Sacred Heart to carry on the school in 1828.[89] The next year, she was joined by Therese Detchemendy,[90] while the two former Loretto sisters, Regina Cloney and Rose Elder, continued there. By September 1830 there were signs of trouble.

---

88 Eventually, one of the Sisters entered the novitiate in Missouri but soon left; the two others were part of the community at Grand Coteau by 1832. Agnes Regina Cloney was there until her death on October 11, 1835 (see her letter to Bishop Dubourg of February 24, 1835). Rose Elder was Xavier's faithful nurse in her last illness and herself died just days later. What can be known of this complicated affair is outlined in Callan, SSHNA, p. 164-80, and the background detailed in "Loretto in Louisiana: The Legacy of LaFourche," by Joan Campbell, S.L. (Nerinx: Sisters of Loretto, 1987).

89 Helene Dutour, RSCJ (1787-1849), a Savoyarde, entered the Society in Grenoble and made final profession in 1818. She arrived in Louisiana in 1827, was founding superior at LaFourche but was forced to leave it in favor of Grand Coteau in 1831 when the school was failing. She died later in Natchitoches.

90 Therese Detchemendy, RSCJ (1802-1833) was born in Ste. Genevieve, Missouri, daughter of one of the wealthiest families in the area. She made first vows in Florissant in 1825, went to LaFourche in 1829, then to St. Michael, where she died of cholera.

As reported by Father Jeanjean to Bishop Rosati, Mother Dutour was building a house 75 by 51 feet, with two stories, an attic, and a gallery. The first payment of $4,000 was due August 15 and as yet unpaid, "and they do not have a *sou*." Mother Duchesne will not learn this with pleasure, he wrote, and when asked, Mother Dutour says she builds only out of obedience.[91] The debts were to continue accumulating, and the next year, Julie Bazire[92] was sent to try to do something about it.

Not only were there financial problems at LaFourche. Helene Dutour's aim was to provide the same level of education as at Saint Michael and Grand Coteau, for children of poorer families, and thus at less cost. This was seen by Eugenie as a threat to the enrollment at Saint Michael if it accepted students at the same academic level but for lower cost. The superiors of the two other houses preferred that LaFourche give up its boarding school and be the center for raising orphans, who, in the customs of the day, would not receive the same level of education. But Helene Dutour had strong episcopal support from Bishop De Neckere.

Back in Saint Louis, Philippine Duchesne was hearing the complaints, especially from Eugenie Audé at Saint Michael, that the attempt to place the school at LaFourche on the same footing as that of Saint Michael was causing unwelcome competition. That was certainly not the perception everywhere. Xavier was less worried and Bishop De Neckere held to the good accomplished at LaFourche. In France, Madeleine Sophie asked Philippine to moderate a meeting of the three superiors to come to an agreement. At first, the plan was for the three, Xavier, Eugenie Audé,

---

91 Letter of Father Jeanjean to Bishop Rosati, September 11, 1830. Autograph. Rosati collection.
92 Julie Bazire, RSCJ (1806-1883), was born and entered the Society in France. She arrived in St. Louis in 1829. She replaced Helene Dutour at LaFourche when the latter could no longer continue. After closing that house, she was superior at St. Michael after the departure of Eugenie Audé for France, and at Grand Coteau in 1837, after the death of Xavier Murphy. She returned to France in 1843, back to America 1847 to 1850, then left the Society and died in France many years later.

and Helene Dutour, to travel to Saint Louis for the conference on neutral ground. This proved to be impossible and dangerous for the welfare of the schools; each was governed by a strong leader whose absence for that long a period would weaken the school. On August 27, 1829, Louise Dorival wrote to Madeleine Sophie:

> Mother, I want to confide to you a little fear that I have: Mother Xavier is thinking of going to St Louis at the beginning of next year at the latest, to confer with Mother Duchesne, who could not come this year to Lower Louisiana, but I fear that this absence will hurt the establishment because of the Americans, who have so much connection here. Nevertheless, I am resigned to everything.

The journey north for the three superiors was not to be, so in late November-early December 1829, Philippine Duchesne traveled south for the second time at the direct instructions of Madeleine Sophie, who asked her to convene a council of the three to settle the problems among the three houses and work out an agreement. Grand Coteau and Saint Michael were at a sufficient distance from each other that they could exist harmoniously. The perceived threat was LaFourche.

The meeting took place at Saint Michael, attended by Philippine Duchesne, Eugenie, Xavier, and Helene Dutour. It was hardly the council that Madeleine Sophie wanted, largely because Philippine was incapable of asserting her authority over these three forceful women. Instead of using her authority as explicit delegate of the superior general, she told them that she came with no authority, as a sister. The lack of consensus was predictable. The question of the comparative curricula was never settled, but LaFourche, under Helene Dutour's unwise leadership, accumulated more debt than it could handle, and was forced to close in 1832.[93] Xavier reported

---

93 Philippine to Madeleine Sophie, December 11 and 22, 1929, January 20, February

to Bishop Rosati on April 30, 1832, that nine students had come to Grand Coteau at the closing.

Although Xavier had felt quite at home with Mother Duchesne when she met her for the first time soon after Xavier's arrival at Grand Coteau in 1822, Philippine in the intervening seven years seems to have suffered more loss of physical and mental ability than is often realized. Her visit to Grand Coteau at the end of the meeting at Saint Michael caused more difficulties. She stayed for three weeks and left on January 19 back to Saint Michael, on her way back to Missouri.

> Mother Duchesne was not happy with the cloister that she did not find sufficiently strict, because of the prairie that is in front of the house. I have changed the dimensions and the arrangement; I have asked Mère Dorival to explain to you. While awaiting your decision, Mother Duchesne has allowed the boarders to continue to walk there but not the community. She also found it bad that I have not made English the predominant language in the house. I do not know why this holy mother holds to that language in which I speak with all our children, carry on correspondence and keep the accounts, but our sisters being French or Creole, I speak with them habitually in their language. Besides for our rules and usages, French is much better and I would fear making any innovation in our practices.[94]

She added later in the letter: "As much as I venerate and greatly esteem Mother Duchesne, I am not completely at ease with her as she is in charge, as she is exhausted by mortifications and

---

1, 1830; PDCGO L. 348, 349, 351, 352. The next year, the Tertiary Sisters of Mt. Carmel attempted to continue the school, but it lasted only a few years. The Vincentians then tried to have a seminary there, but the building was destroyed by fire in 1855.

94 Xavier Murphy to Madeleine Sophie, January 20, 1830. All of the community spoke French, and Marguerite Manteau probably understood little English.

frustrations." Louise Dorival was even more candid about her first encounter with Philippine, finding her lacking in the capacity for relationship that Louise expected from someone with her reputation for sanctity. She found that Philippine sometimes forgot what she had previously said. She seemed to want the houses to prosper but did not approve of the very things that would make this happen. Louise surmised that Philippine was "worn out and broken," and, as much as she revered her, was thankful that she did not have to live with her.[95]

Safely returned to Saint Louis, Philippine wrote in her usual terse style when assessing people, to Madeleine Sophie about the religious in Grand Coteau:

> It remains to tell you about Mother Xavier's house. I found her sometimes a bit sharp and very tolerant of the Protestants....It seems as if she would change houses easily. She could be useful in New York without her house suffering any harm, if Mother Xavier Van Damme went there or if Mother Felicity [Lavy-Brun][96] were capable of teaching English.
>
> Mother Dorival is very lively, very amiable when she is in good form. It is said that she has a need to be in charge.
>
> Carmelite, a professed, is quite necessary for business affairs, as the two other mothers understand very little about it.[97]

As successful as Xavier seemed to be in raising money, Philippine's assessment of her as not understanding business hardly seems credible!

---

95 Louise Dorival to Madeleine Sophie, January 28, 1830.
96 Felicity Lavy-Brun, RSCJ (1802-1866) entered the Society in Besançon, France in 1824. She came to America in 1829, first to St. Louis, where she made her profession in 1830, then to Grand Coteau and later Natchitoches. She returned to France in 1856 and died in Armagh.
97 PDCGO L. 357. March 14, 1830.

As uneasy as both Louise Dorival and Xavier felt about Philippine at this second visit, they felt completely at ease with Madeleine Sophie. Both wrote frankly about difficulties in the community and problems with some of the religious. So much did Xavier relish Sophie's support that in a letter in May 1832 to the treasurer general, Mother Ducis, who looked after the affairs of the convent in Paris, Xavier asked her, "Please put with the letters a piece of veil for choir religious. Add one of our mother's veils for my use. You said there was one in your last packet but you forgot."[98]

With regard to the issue of walking in the prairie around the house, Louise Dorival followed up as directed by Xavier in a letter to Madeleine Sophie on January 28, 1830. She explained that they had both prairie and woods, the latter of which they had not even explored the boundaries. The daytime heat made it impossible to go outside, but after sunset, it was the delight of both students and religious to walk in the prairie, and this was one of the great attractions for parents; otherwise, the children had little space for recreation, and getting out was good for their health. Mother Duchesne objected to the open spaces without defined limits of cloister, in spite of the fact that she herself had observed upon arrival in Missouri that not even the cows and chickens were fenced in. She wanted the religious to have an explicit permission from the mother general to continue walking there—another indication of Philippine's mental fatigue and uncertainty, for she herself could have given the permission. Mother Dorival in her letter to Mother Barat explains that fencing in this great space would be more expensive than they could afford. While waiting for the permission, the religious would discontinue walking there, but the children would continue. However, when Felicity Lavy-Brun arrived from Saint Louis in March, she wrote to Mother Desmarquest in Paris on

---

98 Xavier Murphy to Mother Henriette Ducis, May 2, 1832. Elsewhere (February 22 and August 15, 1829) she requested a pelerine (cape) or veil of the mother general directly from her. It is difficult to imagine Mother Barat complying knowingly.

March 28 (too early to have had a response from France) that the house was surrounded by prairie and woods that she had not had time to explore; no mention of any prohibition of movement! Unfortunately, since only one much earlier letter of Madeleine Sophie to Xavier has survived, we do not know what the answer from France was.

Louise Dorival, who had arrived from France in 1827 to join the community in Grand Coteau, had during the next five years been a great support for Xavier as her assistant, and everything indicates that they got on well together. By 1830, it was clear that she was ill with tuberculosis. In August of that year, she wrote to Madeleine Sophie:

> My health is weakening visibly. Since last December, I have coughed up blood twice rather abundantly. For eight days I have had chest pain and a tiring cough. Mother Xavier thinks with me that perhaps a visit of several months at S^ت Michael would make me better. The doctor says that the trip would probably have that effect. So it seems that she will propose to Mother Eugenie to send me there for the winter, where it is even milder than here.[99]

In the summer of 1832, Louise died of tuberculosis at the age of thirty-seven. The obituary letter announcing her death on July 11, written by Xavier but in the third person, explains that Xavier had been very ill in 1828. At that time Mother Dorival "secretly offered herself as victim in her place. The Lord accepted her sacrifice; Mother Xavier recovered, but from that time, Mother Dorival felt the first signs of consumption that silently undermined her and finally let her to the grave."[100] This illness of Xavier in 1828 is

---

99 Louise Dorival to Madeleine Sophie, August 31, 1830. It is not known if she actually went to St. Michael then.
100 Death notice to Philippine Duchesne, July 11-12, 1832.

not noted in the house journal, but her frequent attacks of fever were perhaps too numerous to mention. In these years, Xavier kept the treasury journal herself, in English, but the house journal is in French so kept by someone else, though she may have supervised it.

When Louise died in July 1832, the house journal records the creation of the convent cemetery at this point: "Mother Xavier has had a cemetery made at the entrance to our woods. Father Rossi blessed the body of our dear Mother Dorival and buried it there, the first of all those who repose there now."[101] On February 24 of the next year, Xavier wrote to Mother Barat: "Undoubtedly you already know of the death of dear Mother Dorival. It was an irreparable loss here. Her death was worthy of a spouse of the Heart of Jesus. I am without an assistant and the burden is too much for poor me."[102]

In addition to the loss of Louise Dorival in 1832, that same year brought to a head the difficulties with the house of LaFourche. It was closed in the spring of 1832. Nine students went from there to Grand Coteau, along with Regina Cloney, Rose Elder, Julie Bazire, and Helene Dutour. Xavier wrote to Henriette Ducis in Paris on May 2, 1832, that Grand Coteau carried the greater part of the debt. To Madeleine Sophie on October 11 of the same year, Helene Dutour wrote that the house was still legally hers. Xavier was pressuring her to sign it over to her in order to give it to the bishop, but Helene Dutour refused without an express order from Madeleine Sophie. She reported that the bishop had put up 7,500 francs toward the building, then another 3,000 toward the debt, but the property was worth 40,000 francs.[103]

Even the joy Xavier had in corresponding with Madeleine Sophie was curtailed as she explained in her letter of February

---

101 Mary Ann Summers, the first who had died in 1826, was buried in the parish cemetery, as Lucille Frances Roche must also have been in 1830.
102 Xavier Murphy to Madeleine Sophie Barat, February 24, 1833.
103 Helene Dutour to Madeleine Sophie Barat, October 11, 1832. Xavier later wrote to Madeleine Sophie (August 22, 1834) that at the time of the suppression, the house owed its priest 4,555 francs.

24, 1833, "At present I have so many things to tell you concerning business that I see that it will be in eternity that I will have a chance to speak to you from my heart of God and my poor soul...." But these moments of vicarious conversation with her mother general in French were also a burden; her letter in January 1834 concludes:

> Finally, I must leave you and my dictionary, too, because I must hold in one hand my heart, and in the other my pen, and in spite of it, these three things are not enough to share with you my sentiments, my thoughts, and my wishes. So read in the heart of our spouse, him only. There you will find my thoughts, my labors, and my devotion for you and yours.

In May 1833 Xavier's "pole star," Father MacCarthy, died; there is no record of when she learned of the loss of this trusted spiritual guide. In the following months she experienced other losses. Bishop Leo De Neckere, whom she characterized in a letter to Madeleine Sophie as "with me like a brother...," died in mid-January 1834, and Eugenie Audé, appointed assistant general for America, was called to France, leaving Louisiana in February 1834, ostensibly for a few months but actually never to return to America.

Xavier wrote to her on November 4, 1834, in English concerning a recent letter giving directives to superiors; she was especially concerned about conferences to be given to the community every fifteen days. "Now this I have not done on account of the difficulty of expressing myself in French. I give them previous to all our great feasts, when there is any particular observation etc. etc. to be made, but to make them every fifteen days is more than I can promise. It is for this that I have been so long calling for a suitable assistant." One of the French nuns had been giving instructions on the Gospel, the rule, etc. and "she can do it in a masterly manner."[104]

---

104 The French religious in the community that year who could have done this include Felicity Lavy-Brun, Adele Toysonnier, and Prosper Prud'hon.

As always she was striving to fulfill her responsibilities, however difficult, and trusted Eugenie to explain her situation better than she felt she could in her limited French.

The last extant letters of Xavier Murphy are from 1835. On January 27, she could report that "the receipts of this house for the year 1834, being so considerable all our debts are paid and there are due to us 22,300 francs tuition sure, and we have deposited for the building 17,740 francs." On June 9 she wrote to Eugenie Audé, understanding that she would translate for Mother Barat:

> You are basking in the presence of Our Mother General whilst I poor Xavier am fighting alone the battles of the God of Israel. This country is in the greatest commotion. Bishops laity all assailed by sectarian practice. They have used every engine that malice and jealousy could suggest to injure Grand Coteau, the rapid improvement of which excites their envy... they accuse me of being the queen of Louisiana and that I have more power to make laws and have them observed than General Jackson, ... that I have infatuated the American gentlemen so as to be able to propagate my Religion. Finally, that this convent ought to be burned down as that of Boston[105] for the public safety – they even have gone so far as to report that I had fled from the Institution – several respectable parents have come to assure themselves of my being here & to entreat that such foolish reports would have no effect on my mind. I responded that they had nothing to dread, that I looked on myself as representing our Society in Louisiana and that with my diadem, holding up my cross, they may be sure of my holding firm to my post & of my not relinquishing my loyalty – we have 90 boarders.

---

105 "Burning of the Charlestown Convent," *Boston Evening Transcript*, 12 August, 1834. Gilder Lehrman Center, Yale University.

Anna Xavier Murphy, RSCJ (1793-1836)

She goes on to report on the progress of the buildings, then:
> I feel that the Heart of Jesus will be more & more glorified in the new building. Seeing that the Devil is using all efforts to contradict the undertaking suffices to give me courage, indeed supernatural, for I have scarce a puff of life in my body but my mind is full of peace & confidence, and I feel how delicious to suffer for the name of Jesus. The church of Saint F. Xavier in Rapides is nearly finished, the first in that section. Another is going to be erected in New Iberia all to satisfy the children raised with us.... The Presbyterians are taking firm root here & the ignorance of Catholic population with their depravity of manners give scope to their zeal & biblical knowledge. The Americans are some of them of opinion that the Religion of Grand Coteau, as they term it, and that of the Creoles cannot be the same.

On November 30 of the same year she wrote to Madeleine Sophie, "Very different from the rest of the world – it is not money that we lack because we received an abundance of that last August being 10,000 francs." Continuing her habit of generosity, "For you, dear Mother, I sent last year to the house of Saint Charles 2,100 francs; and Bishop Rosati being very hard up after this glorious enterprise that he does for our religious, I gave him 2,000 francs."

This letter gives a picture of her situation:
> He said once upon a time: "Think of me and I will think of you." For me, I am an agent for life, for after my class, I have to do the accounts and write letters to the parents and guardians of our children who are surely coming, and all the letters of exchange are done on businesses from New Orleans and all that in English. That gives me enough to do. If it were not for the promise to my star, to do everything against nature, never would I be engaged in this kind of work, for since I took the

books ten years ago, I did not know how to do the accounts, but I asked God and he showed me; consequently it is he who acts. You alone, venerated mother, are able worthily to thank him.

Later in the letter:
… my soul is often pushed to the end for lack of encouragement and advice. These last years I count very much on Father Lallement[106] with my constant friend the Imitation [of Christ]. For the rest, dear mother, I believe that it is in heaven that we will speak or that I can open my heart. Let us go there in the Heart of Jesus, true center of light and understanding; we will see all that this heavenly spouse accomplishes in us for A.M.D.G.[107]

This letter also told of a young woman twenty-two years old who spoke of her hatred of Catholics when she arrived for the year, but on Pentecost with the agreement of her family, she was baptized, taking the name, Maria Xavier. Both the house journal and letters show that many children were baptized. Heading a notebook listing baptisms is the following: "As there is not a Baptismal Register, the notes here are not detailed." The influence of Xavier Murphy is clear as in the years 1826–1836 sixteen of the forty-nine baptized took Xavier as their baptismal name.[108]

The year 1836 opened with the presence of Bishop Rosati, Fathers Auguste Jeanjean, and John Blaise Raho, CM, so that there were three Masses daily, instructions for the community and also for the children; on January 4 Father Tyman [Timon], CM, joined the priests in the cottage. There was a High Mass in the study hall, transformed into a chapel for the Feast of the Epiphany. The

---
106 Louis Lallement, a seventeenth century French spiritual writer; *Imitation of Christ* by Thomas à Kempis, a fifteenth century spiritual book.
107 *Ad Majorem Dei Gloriam* (For the greater glory of God), the Jesuit motto.
108 Ledger "Grand Coteau Baptisms." USCA.

Bishop remained until the 19th as did Father Jeanjean, according to the house journal.

Father Jeanjean was a respected priest of the Diocese of New Orleans who had, the year before, received bulls of appointment as Bishop of New Orleans; but he declined acceptance and left Louisiana for a time. At some point in this period, he received for review the plans for the chapel that Xavier was eager to build. As she wrote to Bishop Rosati in November 1835: "I allude to our embryo Church for the plan & particulars of which I refer you to our dear friend Jeanjean; discuss the matter *ensemble*. Your results cannot be but advantageous ... I prefer his giving your Lordship an idea on our plans, etc. he is so concise and clear-headed." This is the background to an unusual episode showing Xavier's concern for this young priest and for the wider church.

In early April 1836, Xavier was at Saint Michael. She detailed the situation of her return on April 12 in a letter to Bishop Rosati on April 30:

> Now for a little history, father, *entre nous*: since my last, which I wrote on leaving St Michael's after making my adieus with my dear bishop to whom I consigned the letter for your Lordship. As I expected, the S. boat called to take me, when judge of my surprise to see Father Jeanjean accompanied by another gentleman whom I after discovered to be Bishop Portier. The latter remained at St Michael's, whilst Father J. with the captain conducted me to the boat. It was late at night. In the morning, I learned with pain from Father J. that he had escaped from the city, having left a letter to explain himself with the bishop,[109] that he would leave me at Plaquemine and continue his route to Point Coupee. From his air and feelings, to which I

---

[109] Antoine Blanc, recently consecrated Bishop of Louisiana, planned to leave for Europe to recruit priests for the diocese, having appointed Father Jeanjean administrator in his absence.

could not administer any soothing palliative, aware of the anguish and confusion his step had occasioned the poor bishop, yet I feared his going with strangers who would not be acquainted with his situation. I proposed his continuing on to G. Coteau, to which he assented. From Plaquemine I wrote the bishop informing him of the determination of our fugitive, who on our arrival got sick, lost sleep, quiet, etc. By the first mail came a letter from the bishop to my address enclosing one for Father J., which I presented and on my knees demanded he would return the next day by the S. Boat. After perusing the bishop's letter, he consented, left here the following morning....[110]

While Father Jeanjean was at Grand Coteau for those weeks in April, he presided at the first vow ceremony of Mary Knight on April 14.[111] There were five baptisms in the course of the first five months of the year. The devoted Father Rossi came for Mass once a week and also for the Feasts of the Sacred Heart, the Assumption, and the Holy Heart of Mary, August 28.

The End

But by that date Xavier Murphy was kept in bed by a bilious fever and on August 30 was not able to attend the Prizes (the ceremony to close the school year), which were followed by vacation. She renewed her vows that day and begged pardon for her omissions and failures, while the community surrounding her wept. On September

---

110 HJ April 30. In 1827 Father Auguste Jeanjean had been appointed to the episcopal council in the absence of a bishop, in 1832 he was secretary of the diocesan synod, in 1838 he was named vicar general. He died in New Orleans, April 1, 1841.

111 Mary Knight was born in LaFourche in 1819 and entered at St. Michael as a coadjutrix novice in 1832. Her sister Rosa had left the Society two years before. The house journal notes: "far from being disturbed by her sister's departure, (she) has only been more strongly confirmed in her own vocation." She made first vows at Grand Coteau in 1836, but she returned to St. Michael and left the Society from there in 1837.

3 Father Rossi was summoned but was not able to arrive until 11:00 p.m. to give her the Last Sacraments. The next day doctors "versed in the medical ignorance of the day, prescribed a series of blistering plasters to counteract the raging fever of the patient."[112] As a result, "She was covered with sores, and her poor body was just one wound. Her patience and resignation in the midst of such great suffering, her obedience to the infirmarians and the doctors, her abandonment into the hands of God are far above any of our praises."

On September 6, the house journal records:

> We have no more hope of keeping our Mother except by a miracle; God does not wish to answer in this way the ardent and almost continual prayers which we have addressed to Him, especially ever since she has been in danger. The children are also trying to storm heaven, and wish to pray in the chapel two by two, replacing each other in this holy exercise, almost without any break. Candles burn constantly before the Blessed Sacrament, the picture of Our Lady and of St. Francis Xavier. But God knows better than we do what is best for our Mother; He wishes to have her with Himself, and it is in vain that we attempt to keep her longer with us in this land of exile and of tears. M. Rossi is sent for from Opelousas, and he comes in haste, but she is no longer able to receive Holy Viaticum, although she retains full consciousness. This privation, which is very painful for her, increases her merit and renders more touching the sight of her virtues, gained under trials and suffering. She is confessed, receives the Plenary Indulgence, and remains resigned and peaceful in the hands of God.

---

112 Louise Callan's phrase, SSHNA, p. 147.

She remained in peace until her death five minutes before midnight. She was forty-three years old. At daybreak on the 7th the mournful tolling of the bell bore the sad news to all in the house. Faithful Father Rossi gave the eulogy on the 8th, saying that the religious had lost an excellent superior and the area a wise administrator.[113]

As was the custom, soon a death notice was sent to the other houses of the Sacred Heart. On the outside of the notice sent to Mother Duchesne in Missouri, Helene Dutour, now in charge, made the following notes:

> I do not have the time, Reverend Mother, to treat in greater detail as I would like the virtues and sufferings of our holy and excellent mother, wishing to write to our mother general for tomorrow, but I will not fail to do so as soon as possible. Sr. Marguerite is dying of the same illness, and Sr. H. Mayet is also very ill.[114]
>
> Our beloved Mother Xavier fell ill on the 22nd of last month of a bilious fever that resisted all remedies. She gave us the example of heroic patience, of perfect conformity to the will of God, and of perfect obedience even to death, allowing the application or giving of the most repugnant and the most painful remedies, without hesitating or showing any repugnance.
>
> H. Dutour, r of the S.H.

On November 19 of the previous year, Xavier Murphy's last will and testament had been filed in Probate Court in Saint Landry Parish. Her handwriting is strong:

> I, Anne Fransis Xavier Murphy, Religious of the Sacred Heart, in perfect health but desiring to

---

113 HJ September 6-8, 1836.
114 Helene Mayet, RSCJ, died February 3, 1837, but Marguerite Manteau, RSCJ, one of the original group with Philippine, did not die until 1841.

precaution against the surprise of death declare what follows to be my sole testament and last will.

I protest that I desire to live and die a docile obedient child of the Roman Catholic and Apostolic Church ... I recommend myself to the prayers of all the faithful particularly to those of my friends – but Oh! my God, here permit [me] to thank you for having bestowed on my unworth the inestimable favor of my Vocation to a religious life ... I particularly ask pardon of this community for all the disedification I have given ... and here express my gratitude for the charity with which they have supported my failures as well as for the attachment they have ever evinced in my regard.

The document is dated September 26, 1835. She names Catherine Thiéfry, superior of Saint Louis, as her principal heir, and Julie Bazire, superior of Saint Michael, as secondary heir.[115]

In spite of Father Rossi's devotedness, he had heavy responsibilities in his parish in Opelousas, and for the rest of 1836 and into 1837, the community had Mass only occasionally and were deprived even on Christmas. But thanks to Xavier Murphy's long desire to build a real chapel for the Academy, some 200,000 bricks, all of the lime, and most of the wood for this project were in hand when, after her death, the possibility of the Society of Jesus locating in Grand Coteau became known to her successor as superior, Julie Bazire. She offered the bricks to the French Jesuits meeting in Donaldsonville in spring 1837 to decide on the location of their venture in Louisiana under their newly-appointed superior, Nicholas Point, SJ.[116] That offer seems to have tipped the decision

---

115 See Appendix 5 for full text and copy of the original document. Since the ownership of all property of the establishment was in the name of the superior, such a document was necessary although Xavier Murphy herself owned no personal property.
116 Nicholas Point's sister, Marie Jeanne, entered the Society of the Sacred Heart in Paris in 1838 and was sent to America in 1840 before her first vows. She was in Grand Coteau by 1851 and died there in 1857 of yellow fever.

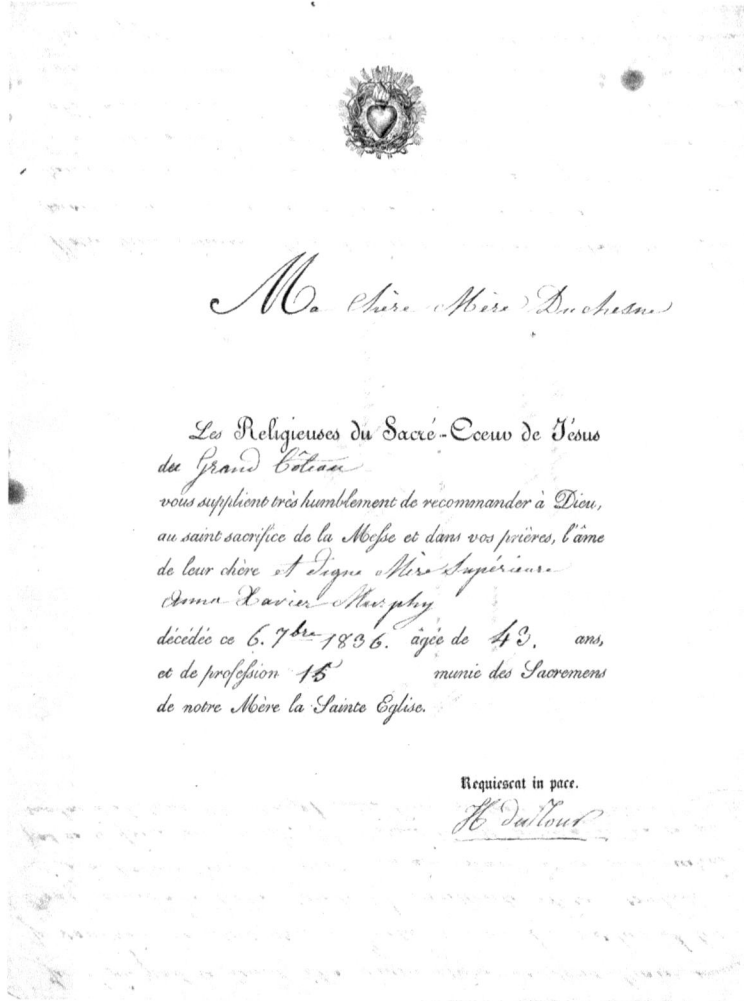

Death notice of Xavier Murphy, the copy sent to Mother Duchesne

in favor of Grand Coteau. So Xavier's long years of prayer, as well as her careful planning, finally assured Mass and the sacraments for the religious and students.

However, Anna Xavier Murphy's influence did not stop there. Just as a former pupil remembered her many years later, as noted at the beginning of this account, almost a hundred years after her death, the alumnae of the Academy were asked to suggest those

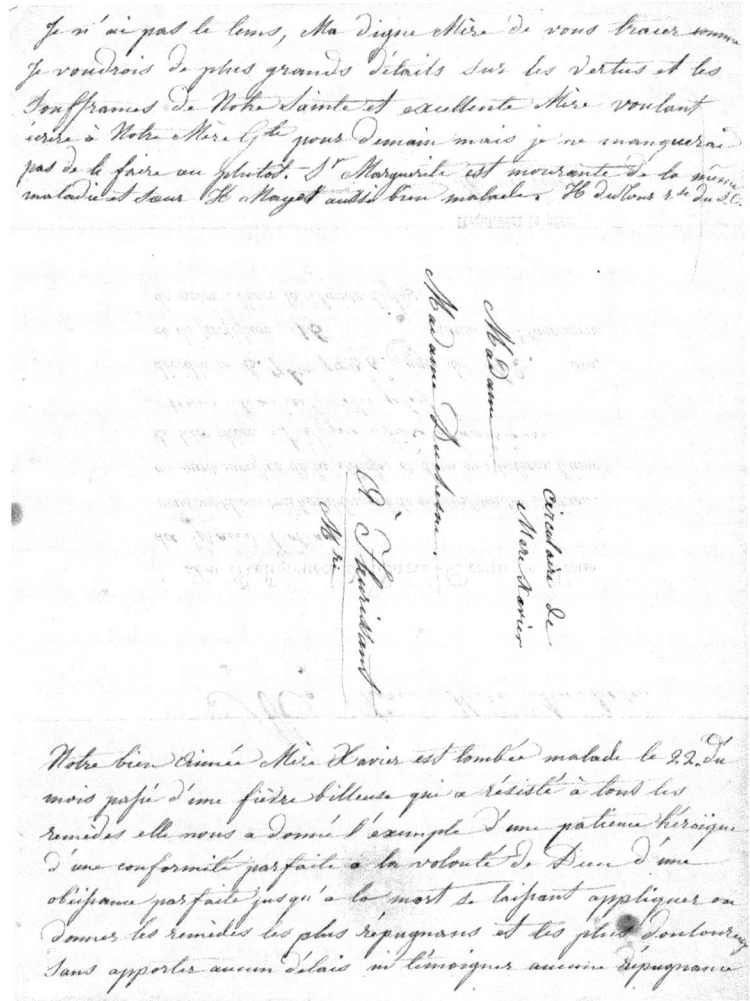

Opposite side of Xavier Murphy's death notice

who should have a special remembrance. One responded, "I would do anything in my power for the Convent at Grand Coteau, for my mother for eleven years knew no other home." Three sisters, Harriet, Emily, and Amanda-Louise Terrell, lost their mother in 1825 when they were aged nine, seven and five, respectively. Their father, Halcott Terrell, though not a Catholic, "entrusted them to the Religious of the Sacred Heart. In spite of their tender age the three little ones were received by Mother Xavier of holy memory and surrounded with every material care. The Convent became truly a home to them."[117] This tribute continues with a description of life at the convent at that time, depicting the laborious life of the nuns and the rhythm of school life. It also pays tribute to the wisdom of Xavier Murphy's care of the children:

> In those far-off days the school year was a solid, substantial piece of work, not ... "open-fancy-work" all shot through with week-ends, Thanksgiving, Christmas and Easter holidays, besides a long-trailing three months' vacation. The pupils entered at the beginning of October, no one leaving before the following September when occurred the month's vacation often curtailed to three weeks. In that atmosphere of peace, study, and piety the sisters grew and were taught to love God, keep His commandments and live according to the principles of convinced Christian maidens. They did not embrace the Catholic Faith until they had left the Convent as Mother Xavier deemed it best under existing circumstances that they should be more familiar with the world before joining the Church. Deep must have sunk the roots of a lively faith in those pure hearts if one can judge by the spiritual fruits that ripened on that family tree, still prolific today in the third and fourth generation.[118]

In the first years of the twenty-first century, the strong educational tradition as well as the iconic façade of the main building, signature of Xavier Murphy, remains the face of the Academy of the Sacred Heart, now joined by Berchmans Academy for boys as Schools of the Sacred Heart in Grand Coteau, Louisiana.

---

117 Although the spelling is different, these girls probably were cousins of the alumna, Rebecca Terrel, quoted in the beginning of this account, as both families were from Rapides Parish (See Appendix 4).
118 Sacred Heart Alumnae, Grand Coteau, *Newsletter*, May 20, 1933. pp. 7-8.

JOURNALS AND LETTERS

Introduction

What follows are three journals and seventy-two letters, of which two journals and fifty-two letters were written by Anna Xavier Murphy herself, the rest by others, added here to provide context. Of Xavier's fifty letters, twenty-two were written to her beloved Reverend Mother Madeleine Sophie Barat in France, and nineteen to her great friend, Bishop Joseph Rosati.

When writing to Madeleine Sophie Barat and other members of the Society of the Sacred Heart in Paris, Xavier writes in French. Though she had done her initial formation in Paris and probably had a good speaking ability in that language, her written French was haphazard and she alludes several times to the need of a dictionary. Grammar and spelling leave much to be desired. When her letters were copied into notebooks at the motherhouse along with those of the other missionaries, her language was corrected. Thus, only the autographs, which constitute the majority, reveal her written style. The translations of these French letters that follow, whether autographs or from copy books, are in modern English and follow recognized contemporary English rules of punctuation and capitalization.

By contrast, her letters to others are written in the English that she knew as an Irish woman of the early nineteenth century. The transcriptions of these letters aim to be as faithful as possible to what she wrote, including frequent capitalization and very little punctuation. In some cases, however, it has been necessary to add some punctuation to facilitate reading.

Xavier's written style includes numerous underlined words for added emphasis, as well as French words scattered in her English letters. Underlining has been retained in both translations and transcriptions as she wrote, and italics used for foreign words, French and Latin.

Though the school was founded in 1821 with the intention of serving the Catholic population of the area, it becomes clear after a few years that there are also many Protestant students, as well as Protestant boarding schools. Competition for students was fierce, and antipathy between Catholics and Protestants reflected the religious feelings of the day.

A few letters written by others have been added to provide context. Most come from other Religious of the Sacred Heart in the Grand Coteau community. The letters are arranged chronologically. Reading them in the sequence in which they were written provides a much broader view of the life and incredible difficulties that confronted these courageous women on the Louisiana frontier.

CHRONOLOGICAL LIST

Journals and Letters of Anna Xavier Murphy and selected contemporaries

1822
- Journal of the crossing, Mathevon and Murphy, February 1822 (1 letter, 1 journal by Mathevon)
- Journal June 1822-July 1823
- XM to MSB 3.11.1822
- XM to MSB 5.17.1822
- XM to MSB 8.27.1822

1823
- XM to MSB 3.2.1823
    MSB to E. Audé 6.18.1823 excerpt regarding XM

1824
- XM to MSB 5.4.1824
- XM to MSB 5.29.1824

1825
- XM to MSB 10.16.1825

1826
    MSB to XM 2.6.1826
- XM to MSB 4.19.1826
- XM to MSB 10.19.1826

1827
- XM to MSB 2.27.1827
    MSB to E. Audé 10.5.1827 excerpt regarding XM
    L. Dorival to MSB 10.19.1827
- XM to Rosati 12.27.1827

1828
    L. Dorival to MSB 1.14.1828
- XM to Rosati 3.27.1828
- XM to Rosati 4.25.1828
- XM to Rosati 5.27.1828
    L. Dorival to MSB 6.16.1828
- XM to Rosati 11.7.1828

1829
- XM to MSB 2.22.1829
    L. Dorival to MSB 2.22.1829
    L. Dorival to MSB 3.3.1829
    L. Dorival to MSB 6.5/15.1829
- XM to Rosati 6.15.1829
    L. Dorival to MSB 8.14.1829
- XM to MSB 8.15.1829
- XM to MSB 10.19.1829

1830
- XM to MSB 1.20.1830
    L. Dorival to MSB 1.28.1830
- XM to Rosati 2.19.1830
- XM to Rosati 5.11.1830
- XM to Delacroix 6.3.1830
- XM to MSB 6.12.1830
- XM to MSB 8.23.1830

- XM to MSB 10.16.1830
    - L. Dorival to MSB 8.31.1830
- XM to Rosati 12.30.1830

1831
- MSB to E. de Gramont 4.6.1830 re XM, excerpt
- L. Dorival to MSB 11.12.1831

1832
- XM to Rosati 4.15.1832
- XM to Rosati 4.30.1832
- XM to H. Ducis 5.2.1832
- XM to PD obit L. Dorival 7.12/13.1832
    - H. Dutour to MSB 10.11.1832
- XM to Rosati 11.3.1832

1833
- XM to H. Ducis 2.2.1833
- XM to Rosati 2.10.1833
- XM to MSB 2.24.1833

1834
- XM to MSB 1.19.1834
- XM to Delacroix 2.9.1834
    - Sr. Xavier, Sr. of Charity to Bishop Rosati from Grand Coteau 4.20.1834
- XM to Rosati 4.29.1834
- XM to MSB 8.22.1834
- XM to Rosati 10.27.1834
- XM to E. Audé 11.4.1834
- XM to E. Audé 11.25.1834
- XM to Bishop Blanc 12.19.1834

1835
- XM to MSB 1.27.1835
    A. Cloney to Rosati 2.24.1835
- XM to Rosati 3.14.1835
- XM to Rosati 5.26.1835
- XM to E. Audé 6.9.1835
- XM to Rosati 11.14.1835
- XM to MSB 11.30.1835

1836
- XM to Rosati 4.9.1836
- XM to Rosati 4.30.1836
- XM to Rosati 5.25.1836
    H Dutour to Rosati, death of XM 9.11.1836
    H Dutour to PD, death notice of XM

1837
    J Bazire to Bishop Blanc 7.24.1837 (see Appendix 3)

JOURNALS

Journal of the Crossing by Lucile Mathevon

The two missionaries journeyed first to Bordeaux, staying with the religious there; then to Pauillac where they were to board ship. As the elder, Lucile Mathevon wrote their farewell letter to the community in Bordeaux.[119]

Lucile Mathevon to Josephine Bigeu, Bordeaux

Bordeaux, Pauillac
December 6, 1821

For Reverend Mother Bigeu

Dear Reverend Mother,
    I hasten to give you news of us, so you will not worry about us and at the same time to satisfy myself because I have great satisfaction in speaking to you again of France. I did not believe in holding on to this dear country and when I thought of leaving it, I felt great sorrow. But I quickly sacrificed it for our good Master, and I no longer have any sorrow, I am in the joy of my soul. I have no fear, neither of rivers nor of the sea; I have been very content all the time I have been here.
    We have very good passengers, all very respectable; there are three women who all have children of eleven, five and two years; there is an Irish gentleman who knows the family of Sister Xavier

---

119 French autograph. GASSH CVII 2. Transcription Paisant, L. 116, pp. 437-38.
    Josephine Bigeu was superior of the new community there. A post-script added to the first page: "The pastor asks me to offer his respects to Mother Lalanne."

very well; he is very kind to us. Sister Xavier has given him news of his family, as he has not had news of them for a long time. All the merchandise on this ship is his, so that he is like the master and treats us accordingly. The sick woman who came with us manages her fatigue with great courage.

We have been well received by the pastor of Pauillac; nothing has been lacking to us: a three-course meal, coffee, rum, in sum, all sorts of kindnesses. He has an Irish vicar; Sister Xavier is very happy with him. She was charmed to find a compatriot. She is only troubled about leaving too early.

We embark today, December 6th at four in the evening. Please, dear mother, give this news to Mother Barat and to the house at Grenoble. We ask in a special way for the prayers of all the Society. On our side, we will not forget this dear Society, and particularly the house of Bordeaux. Give my regards to Father Barat as well as to all our Fathers. Please give Mother Lalanne all the gratitude we owe her for so much goodness, and the same to Mrs. Fournier and to Mrs. Dubourg.[120] My love to all my dear sisters.

It is in union with the Divine Hearts that I ask you to accept the assurance of my respect and the tender attachment of your unworthy daughter,

Lucile Mathevon

The contrast between the two travelers is better shown by including Lucile Mathevon's journal of the voyage before that of Xavier Murphy.

Journal of the voyage, by Lucile Mathevon[121]

Dear Reverend Mother,

---

120 Victoire Fournier, sister of Bishop Louis William Dubourg, and her sister-in-law, wife of the bishop's brother.
121 French copy GASSH A II 2 j, Box 3: *Lettres intéressantes*, cahier 1, pp. 272-280. Paisant L. 117, pp. 438-46.

It is only on the eighth day that I can write to you; it has been impossible to do so earlier. But fearing to omit any circumstances of our dear voyage, I give them with great difficulty as the rolling of the ship is so strong that at each moment I roll to the side of my cabin. I am sufficiently recovered finally to tell you all that we are doing and the good company that we have had the good fortune to encounter.

We see well that the Lord watches over us and that we are accompanied by the prayers of our good mothers and sisters. It is a blessing of God over us that these gentlemen do not cease to admire and they say that we are children of Providence. We have, however, had much to suffer from contrary winds for nineteen days, but the sea has always been in our favor. Here is a first point of their admiration and they say: "It is astonishing that with a wind so strong and so contrary, all on board have been happy!" It is only I who have experienced great fear. I spent the nights in prayer and sometimes I woke Sister Xavier, who told me to be still, that she never sleeps better than when the sea is agitated. I admire her tranquility.

Finally, I must add a word about our companions, of whom we are the spoiled children: eight gentlemen, of whom six are from New Orleans and two from Philadelphia,[122] and three ladies from New Orleans. They are very respectful and do not permit any bad language in our company. They are very reserved and show us great respect. They wanted us to be placed at table next to the captain and each tries to give us the best morsels of food. Finally, we must receive new compliments at every moment. They tell us unceasingly, "We love you very much, madams, your manners toward everyone give us a good impression of your Institute." Another says: "I love to see you laugh, you laugh from your heart." And to me:

---

122 Apparently, the two servants are not counted, nor is there mention of whether they are slave or free; see Appendix 2.

"You are a good sailor, but you will remember Cape Finisterre[123] for a long time." It was there that I experienced the greatest fright.

They love Sister Xavier very much, above all, the captain, who tells her his successes and losses and all the story of his life and that of his family. He is an admirable man; we have nothing but regret that he is Protestant; he has all the moral virtues. We do not give up hope of claiming him. Sister Xavier speaks to him from time to time. He loves the Catholic religion very much, but he has a prejudice against Catholics that it will be difficult to counter, having seen the horrors committed by the Spanish Catholics of Cuba. They have given him such a bad idea that it will be difficult to change it.

We also had several little discussions with another Protestant. He told me that he would be Catholic if it were not necessary to go to confession, but he did not wish to discuss this again. He always seeks us out; he always finds us happy and our happiness troubles him. Grace urges him, and I do not know if he will respond. After he had spoken for a long time with Sister Xavier, she said to him: "Know, sir, that you will not be happy and peaceful until you are a Catholic." That thought tormented him all day; he remained in a corner reflecting and in the evening, he approached me and asked if I was never worried: "No, sir, never, since I belong to God." He asked us permission to come to see us at the Ursulines. If he becomes Catholic, he will not be half-hearted. He says to me sometimes: "Is it necessary for me to be a priest or monk?" "No, sir, be a good Catholic in the world; God will not ask more of you."

We spend our days on deck with no difficulty, having such good fellow passengers. There we can make our meditation, our reading, and say office; after that we work. We always have Mrs. Chapela with us [the passenger who was ill]. We often recommend some little things to these gentlemen. That pleases them and has given

---

123 The northwesternmost point of Spain, thus the last part of continental Europe. We are left uninformed of events there, also referred to in her journal for December 23.

them an entirely different idea of religious than they had before, the captain especially. When told that he would have religious on board, he believed that he would have to do more for them than for the other passengers. He got many expensive provisions, and so we have been too well treated. When he saw that we eat little and everything, he did not know what to think. Finally, one evening when we were on deck, he put his trust in Sister Xavier and asked her many questions about our Institute. He is educated and knows the Bible, so she instructed him and said: "Do you know the evangelical counsels?" "Yes, Madam." "Do you know the passage of the Gospel where Our Lord says to the young man, 'If you wish to be perfect go, sell what you have and give it to the poor, etc.?' That is what religious do, they embrace poverty by choice, obedience, and chastity." Since then he conceived a high idea of us and said to her, "I had formed a completely different idea of religious." He likes us very much and tries to give us pleasure, even coming to tell us when the sun is rising, because it is a charming sight when it appears on the horizon; in the evening he has us observe the sunset. He is teaching me to speak English, etc.

Well, mother, I do not know how to tell you how good these gentlemen are to us, continually bringing us figs, prunes, etc. It seems that we are their children; we live in a family. One also sees Sister Xavier busy mending their suits, vests, ties, hats, caps; I sometimes do it and we do as much as we can since we see that it makes religion loved and gives a good idea of our Institute to the good Louisianians.

We have taken Mr. Nagliss for our mentor. He is an Irishman from Cork, a good friend of Sister Xavier. He is a man of great merit and quite devoted. He lives in Philadelphia, and would really like a house of our order there, and I believe he will do all he can to have us. He promises us two young girls, daughters of one of his friends, for the house in Opelousas.

We often have little surprises that make us laugh unto tears; our gaiety edifies them and they come to tell us: "You are so happy, madams, your lot is worthy of envy! Don't you have any worries?" I reply: "No, sir, since I am God's; never was I more free than since I gave up my liberty."

Finally, it is time to begin my journal.

December 6th at three in the afternoon, we embarked on the ship.

Friday, December 7th at three in the morning, the ship sailed and when we awoke I asked if we were still at Pauillac, and heard the response: "We are ten leagues away." My heart began to palpitate; I felt a great sorrow at leaving France. I would not have believed it, never having had that thought, but our good Master wished to use it for his glory; I made a generous sacrifice at once. The day was very beautiful.

Saturday, December 8th the same. We are at sea; I was the first to be sick and obliged to leave the table. We passed the day on the deck in order not to be sick.

Sunday, December 9th seasickness continues. Beautiful weather, we are making good progress. At night, all were sick; bad weather; I began to be frightened; I trembled during part of the night.

Monday, December 10th contrary winds; the sea is extremely high, but it is in our favor, otherwise there would have been much to fear. I was seasick and terrified. Mother Xavier is less suffering and has no fear; on the contrary, she is very happy with the noise and this furious sea.

Tuesday, December 11th the same. The **12**[th] even worse weather. No one can go on the deck except the sailors. The sea struck the sides at every moment; a wave came up to the window of the cabin where I was sitting. I was covered with water; at that moment, I thought I was drowning. Never will I forget the day of the 12th, and the night; every time I saw the captain I asked for news of the weather: "Bad, madam, bad; but do not fear, there is no danger." Finally, during the night, I thought I heard "danger" – "What is that?!" He laughed at my fear and said to me: "No danger; sleep, madam, sleep."

13th contrary winds. We are not making progress; then the night was even worse. The ship stopped. Then strong rolling; one heard glasses and cups breaking on all sides and even the night pots were knocked over on the gentlemen; I laughed a lot at that event.

Friday the 14th contrary wind, strong sea, the captain restless; the seasickness continued. I began to fear no longer. At four in the evening, a good wind came: great joy, the dinner bell sounded. The captain came to get me saying: "Good wind, madam, good wind."

Saturday the 15th good wind; we made two leagues and half an hour, strong rolling.

Sunday the 16th contrary wind, sea very strong. **Monday the 17th** the same.

Tuesday the 18th still worse, the contrary wind increased during several hours; we were ready to perish at any moment; I suffered very much that day and said: "Ah! If our mothers knew what we are suffering, they would be praying for us!" But I had recourse to the Heart of Jesus and I was helped in a striking manner by the intercession of Aloysia.[124]

Wednesday the 19th beautiful weather, good wind; we made sixty leagues that day.

Thursday the 20th good wind, but the sea was calm.

Friday, the 21st calm sea, we do not make progress. We began to recover from seasickness; it had lasted twelve days.

Saturday the 22nd contrary wind. Sunday the 23rd contrary wind; it increased at each moment. I am no longer afraid, I laugh

---

[124] Euphrosyne Aloysia Jouve, Philippine Duchesne's niece, entered the Society and hoped to be a missionary like her aunt, but she died January 21, 1821, soon after her profession, at the age of twenty-five. She was considered by all to be very holy.

at my fears and they often speak to me of Cape Finisterre. I say that I will never forget it.

Monday the 24th very strong contrary wind. People are beginning to murmur; only the captain remains tranquil. He is an admirable man; he is a lesson to us, even though he is Protestant.

Tuesday the 25th contrary wind and a frightening night. **Wednesday the 26th** the Lord came to our aid; good wind, good weather, all are rejoicing, we are making two and a half leagues an hour.

Thursday the 27th good weather; today we saw the Canary Islands: a cry of joy; they came to wake us up to see the land. At eight in the morning we were opposite the town of Santa Cruz; on the other side we saw the peak of Tenerife, it is amazing to see that height of land in the midst of the vast ocean; it was visible all day. It was the feast of Saint John when I began to enjoy the trip. We passed this day between the Canary Islands and the Trinity [?]. These were the first we saw. We did not see Madeira, having passed it during the night.

Friday beautiful weather, good wind, two and a half leagues an hour. **Saturday the 29th** the same; we entered into the trade winds.

Sunday the 30th at one o'clock we passed the Tropic, the heat is beginning and increases every day.

Monday the 31st the good wind continues. Once we reached the trade winds, there is always good wind and there is only a calm to fear.

Tuesday, January 1st good weather; the wishes for the New Year are the continuation of the good wind.

Wednesday the 2nd the good weather continues. We see a dolphin that swims around the ship. It amuses itself by making itself visible. It is a good twenty feet long; when it is under the water it appears azure blue.

January 3rd good weather; we make only two leagues an hour.

Friday the 4th the same. **Saturday 5th** the same. **Sunday 6th** the same. **Monday 7th** the same. **The 9th** same. **The 10th** calm weather.

11th same. 12th same. 13th good wind. We saw a ship bound for Guadaloupe. We are opposite that island. 14th calm. 15th good wind; we make two and a half leagues per hour.

16th we make only two leagues, and begin to see the island of Saint-Domingue; the heat is excessive. We are obliged to leave the door of our cabin open at night.

17th we make three leagues an hour. 18th the same; at seven in the morning, we see the island of Cuba. 19th beautiful weather. 20th calm; we see a ship coming from Philadelphia; we speak to it with a horn. 21st calm. 22nd contrary wind that slows us down. We make only one league an hour. 23rd calm. 24th the same; contrary wind in the evening.

25th feast of the Conversion of Saint Paul, a day forever memorable because of the sad event that happened, but by the grace of God it was only a fright. The contrary wind during the night had pushed us too near the land of Cape Saint Anthony[125]; toward ten o'clock in the morning, we saw coming toward us a canoe of Spanish pirates. They were easily thirty armed people; they had guns and we did not. They rowed forcefully and we were becalmed. We could only wait to fall into their hands, if the Lord had not been our help. They raised the Spanish flag; we the American. They also raised an American flag; we had to depend on ourselves. All the sails were raised in order to go more quickly and to put out to sea because they did not leave the shores. Nevertheless, they gained on us and gave us a sign that declared war; we did not respond to them because we saw ourselves as taken. They were a quarter league from us. Everyone immediately began to hide their money, the silver tableware, watches, etc. Everyone was frightened, trying to make arrangements with them so that they would not do us harm; we were ready to give them whatever they wanted provided they spared our lives. Finally, someone said: "If a good wind came, a great breeze, we would not need to fear them." I immediately threw

---

125 Cabo San Antonio, the westernmost point of Cuba.

myself at the feet of the holy Virgin to obtain by her intercession and that of Aloysia, the grace of a good wind and to deliver us from these pirates.

Immediately I was heard: a strong wind came, a good breeze that was against them and took us beyond them. They were obliged to turn back. What joy for all of us! How much I have thanked the Heart of Jesus, Mary, my good mother, and Aloysia. These gentlemen also cried: "It is only God who could have delivered us from such great danger. We would have preferred shipwreck rather than to fall into their hands." Others said: "How can we thank God? The grace is too great, it silences us, it is impossible for us to express in words."

This is what happened that day. As for us, we were calm, tranquil, we laughed a lot and you see that the Lord came to our rescue. As I obtained that grace through the intercession of Aloysia, I promised that I would tell you and give you all the details.

26th good wind, beautiful weather; we entered the Gulf of Mexico. **27**[th] good wind, but very little. **28**[th] the same. **29**[th] fog, which prevented us from seeing the land of America; we did not run aground; it seemed unavoidable any moment, but the Lord again came to our aid; they were able to anchor the ship and we remained there until ten o'clock the next day. The pilot saw us and came to get us.

30th we are at the mouth of the Mississippi, but the wind is against us; we cast anchor to await a good wind. The pilot told us that the same pirates that we had seen, and from whom the Lord delivered us through the intercession of Aloysia, had a few days earlier taken an American ship. They had hanged the captain as well as the second in command, but they released the latter before he died and he was saved. They had shot the dining steward, then took everything that was on the ship; they left nothing, neither clothing nor food. All the men said: "We got out of there only by a miracle." They attributed this to our prayers, and we to Our Lady and Aloysia.

31st we are still at the mouth of the river; impossible to go up river.

February 1st a steamboat came from New York; seeing that the ship could be here a fortnight, we decided, as did all the passengers, to take the steamboat to go up river.

February 2nd we arrived in New Orleans at ten in the morning. Our good Mr. Nagliss, our mentor, took us quickly to the Ursuline sisters, who received us like their children. They were endlessly kind; we were overwhelmed by their care, by their foresight. Sister Xavier's soul is filled with joy; she has found several of these nuns who speak English. The Bishop [Dubourg], who happens to be here, came to see us an hour after our arrival. What joy to see that respected prelate! He quickly told us our destinations: "Sister Xavier, you are for Opelousas and Sister Lucile, I will take you with me to Florissant." I felt a great sorrow to be separated from my good Sister Xavier. It seemed to be Paul and Barnabas who were separated, if I can make that comparison, though we are far from them.[126] I will remain here more than a month to await the trip. Sister Xavier will leave at the first opportunity for Opelousas.

We are in very good health. America is our element. I am enchanted by the Americans, and I cannot pass over in silence that though we remained in the steamboat for twenty-four hours with more than fifty persons, we did not hear a single swearword. I admired their silence; if they spoke it was very quietly, with propriety, with refinement. They are amused with a nothing; they gave us much polite attention. When we entered the room, all rose, someone brought us a stool, another oranges, pineapples, etc. We had the first places at table everywhere. On the steamboat, they said the grace aloud; all were standing with their hats off. It was the captain who led the grace, but in the Protestant version; we

---

126 Acts 15:39.

said it as Catholics. I regretted that these good men, so perfect in their religion, were not Catholics.

Sunday February 3rd Bishop [Dubourg] preached in our chapel. There were many people. I admired the silence in the chapel. In the evening at five o'clock, it was full of young people and above all the Negroes. The rosary was said and all responded with such great fervor that I could not keep back my tears. I think that never in my life have I said my rosary so well. Afterwards the religious intoned a hymn, the congregation sang with us with all their heart, and I sang with all my voice and all my soul. The blessing followed; they remained a long time after in prayer. What is good here is very good, but there are the two extremes.

We just saw Father Martial a moment ago.[127] He told us that it is necessary to have more than supernatural prudence; one cannot say from the pulpit all that one wishes. New Orleans is a true Sodom, but it is not the same in Saint Louis. When one preaches to Catholics, they leave the church; immediately it is full of Protestants to whom he preaches in English. When they leave, they say: "What he tells us is very true."

Journal of the Crossing by Xavier Murphy[128]

New Orleans, February 6, 1822

S.C.J.M.

---

[127] Father Bertrand Martial, a secular priest, accompanied Philippine Duchesne and her companions on the *Rebecca* in 1818. Born in Bordeaux in 1770, he exercised his ministry in Saint Louis and New Orleans, where he died in 1832.

[128] From copy in A II 2 j, Box 3: *Lettres intéressantes*, cahier 1, pp. 293-302. Paisant L. 118, pp. 446-454. Other copies noted there. All surviving copies are French, though the original, like the one that follows, was in English and has not survived. It would have been quickly translated when it arrived in Paris (see comment to that effect near the end).

Anna Xavier Murphy, RSCJ (1793-1836)

Here we are, very dear reverend mother, safely disembarked on the American shore, after a delightful trip of fifty-five days. We are settled with the Ursulines, who are literally weighing us down with their kindness. But to tell you all my adventures since departure, here is a little story.

The seventh of December, at two o'clock in the morning,[129] we left the French shore under the auspices of the Sacred Heart (It was the first Friday of the month and the octave of my glorious patron [St. Francis Xavier]). We remained until 11, turning around the Bay of Biscaye, then at last we were completely on the open sea. As I contemplated its unlimited extent, I was filled with an astonishment and an admiration that I cannot express, but which brought me a delightful sensation. Nevertheless, a very strong wind thought it good to come greet us, and it continued to trouble us for three weeks. Everyone suffered.

I was sick for several days, but I was never afraid. Mother Lucile was afraid of dying, and nevertheless I couldn't help myself from laughing at her exclamations. She invoked all the saints in the calendar. Sometimes she thought she was so lost that she jumped from her bed and, like Moses, she stretched out her arms and cried "Mercy!" I was too sleepy to take the place of Aaron; I slept through the worst of the storm. I am sure that Mother Lucile wishes herself more than once on the hill of Sainte-Marie [d'En-Haut]. The chickens died by the dozens each day; the poor cow added to the number of victims and was thrown overboard. I try to imagine, dear mother, how you would have been to see this. If we had another week with such heat, all our living species would have perished. To avoid being sick, I remained on the bridge, enveloped in the captain's ample coat.

One day I saw the ship nearly swallowed up. The waves came so high and so quickly around our boat that the prow and the lower

---

129 Lucile's journal gives December 6 at four in the afternoon. That would refer to setting sail, and this to actually leaving the channel and setting out on open sea.

cabins were flooded; our room was well washed and in an expedited manner. You will agree, dear mother, that all this was very appropriate for Christmas time. I will tell you frankly, what this scene produced in me: it was a feeling of devotion more real than at the foot of the sanctuary, so true is it that for the shorn sheep, God measures the wind.

The 26th the wind changed; the following day, feast of Saint John the Evangelist, we saw the famous peak of Tenerife and the other Canary Islands; the calm kept us there twenty-four hours, so that the peak ceased to be a curiosity.

Sunday 30th we crossed the line [Tropic of Cancer]; we soon found ourselves in a very different climate; we had the Trade Winds that rarely change. The heat became so excessive that I could only wear a little skirt with dear Mother de Marbeuf's coat, which I did not decide to let go until after we had landed in Opelousas. The delight was continuous all the way to our arrival at the channel marker (That's where we left the ship to take a steamboat).

During the crossing, I was often ravished by the magnificent nature scenes visible at every hour; I could only contemplate them in an astonished silence and humble myself before the great author of so many marvels. I needed no book for meditation, because when one crosses the equator, the rising and setting sun is the greatest natural spectacle; then when the moon and the stars light the ocean with their silvery light, I was so carried away that I could not think of anything else. Surely if I had the misfortune to be unbelieving, such prodigies would have convinced me at once of the existence of a God. How often when I was looking at the polar star, I believed I was seeing my polar star, and I imagined hearing him reproaching me for so many faults that I have committed during the voyage. But I am forgetting, dear mother, that this is a journal and not a letter of spiritual direction.

January 16th we entered the Caribbean Sea and were opposite Saint-Domingue. How I thought of my dear Neline [Bruhier] and of all the horrors committed there.[130]

The 18th we had the island of Cuba in view; we sailed between it and the island of Jamaica; since that one is to the south, we could not discover Havana, which is situated to the north.

The 21st a contrary wind came to visit us again and lasted three days.

The 25th after leaving Cape Saint Anthony, we were pursued by a corsair; our deliverance was truly miraculous. They followed us for four hours. Nothing was as amusing as the agitation of the passengers. Everyone tried to hide what they had. I smiled every once in a while at their worry and fright; do you know, dear mother, why I was so peaceful? It is because my polar star assured me of the special protection of my adorable Spouse. Eh! What could a daughter of the Sacred Heart have to fear? My dear father's promise was so firmly engraved on my spirit that I had not an instant of malaise from the moment when I got on the ship, until the moment when I got off. They said I was a great sailor, but they [the passengers] hardly knew by whom I was sustained during the voyage; every night I slept in a profound tranquility, wearing on my heart the cross that he blessed, where I found all the resources that I needed, either for moments of danger or for temptations. But to return to our pirates, a light wind happily came to our help and put us out of their sight. We obtained that favor through the intercession of our Holy Mother Aloysia. All our company cried that our deliverance was miraculous and they attributed it to our prayers.

The 26th we crossed the line for the second time and found ourselves in the Gulf of Mexico. There we were tormented in turn by the agitation and the calm of the sea, which kept us several days.

---

130 Xavier refers to the long years of revolution in Saint-Domingue (Haiti) in the 1790s. Lucie-Celine Bruhier de Warvillier, RSCJ, was born there in 1791, entered the Society in Paris, and made vows in 1820; this is where Xavier would have known her. She died in Bordeaux in 1841.

The 29th feast of my good and very dear Saint Francis de Sales, we were close to the channel marker situated at the entrance of the Mississippi. We were in great anxiety when, all of a sudden, we saw arise a thick fog that lasted sixteen hours. We cast anchor to be sure, because we didn't know where we were.

The next morning, the fog dissipated and we had the pleasure of seeing the captain [river pilot] come on board. That happy event was followed by a northwest wind that stopped us for three days and probably would have for three weeks without our ability to get to the shore, if we did not have the good fortune to encounter the liner from New York, which led us in twenty-four hours to New Orleans.

But before leaving our vessel, the *Hector*, dear mother, I must give you some idea of its passengers and our situation on board. Our group was composed of twelve people,[131] mostly from New Orleans, and the rest from the northern United States. Among the latter, I had a compatriot; it was an elderly man full of good judgment and knowledge, and besides, a perfect Christian. He treated me like his daughter, and gave me salutary advice that my inexperience needed. Really, he was the greatest of mentors for me. He insisted that I speak French, which is as familiar to him as English. There was also a woman, whose death we awaited at any moment, but thanks be to God, we saw her off still alive. Since her arrival, she has received the Last Sacraments with the most edifying dispositions. The captain, an excellent man, gave us all sorts of attention at table. We were placed, my sister and I, at his right and his left; on days of abstinence, which we observed with no difficulties, he always had something sweet prepared for us.

---

131 The ship's log list contains seventeen names. The four minor children and two servants are probably not counted here, but the number still does not match unless the captain is counted. He played a large part in much of the conversation, especially at table. Also, Mr. Nagliss is not listed, unless by another name. See Appendix 2.

I can truly say that we were treated by all the passengers with the most distinguished deference, and I am completely charmed by the American character. I am not speaking of the southern part, but of the United States; they form a people that is very different; the former are as remarkable for luxury and indolence as the others are for the contrary virtues. During the whole crossing, I never heard swearing, nor even a voice too loud on the part of the sailors; and as for the conversations of these gentlemen, they were polite, reasonable and instructive.

Every morning before leaving my room, I greeted my guardian angel and my favorite saints, after the example of dear Mother de Marbeuf, asking them to obtain for me the grace to say or do nothing during the day contrary to the perfection that my identity imposes, and that I have seen is expected of us. One day, a French child said lightly: "O God!" The captain took it up, and asked me to know if this was a fault. Such is the American sensitivity to perfection.

The day that the pilot came on board, we all conversed with him, and imagine our terror and our gratitude at the same time, when we learned from him that the last fourteen ships that came to the port were visited by pirates and consequently robbed. They killed the captain and broke the mast of an English ship because they didn't want to give them their money right away, which they had hidden. After this story, I went back to my room to throw myself on my knees to say the *Te Deum*, and I felt with all its force the inappreciable happiness of belonging to *God alone*, who protected us so clearly and gave us refuge in the adorable sanctuary of his divine Heart, *Dominus custodit te.*[132]

On Friday, February 1, we had not yet risen from bed, when the steamboat was announced at a short distance; immediately all the passengers got ready to go to the bridge. We hoisted our American flag, and an hour later, the steamboat pulled up alongside. Mother

---

132 May the Lord keep you (Num 6:24).

Lucile and I got into the steamboat's launch under the protection of my compatriot, who took charge of everything and delivered us into the hands of the Ursuline superior. Can you believe, dear mother, what I felt when I left the ship? I had a sort of affection for it. I raised my heart to God, I asked pardon for the numerous faults committed in the last fifty-eight days. It is remarkable that we left France on a first Friday of the month, and that we entered America on the same feast day.

When we had embarked on the steamboat, which is a masterpiece of invention and a second Hotel de Biron (at least for the mirrors and gold trim), I found myself in a completely different world. There were about a hundred passengers, nearly all American and speaking only English. They were coming directly from Havana, and they had all the exquisite fruits of that country. They gave them to us in abundance, and I ate so many of them that my mentor, who missed nothing, forbade me to eat any more. How I would have liked to pass on some pineapples to my beloved sisters at the Hotel de Biron!

We were about a hundred people at dinner. Sister Lucile and I were placed next to the master of the boat, a Protestant minister. He said grace, during which everyone remained standing. I've never seen anything like the order and tranquility that reigned in that great assembly and everywhere. I assure you that in our novitiate at our recreations, the noise was much louder; in the evening at tea and at supper, the same order was observed.

When I went to bed, I noticed that Morpheus was not disposed to visit me, so I began to prepare my confession, and after an examen of the two months, I found that I needed to tell my story in English. After I arranged my conscience, I looked at my watch, and calculating the time it was in France, I united my intention with that of dear Father Perreau and I communicated in spirit with all my dear mothers and sisters of the house of Paris. It was the feast of the Purification; how I envied the holy old man Simeon.[133]

My disappointment was great when I saw the father of rivers, the Mississippi, so narrow, and the lands around it so low that they are sometimes inundated. When I remembered everything that M. de Chateaubriand said about the enchanting banks of the Mississippi, I had to remember that he was a poet who made an idealized description. The only thing I thought worth looking at were the fields close to the shore that were burned at night, which produces a magnificent effect, reflecting in the water like a mirror. They burn these fields to destroy the weeds.

Saturday morning at nine o'clock, we disembarked on the wharf at New Orleans; I had hoped that with the holy old man Simeon I could say: "*Nunc dimittis,*" etc. It wasn't like that; a different feeling took hold of me; all my friends in Europe suddenly crossed my mind and my heart fell like the pendulum on a clock. Nevertheless, I asked God to strengthen me and to accept the offering that the higher part of my soul was making; I united myself with the offering he himself made in the Temple; I also asked the Blessed Virgin to present me in the same way that she offered her child Jesus that day.

With these thoughts, I arrived at the convent, which is about forty yards from the port. I assure you, mother, that the first sight is not attractive for someone recently at the Hotel de Biron. The darkness of the cloisters frightened me. My compatriot asked for the superior and was told that she was dangerously ill. So he asked for her representative and the assistant came with a long veil very lowered. We were presented and she ordered the door opened. It was only the evening before that one of our sisters [Josephine Meneyroux] had left this house for Opelousas.

So finally, dear mother, here we are cloistered with the Ursulines, where I can only laugh at their quaint customs. I had

---

133 Luke 2:25-30.

scarcely arrived when I had the happiness to learn that the bishop was in the house, and we were quickly presented. I have never seen anyone with whom I could so easily get along; he filled me with such confidence that I imagined myself speaking with my polar star. I asked his permission to go to confession to him, he consented, and the next morning, he came very early; he told me he would be always for us, any time I wished to call on him. If I stay here for some time, I will ask him to make a retreat, in memory of that so memorable retreat of last year, of which though few in days, I will often think. At his first visit, he announced our destination, which, according to the Sacred Heart, is to be separated, after having for so long traveled together. Naturally, I feel this a little for Mother Lucile, who was full of attention and indulgence. I gave her more trouble than all the rest during the voyage, and nevertheless, she never complained and never seemed unhappy.

We were present yesterday evening for the elections in this community: the superior [Mother Gensoul], whose six years as superior were ending, was elected assistant, and Mother Saint-Joseph who was assistant, was elected superior. She is an older, delicate woman whose manners and appearance are completely different from the other. Thank God, we do not have this terrible annoyance of elections. They lack religious; they are sixteen in all, half of them old and infirm. They prefer Americans to French. The latter give them too much trouble.

She told me that I was destined to be an Ursuline, that I fit in so well with them, that I knew their Rules as if I were there for five years. But I answered them that I was born to be a Jesuit. They tried to get the bishop to let us spend Lent with them. But despite all their attention, that would not have pleased me and he [Bishop Dubourg] did not want to consent because he is now working on our departure. There is a coadjutrix sister here [Carmelite Landry] whom he praises highly; she is supposed to accompany me. She is in this house, but with his approval, she will leave it. There is also a charming boarder, fourteen years old who has been here since the age of five and who wants to join us. Today she wrote to her guardian to ask permission to come with me; she is American, but she speaks French as well as she does English. Another religious left with Mother Josephine [Meneyroux] and they say she will be a good acquisition.[134]

My companion wanted me to stay here until the arrival of a ship that left Bordeaux a day before us, because there is one of her friends on board who lives in Opelousas. It is a man of high status and member of the legislature of this country. When he learned in Bordeaux that we were coming to settle here, he said that he wanted to confide to us his two daughters. I told the bishop, who seemed delighted and said he was his close friend, but he did not want me to wait. I told him: "Bishop, I came from France, not only from France but Ireland, to be your obedient daughter; so do with me on every occasion what pleases you."

They have given me here many compliments on my good health; it is true, and I thank God. I have never been so well, except for five days on the ship. I am completely changed; I eat with an appetite like I have never had; I sleep very well, because I lose all the noise of the storm. Here, I take all the good things given to me in profusion and I follow all the observances except that of Friday, for which I have told them that I have no attraction, and besides, as a traveler, I claim an exemption. They find the winter extremely harsh; for us, it is light. The Mississippi at Saint Louis is entirely frozen over. The climate of Opelousas, although on the same river, is much lighter, and the countryside resembles Europe.

Our ship could not enter the river, which is extremely difficult to navigate upstream because the current is always very strong and prevents it. Our baggage is on board.

---

134 The "charming boarder" to whom she refers above is undoubtedly a certain Augustine; the coadjutrix sister who left with Josephine Meneyroux is a certain Adelaide; neither one would stay in the Society.

I have written to Mother Duchesne as you wanted. Sister Lucile is very happy about her destination. For me, it's all the same, wherever, as long as it is America.

So here, dear mother, is the journal that you ordered me to write, a little large so that my sisters who know English will be able to translate it easily. I hurried through in writing it like a hunter who fears to be chased, because the ship sails this evening, which is a great disappointment because I had hoped to have the pleasure of writing to my dear Father de McCarty [sic], to whom I have a thousand things to say. Dear mother, please tell him a thousand things for me and to dear Mother de Marbeuf, for you know how my heart feels for those two friends, whom I know well to appreciate, and say it to my sisters, about whom, even in another hemisphere, I feel often that our hearts are united in the Sacred Heart of Jesus. Thank you and them for your prayers that are happily brought to us. I ask you to continue them for the good of the Society to which I hope to be useful. I feel that I can do nothing but to say with the prophet: "When I was exalted, that is when I became humiliated and troubled."

Our profound respects to Fathers Perreau, Varin, and Barat. If my dear children are good, please, dear mother, embrace them for me.

Goodbye, very dear and reverend mother. I throw myself at your feet, I ask your blessing and embrace you with all my heart. Believe me to be your devoted daughter in the Heart of Jesus.

Anna Francis Xavier

The 1822 portion of this journal is given here.
The 1823 portion follows the 1822 letters.

Journal of Grand Coteau[135]
June 1822 to April 1823[136]

A.M.D.G

[*other handwriting*:] Grand Coteau 1822

June 22, 1822. The journal of April and May I sent to Paris by Madame Josephine [Meneyroux] who left the Grand Coteau for France the 29 of May 1822.[137]

June 6th: On the *fete de Dieu* [Corpus Christi] we had our procession before Mass at which several persons assisted – the *Repositoir* was tastefully arranged in the wood rear of the House. This was the first ceremony of the kind seen in this quarter of the Country. We had exposition [of the Blessed Sacrament] all day.

The 14th Feast of the Sacred Heart. Mother Gerard took the habit and Sister Mary (an American) [Layton] made her first vows. Before Mass the Chaplain said a few words on the *sweet feast* (not to be sure in the energetic warm style of our *Père* Varin) and on the several ceremonies that were going to take place. *Ensuite* at the usual hour Mother Eugenie *et moi*, united with *toute notre chère Société* in renewing those solemn engagements which we had made at the foot of the sanctuary had exposition all day, vespers at the usual hour, and *Salut* [Benediction] at ½ past 6, which terminated with a *Cantique* that so engaged priest and children that they continued singing until the bell of supper.

---

135 This is her own journal sent to the motherhouse, but beginning on June 6, 1822, the house journal, previously in French, begins to be written in English in a hand that is probably Xavier's. It continues in English until August 31, 1827, then resumes in French. The two journals record the same events, but are not identical.

136 Eight handwritten pages on legal size paper, covering June 1822 – April 1823. English original interspersed with occasional French: C-VII, 2 Box M-3, Env. Murphy, Anna Xavier. French translation: A-II, 2 g, Box 2 *Lettres intéressantes*, pp. 324-330. Partly in Paisant, L. 136, 166. Another partial copy A II 2 j, Box 3: *Lettres intéressantes,* cahier 1, pp. 325-327, Paisant L. 153, pp. 543-545.

137 This document has not survived, but it is probably the one for which Madeleine Sophie acknowledges receipt in her letter to Eugenie Audé of June 18, 1823.

On the **18**[th] our Chaplain [Fr. Jeanjean] took his *congé*, leaving us like the once solitary daughters of Jerusalem without priest or sacrifice.[138] For some days we were in expectance of the person whom the Bishop had at his visit of May formally introduced to the community (whom he assembled for the purpose) as our future chaplain [Valesano]—when behold, the first intelligence we got of him was that of his having sailed for France. When I heard it I said perhaps to escape the <u>torment of direction</u> – be it as it may, I hope he may be safely wafted to the gallic shores. The good *curé* of the adjoining parish which is 8 leagues off has taken pity on us. He comes to give us Mass as often as his multiple avocations. What a missioner this is. It was of him I gave the account in May.

July 19 Feast of St. Vincent de Paul. No <u>Mass</u>. Gave the prizes to our little externs - *apropos* I believe I have not described our extern school. It is about the size of the Novices Infirmary (at the Hotel de Biron) the *chiminée* occupies one side – on the other is the door which also serves as a window (as it is the only means by which light is given). Of course we have a hospitable appearance as the door is always open – in fine the whole is made of mud which the rats nearly destroy *malgré* the industry *de nos enfants* who each day fill up the holes made during the night. In this chamber I feel more real content than if I were an inhabitant of the Tuileries. A few days ago one of the externs brought a large bale of worstead [*sic*] – and presenting it without preface says "M. Xavier, my cousin says will you knit her some socks" – I laughingly told the girl that even if I had the time I did not have here, there is no occasion for *point cérémonie, s'il vous plaît*.

The 22nd – Sweet *fête de notre chère Mère Barat* – during this day of remembrance how often did my spirit bound to the Hotel de Biron, there mingling with the idolizing group I embraced and offered <u>this</u> cherished, <u>this</u> Venerated Mother the best and ardent wishes of my heart, which never ceases to repeat: may she last <u>long</u>

---

138 Luke 23:28; Dan 3:38.

long. May she continue to constitute the pride and delight of our little Society – No Mass – in fine no exterior memento whatever to celebrate it – but the first Communion I shall have the happiness of making will be undoubtedly for her.

The 26th Feast of St. Anne *(jour de ma naissance)* No Mass but every privation has a *je ne sais quoi pour moi* in this cherished land of my adoption A.M.D.G.

The 31st Feast of our dear holy Father – had the consolation of having Mass consequently paid my debt to *notre chère Mère Barat* – The postulant [Carmelite Landry] who came with me from New Orleans took the habit. She is Creole and a valuable subject – this soil if cultivated could produce excellent fruit and will ere long, I hope, form a bright gem in our little Society. This idea at times transports me when I see the children commence to feel a devotion to the dear *Coeur de Jésus*. AMDG.

August 3rd The examens which finished the same day the following day (Sunday) the prizes were given at which our good friend the *curé* and Mrs. Smith assisted. They were highly pleased with a little piece which the children repeated extremely well.

The 7th What a memorable day – just as we were going to breakfast arrived our *digne mère* provincial[139] accompanied by *une Dame* [Emily Saint-Cyr] *et une Soeur Coadjutrice* [Mary Mullanphy][140] both young – the day after the children went home for the vacation which lasts 15 days – their absence procured us the delightful gratification of being entirely *avec notre chère chère mère*. How I did look with pleasure at this cherished mother whom for years I had been accustomed to see in spirit. She had the mortification of

---

139 This was Philippine Duchesne. There were no provincials in the Society at this time, but Philippine had been given some powers other than local superior, because of the distance from Paris.
140 They had left Saint Louis on July 20. The choir religious, Emily Saint-Cyr, had just made her first vows on July 19. The coadjutrix novice, Mary Mullanphy, was a distant relative of their Saint Louis patron John Mullanphy. She did not remain in the Society.

being without Mass the Sunday after her arrival – "But the just one lives by Faith"[141] – the only nourishment congenial to this climate.

22nd The return of our children who appeared quite satisfied at their being restored to us. *Mère* Duchesne read the rules for the *rentrée* of the class. Made the appointments etc.

25th Feast of Saint Louis – Sunday – no Mass – *fiat fiat*.

29th *Jour de la naissance* of *mère* Duchesne – no Mass – but she passed the entire day at the foot of the altar in the sweet sanctuary of the Heart of Jesus where she reconsecrated that valuable life pour l'A.M.D.G. It was at the recreation at night she told us she had that day accomplished her 53rd year. On account of not knowing it we were deprived the pleasure of expressing the sentiments which such an event necessarily excited in the hearts of her children – may her valuable life be <u>long long</u> preserved, may she live to see her children's children's peace established in America.[142]

September 2[nd][143] *Notre chère mère* left us. Judge of our feelings on the occasion but it is unworthy *une fille de Sacré Coeur* to express them. *Dieu Seul – Ita Pater.*

September 14th *Mère* Duchesne left New Orleans where she was obliged to go to take the Steam boat for Saint Louis – may the Heart of Jesus waft her safely to her destination.

28th Our long looked for Chaplain arrived, an Italian a Lazarite he was seized by the epidemic fever 10 days after his arrival. Once more were we deprived of Mass on a Sunday. During the 4 months that we were without a Priest we were but 5 Sundays deprived of Mass owing to the zeal and goodness of the *bon curé* who never failed giving us Mass one day in each week. Heard our Confessions and the Sundays that we had not Mass was in consequence of his being obliged to say it in the church after which he had 9 leagues to go to say his second Mass in his own Parish.

November 1st We had high Mass – exposition all day –

---

141 Hab 2:4.
142 Ps 128:6.
143 The manuscript seems to give 3rd or 9th, but the house journal gives the 2nd.

2nd No Mass the priest was obliged to say it in the church – this was a practice for the Souls in purgatory.

December 8th Feast of the Immaculate Conception had High Mass – exposition for the day – *salut* [Benediction] in the evening – after which a little altar tastefully arranged was placed at the foot of the sanctuary. *Nos enfants* entered two & two holding in one hand an olive branch as a link between them – in the other a lighted taper – the act of consecration was audibly read by one of them *ensuite* a *Cantique* with the Chaplet which terminated this interesting ceremony.

25th Feast *de Noel* – had *la grande Messe et Sermon* at *minuit* all of which lasted until 3 o'clock. You may suppose we had no objection to go to bed after – all did except *Mère* Eugenie who remained before the Blessed Sacrament which was exposed all night and during the day until the *Salut* [Benediction] in the evening – at 7 o'clock in the morning had the second Mass – at 9 vespers and at the usual hour *Salut*. The Chaplain with Mrs. Smith remained all night; one slept in the parlor – the other in the class. There were 26 persons communicated in our little chapel among whom were several black men and women. There was a crèche tastefully fixed up which seemed to have excited universal devotion.

27th Saint John the Evangelist, everything corresponding with a feast of the first class – often I thought of my *chère chère amies de Paris* and of dear Neline who made her first vows on this sweet day. She is now in possession of the emblem of our Society.

29th No bread for breakfast but the strong nourishment of doing the will of God and of promoting his glory gives here a *je ne sais quoi* to all our privations.

The 1823 portion of this journal continues after the letters of 1822, starting on the next page.

LETTERS

1822

Xavier Murphy to Madeleine Sophie Barat [written by L. Mathevon][144]

I am writing for Sister Xavier. She is dictating.

New Orleans, March 11, 1822

My very dear Mother,

Here I am, greatly impeded because I do not find it possible to open my heart to you. I have many things to tell you, and I hope that when I reach my destination, I will be able to speak heart to heart with you.

I made a ten-day retreat with the bishop [Dubourg] whom I love very much; he is after my heart. I made this retreat as an anniversary of the splendid retreat that my pole star[145] gave us. Since I came down from the mountain, I have been very busy, and I find myself completely centered. I am already quite accustomed to this country and I breathe only *Ad majorem Dei gloriam*, although I am obliged to say with the prophet, "Lord, I cannot speak, I am like an infant,[146] I need you to pray for me, you know all my faults."

---

144 French autograph. Sent at the same time as letter from Lucile Mathevon of the same date. Copy GASSH CIII USA Foundation, Box 2: *Lettres de la Basse Louisiane,* vol 2 (1822-1827), p. 76. Paisant L. 122, p. 463. Cf. for other copies.
145 Her spiritual director during her novitiate, Nicolas Tuite MacCarthy, S.J. (1769-1833), known in France as Abbé de Lévignac. He grew up among the nobility in France, was ordained in 1814, joined the Jesuits, and was a renowned preacher.
146 Jer 1:6.

And the bishop has found that I did nothing during my novitiate; I answered that all my thoughts were about America. I promised that I would turn a new leaf for the future.

Farewell, very dear mother. I embrace you with all my heart and with all my soul, as well as dear Mother de Marbeuf.

I am at your feet, your daughter entirely devoted in the Heart of Jesus.

Xavier.

Xavier Murphy to Madeleine Sophie Barat[147]

S.S.C.J.M.
Convent of the Sacred Heart
Grand Coteau May 17, 1822

Here I am, my very dear and reverend mother, in the joy of my heart now completely enrolled under the standard of St. Ignatius, finally a spouse of the Heart of Jesus always and forever–on the fourteenth of this month, our reverend Bishop gave me the symbol of our dear Society.[148] But a little history is needed to explain how it happened.

Last Sunday, the bishop arrived. Monday I had a private visit with him when he decided that I would make my profession the following day so that I would be his first daughter of the new world. He also decided that I would make my vows in English. The same day, we had the First Communion of the niece of Mrs. Smith. She and the father of one of our children (and another gentleman) were confirmed; all the ceremonies were done at Mass. Undoubtedly Mother Eugenie will have given details of all the circumstances

---

147 French autograph GASSH CVII 2 A. Paisant L. 133, pp. 491-92. See note there for further copies.
148 Anna had left Paris without making her final profession, which she made at Grand Coteau on May 14, 1822.

of this truly interesting day. You know, dear mother, that I am not able to relate them to you. But in this solemn moment, what a range of feelings I experienced when I spoke your name! And at the moment when I embraced our little community, in spirit I prostrated myself at your feet and it seemed to me that once again you embraced your poor Xavier with all my dear mothers and sisters of the Hotel Biron.

My dear mother, since I have been here I have experienced a great combat between the inferior and superior parts of my soul, a distaste for everything, not at all my usual facility for prayer. In a word, deprived of any space for consolation on the part of the Creator and creatures, but the sweet certitude of doing the will of God enhances all my privations. I try in all things to act according to the promises I have made to my dear pole star, "to do everything against nature," and to act only according to the spirit of faith.

I discussed all these things with the bishop in confession and outside of confession. He assured me that I need not have any concern, having done what God asked of me, because he tested me in many ways. He was satisfied that all was well with me.

Farewell very dear mother, pray for your poor Xavier who embraces you with all her heart and with all her soul. I have written a journal in English that I will send you by opportunity.[149] I am at your feet, your child entirely devoted in the Heart of Jesus.

Anne Françoise Xavier

---

[149] This is presumably the journal of the voyage (Paisant L. 118), for she notes in the next journal, that of June-July 1822, that she sent the previous one for April and May with Josephine Meneyroux, who left Grand Coteau May 29, 1822, to return to France. That journal of the crossing is preserved in at least two English copies and a French translation.

[*On the outside:*]
>To Mother Barat
>Superior General
>of the Religious of the Sacred Heart
>At Paris

[*On the fold of the envelope:*]
Dear Mother,
I would like for you to write a few lines to the Ursulines in New Orleans. They would be flattered. I told them that I would let you know about the death of their superior, Mother Saint-Michel, whom they ardently recommend to your prayers, as well as their house, to all the Society. It is Mother de Saint-Joseph who is now superior. They often send presents here to our Mother Duchesne, and when I was in New Orleans they made me promise to ask them for anything I needed.

Xavier Murphy to Madeleine Sophie Barat[150]

SS.CC.J.M.

>Opelousas
>27 August 1822

Behold, dear mother, your prediction already accomplished: the 7th of this month, I had the sweet consolation of embracing our dear Mother Duchesne. You can easily understand my delight on this occasion. Like the old Simeon, I would almost have said that I had nothing more to desire and that I was content to finish my pilgrimage.[151] I had made a novena to the Sacred Heart of Jesus that she would arrive.

---

150 French autograph GASSH CVII 2 A. Paisant L. 137, pp.503-504. See there for further copies.
151 Luke 2:29.

I needed to speak and open my heart to someone in whom I had confidence. [several lines scratched out, but recoverable:] ~~because unfortunately I have none in Mother Eugenie, whose character is so completely opposite of mine that I had distaste for the Rules that I so esteemed and admired under your government. When I tried to act in opposition to what I felt in my heart, she seemed happy with my conduct, but that did not put my conscience in peace, which at several points I found guilty, and that was still the source of my unease.~~

However, even in that state I found that there is no sacrifice that I would not make for the greater glory of God, no privation that I would not endure in this dear land of my adoption. But the fear of offending God and of breaking the solemn promises that I made at the foot of the sanctuary alarmed me. But Mother Duchesne to whom I disclosed my thoughts eased my fears. She understood me in English, and never have I opened myself with greater facility, and never felt greater peace and consolation than when she gave me her decision. She is a woman totally after my own heart.

With regard to prayer, dear mother, I could not apply myself. This trial began before my departure from Paris; it has grown since I have been here and now I am at the point of finding myself a statue. The only inclination that I experience in that state of dereliction, is to offer myself with Jesus Christ abandoned in the garden and on the cross, repeating with him: *May your will be done in time and in eternity*. However, I perceived that when in prayer I found myself in a state of apathy, when it is finished, I find myself full of vigor to carry out my duties and more courageous to do everything against nature.

I have written in English and our dear Mother Duchesne translated my letter and will send it to you.[152] I have written to you and to Mother de Marbeuf and my dear pole star by Madame

---

152 The autograph of this letter is, however, in French, in a hand and a style much more similar to Xavier's than to Philippine's.

Josephine [Meneyroux]. I received letters from Mother Bigeu and Neline. With old dates; they had not received the journal that I wrote on my arrival in New Orleans. I am really disappointed that they do not have boarders; we have 16 here and more are announced. Mother Duchesne will give you details about our little establishment.

Dear, dear mother, pray for your poor child who embraces you most respectfully, as well as my dear Mothers de Marbeuf and de Gramont, and finally all the mothers and sisters of the Hotel Biron.

I am in the Sacred Heart of Jesus, your

Xavier

A thousand greetings for Fathers MacCarthy, Varin and Perreau.

1823

Continuation of Journal[153]

January 1823 The last day of the year had the examines *le jour [de] l'an* gave the prizes. *Nos enfants* were ornamented with the trophies of their industry by the Chaplain and our good friend the *curé* of the adjoining parish. Our revered foundress who joined in decorating the interesting little group of whom she seemed to exclaim by her approbationary look of satisfaction: *Voilà mes bijeux et ma plus belle parure* – But the most amusing part of the ceremony was the description the children gave of their feelings at the moment the crowns were placed on their heads. One says "Indeed, Mother Xavier, I thought when the crown was put on my head that I was going <u>right up</u> to Heaven." Often I think how charmed *chère chère Mère* Barat would be with the native simplicity of the children here. I lately desired them to pray that I may obtain a favor I wanted

---

153 Handwritten English interspersed French. For complete information, see 1822 journal, above.

– they lost no time and at their return from Mass some of them call out, "Mother Xavier, I asked of God to grant you what you desired except that you wished to die, and in that case I told him not to grant your request." They often tell me that they have vocations, to which I answer that they must eat & learn a great deal more before I believe it – tho' I do really believe at present there are a few whom the Heart of Jesus has selected to bide in his adorable Sanctuary.

March 30th On Wednesday in Holy week the retreat for the first Communicants commenced, 15 boarders & 5 externs. The later [sic] remained entirely in the house *tout ensemble* (you know in this Country there is no distinction, all are equal). *Nos enfants* appeared to have the fervor of angels. After receiving absolution they all entered the class and on their knees asked pardon, not satisfied with this (which was a great effort for the American character) they requested to kiss the feet of a few of their companions to whom they had given most pain. This had a great effect on the others – On the happy morning all rose (if not glorious at least they did triumphant) to meet their Saviour. Our little little chapel was most tastefully arranged by *Mère* Eugenie who is *au fait* at everything in this way. At the Gospel, the Chaplain turned to address his little doves, whose appearance so affected him that he commenced by tears – this had a good effect at the moment – when the favored time after which they for days sighed came, all approached in order and recollection – for my part it was one of the happiest moments of my life to witness which I would cross the 5 oceans. In the evening *avant salut* the usual ceremony of the Baptismal Vows was *selon notre usage* performed. Some of them expressed themselves in a manner so touching that all were affected. Once more the Chaplain addressed them on the solemn engagements they had so feelingly so sacredly ratified.

On Tuesday morning they reentered the class weeping after their dear solitude – all the other children with one voice demanded, when will they be permitted to participate in a similar happiness.

How consoling – how gratifying *à notre chère chère Mère* Barat this account must be. See what a people she has formed – even in another Hemisphere are the rising generation taught to lisp the praises of her whose panegyric has been already pronounced – "Let her works praise her in the gates."[154]

April 6th Low Sunday. My black men and women made their first Communion. But one of my little boys was old enough – they all came after Church to thank and tell me how happy, happy they felt – this you will easily conceive was mutual on both sides. I brought them into our little chapel to renew their Baptismal vows. I hope by Pentecost to have another band and to have them all ready to present *notre digne Eveque* at his visit to make them perfect Christians. Some time ago *un petit frère d'un de nos enfans* came with his mamma *pour voir sa Soeur*. *Mère* Eugenie was in the salon and seeing this *petit bon homme* tormenting his sister, she asked him what he desired. "To see Mother Xavier, for she will teach me my Catechism." But, said his sister, this is Mother Eugenie; won't she do – "Oh, no, Mother Eugenie is very good for girls, but Mother Xavier for the boys." So *Mère* Eugenie came to call me saying there is a little boy who absolutely says he must see you. *Apropos* to boys, our worthy Foundress [Mrs. Smith], not content with all she has done for the Church, is now planning an establishment for the education of Boys. No final arrangement has yet been made, but I think it will be the Lazirites who will be changed with it. With justice the Bishop calls her the pillar of his Church. She is in the joy of her heart at seeing *notre maison* increasing. It seems to be her pride & her glory – did *notre chère Mère* Barat know her she would be embalmed [fascinated] with her – she is indeed *une femme de Foi*. Had I time, *ou plûtot le moyen*, [I] would send you a sketch of her life which is both remarkable and edifying – she is a convert *mais voilà une histoire courte – pour un bon curé nous a dit que souvent il avait aperçu un vieux homme*

---

154 Prov 31:31.

entre l'église pendant le jour mais jamais pour la Messe. Il lui dit, Mon ami, pourquoi ne venez-vous pas à la Messe? Connaissez-vous Jésus-Christ, le Saint Esprit, etc.? "Moi je connais pas de tout ces jeunes Dieux. Je connais et je prie seulement à mon vieux vieux bon Dieu que je connais toujours."[155]

April 9th *Je suis dans la joie de mon âme en voilà pourquoi. Monseigneur notre digne Evêque en a accordé par le Congrès 200,000 francs – et 100,000 arpens de terre pour les mission chez les Osage (tribu de sauvages). Aussi 4 Jésuites pour cette grande œuvre. Savez-vous que nos Pères ont à Washington un établissement superb.*[156] It is the oldest Catholic literary establishment in the U States and has been raised by Congress to the rank of an University and empowered to confer degrees in any of the faculties. There are at present 26 Fathers, 45 scholastics in the different branches and 22 lay brothers – about 20 miles from Washington they have a probationary House. How delighted I was on hearing the sweep and indefatigable labour of the sons of St Ignatius, illustrious even in the New World. The Bishop has passed all the winter at Washington for a Synod called by the Archbishop on his return from Rome, invested with the power of Legate.

I believe I have not mentioned how we are with regard to spiritual matters – have mass every day, sometimes 2 (when the good *curé* comes) – exposition all the days appointed *par le règle. Salut tous le dimanche et fêtes. Tous va bien dans le Coeur Sacré de Jésus.*[157] Since the 1st Communion we have lost one *de nos enfans*. She was

---

155 But here is a short story. A good pastor told us that often he saw an old man enter the church during the day but never for the Mass. He said to him "Friend, why do you not come to Mass, do you know Jesus Christ, the Holy Spirit etc.?" "Me, I do not know all these young Gods. I know and I pray only to my old, old good God whom I have always known."

156 I am overjoyed and this is why. Our reverend bishop has been granted by Congress 200,000 francs and 100,000 arpents [approximately the same as acres] of land for a mission to the Osages (an Indian tribe), also 4 Jesuits for this great work. Do you know that our Fathers have a superb establishment in Washington?

157 ...by the rule – Benediction all the Sundays and Feasts. All goes well in the Sacred Heart of Jesus.

quickly replaced by one who has not yet made hers. *Nos enfans sont* 27 children and 6 or 7 announced for the next month. *Les dames Ursulines* have got a valuable reinforcement from Canada: 5 professed religious and 3 postulants all Veterans in age and Religion they are preparing to inhabit their new establishment. Our Community consists of 7 – 5 *dames et 2 soeurs.* We want a few more + I think there are a few vocations *parmi nos enfans mais ells sont trop jeune pour déterminer.*[158]

Adieu ma [sic] *très très chères Mères et Sœurs. Je vous embrasse de tout mon âme et de tout mon cœur.*[159] If I could gratify myself I would write to several but the time not the inclination deprives me of this sweet consolation. I hope some person will translate this for *chère Mère Barat.* I recommend to your prayers 2 Protestant children – one of them has already asked Papa for permission to be Baptized; he refused but *le Coeur de Jésus* will arrange that *comme toutes les autres choses de notre petite Société.*[160]

A.M.D.G.

Xavier

Xavier Murphy to Madeleine Sophie Barat[161]

SS.C.J.M.

(N° 3)
Grand Coteau [2] March 1823

Your esteemed letter of September, dear and reverend mother, filled me with the sweetest joy and consolation. Truly in reading

---

158 ...among our children but they are too young to decide.
159 Good-bye, my very dear mothers and sisters. I embrace you with all my soul and with all my heart.
160 Like all the other things of our little Society.
161 French autograph GASSH CVII 2 A. Paisant L. 164, pp. 570-71. See there for further copies.

it I felt that I was your child, and a child devoted to you and to our dear Society.

I hope that the letter I confided to Mother Duchesne reached you. Since that good mother left I find myself in general more at ease, even though I experience difficulties with obedience. [*Crossed out:*] ~~My confessor grants me daily communion, however I do not feel sensible devotion; I am in the desert, without even being alone with God. If you remember our last conversation, I told you that God willed for me a life of sacrifice; it is, you know, the promise that I made to Father McCarthy, to do everything against nature.~~

Perhaps Mother Duchesne told you all the roles she gave me, and I am not able to fulfill them. My principal work is with the children, who give me the greatest satisfaction; even in times when I was weakened by fever, when I entered the class I felt a strength that sustained me and that grace I attribute to the merits of the vows. All my attraction is for religious instruction; we have several Americans who give me occasion to give myself to that occupation dear to my heart. I also have black men and women with the little boys.

I am sending you my journal in English; to give you pleasure. I wish that it was in French, but the difficulty that I experience in expressing myself in that language makes me stay away from it.[162]

If my little Irish girls merit your consideration, please embrace them tenderly for me. Good Mother de Marbeuf gave me all the details of the precious part of the Society that the ocean separates from us. Dear, dear mother, pray for your poor child and for the young plants that you have confided to me; since I lack light for myself, I ought to be blinder yet for others. So supply, dear mother, for what I lack, for the Heart of Jesus is not able to refuse you anything.

Perhaps several months will pass before you receive this letter, however, receive, dear and worthy mother, the tender and sincere

---

162 This would have to be the journal of 1822, as that of 1823 goes into April.

wishes which we all have for your precious health and your happiness. I embrace dear Mother de Gramont and all my mothers and sisters, with all the affection of my soul.

I am at your feet, your child totally devoted in the Sacred Hearts of Jesus and Mary.

Xavier

[*On the outside:*]
To Madame
Madame Barat, Superior General
of the Religious of the Sacred Heart
In Paris

Since I sealed this letter, I have had the sweet consolation of receiving an inimitable letter from my dear Father MacCarthy. Dear mother, if you could see it, you would be like me full of gratitude for that precious proof of his friendship. Please have the goodness to thank him for your Xavier.

Madeleine Sophie Barat to Eugenie Audé, June 18, 1823, excerpt:[163]
P.S. I embrace your dear daughters, especially Sister Xavier; tell her that I have just received her packet of letters and her journal. Please tell her to continue doing it. I did not see the gentleman who brought this mail. Unfortunately, he put all these letters in the post at Le Havre, which made for considerable expense. Try to avoid this for us by recommending to the people to whom you entrust your mail to wait or look for opportunities to get it to us.

---

163 French autograph. GASSH.

1824

Xavier Murphy to Madeleine Sophie Barat[164]

Grand Coteau, May 4, 1824

Here I am in the joy of my soul and my heart, face to face with my very dear and honored mother general. Though I am no doubt the last to congratulate you on your establishment, nevertheless I dare to assure you that no one has in it a more fervent joy.

I received the little note that Mother Prevost wrote to me on your part. Be sure, dear mother, that I will do everything in my power to conform to your intentions. I am never so happy as when I know them. I am very consoled in thinking that in general I have acted according to your desires, even in acting contrary to nature, the only cause of all my difficulties. If only I could now follow my inclination and speak heart to heart with you, dear mother, what happiness it would be for your child! But you know that only with great difficulty can I arrange my thoughts in French.

In spite of all the difficulties and all the privations that I have experienced since I am here. I would not, however, change my situation with the happiest person in the world. Each day the love of my state and my predilection for this dear country grows. Though our children are ignorant, simple, and rustic, they have a certain frankness and docility that pleases me very much. They love us and we love them. In general, the parents are content with our house, but they are so constrained now by bad harvests that this impedes them giving us their children. We have 24 at the moment: ten have already left us. Nearly all made their First Communion with us.

I have just written to Mother Duchesne to invite her to make us a little visit this summer and to arrange with her some little

---

164 French copy in copybook *de la Basse Louisiane*, pp. 33-35. GASSH.

business about the establishment projected for us on the river [Saint Michael]. This good mother is full of goodness for me. She has often proposed to me (for the reason that you know) to change house, but thanks to God, I have always said <u>no</u>, even though my heart says <u>yes</u>. But I thought that if I left this establishment, it might hurt it, and I love our dear Society too much to do something that could have negative consequences. Besides that, I sense that God is asking this sacrifice of me in order to eliminate my too strong sensibility and my attachment to nature and independence. I feel that our good Master asks of me a great submission and an absolute stripping of my own judgment; in effect, a life of faith and prayer. In spite of all my infidelities, I have the happiness of receiving Communion every day except those on which I go to confession. It is in this divine sacrament that I find my strength, my light, and my consolation.

I do not know if I can hope that this letter reaches you before the time of your dear feast. Allow me, dear reverend mother, to offer you all the sentiments of which my heart is capable on this beautiful day, when my spirit and all my affection will be at dear Hotel Biron.

I count on having the pleasure to write to *my dear star*. His advice is my compass in these vast deserts. No doubt, the Holy Spirit guided his pen in his last letter.

My respects, please, to our Fathers Varin and Perreau. I embrace tenderly all my dear mothers and sisters, and I beg them to recommend me often to Our Lord. Like my holy patron, here I am, dear mother, on my knees to ask for your prayers and you blessings. Believe me to be, very dear mother general,

Your child completely devoted
in Corde Jesu
Xavier Murphy

Xavier Murphy to Madeleine Sophie Barat[165]

Grand Coteau, May 29, 1824

I have just received your letter, very dear and venerated mother. I find myself at this moment so full of gratitude for all the affection that you have for me that I truly do not know how to express it. Yes, dearly beloved mother, I want to consecrate to this God of my heart, and to the glory of the Sacred Heart, my <u>soul</u>, my spirit, and all my <u>being</u>. I only regret that I have nothing worthy to offer him, but this God who is so great is pleased with our littleness and draws his glory from our impotence. Truly, dear mother, when I think of all the graces that I have received since my entrance into the dear Society, I cry out: "Lord, if I do not love you after everything that you have done for me, what will happen to the glory of your name."

You speak, dear mother, of the sweetness that there is in suffering for our spouse. You are very right, and the spirit of faith teaches us that the secret of happiness in the religious life is there, but nature still acts too powerfully in me to taste this delicious teaching. If I had been more faithful about renouncing the sensitivity of my self-love, I would be more worthy to be the child of Mother Barat.

I will not tell you anything about our very little house. Mother Eugenie will give you all the details, except that <u>peace</u>, <u>union</u>, and <u>affection</u> reign among us. I find in the example of my mother and sisters enough to humiliate me every day. You know, dear mother, that there are many things in me that make me capable of causing myself difficulties, but God is good and compassionate towards this poor soul who is so weak.

Mother Eugenie will also tell you also about the establishment on the river that Mother Duchesne, following your intentions,

---

165 French in copy book *de la Basse Louisiane,* pp. 40-41. GASSH.

had decided to refuse, but several of our friends are of a contrary opinion. God will arrange if all for A.M.D.G. You also speak, dear mother, of coming to the New World, but you will never come here. <u>You will remain to announce the works of God to Jacob, the laws of his lands, and his judgments to Israel</u>.[166] You are already mother of a numerous generation. With what joy, what delight, what satisfaction we receive the news of the rapid growth of our dear Society, and that the boarding school in Paris is so numerous. Here we go slowly in our progress, but I hope, even against all hope, that the Sacred Heart will one day be known and adored along the banks of the Mississippi and the Ohio for A.M.D.G.

> A little remembrance from me to our Fathers Varin, Barat, and Perreau.
> Believe me, dear mother, in the Sacred Hearts of Jesus and Mary
> Your completely devoted child,
> Xavier

1825

Xavier Murphy to Madeleine Sophie Barat[167]

S.S.C.J.M.   Grand Coteau, October 16, 1825

I hope, my very dear and much loved mother general, that you have received my little note of the month of July. A month has passed since <u>fate is cast</u>, because our recent orders have been announced by Mother Duchesne, though they are the most painful that I have ever experienced, nevertheless, since you judge me appropriate for this charge, may your will be done entirely in my regard.[168] You and

---

166 Loose paraphrase of Ps 78:5.
167 French autograph. GASSH.
168 Eugenie Audé and five companions set out for the foundation of St. Michael on

Anna Xavier Murphy, RSCJ (1793-1836)

you alone, dear and worthy mother, know the depth of my heart, because it has not changed since I left you, and in spite of all my faults and infidelities, I have no other desire than to devote myself <u>soul</u> and <u>body</u> to the glory of the Sacred Heart and for the good of our <u>dear, dear Society</u>. But dear mother, [crossed out] ~~I have three character faults that I easily repeat: pride, sensibility, and~~ timidity, but God will be faithful in my regard and I have for guarantee of his fidelity the union that I contracted with Jesus Christ, and I hope even against hope that your maternal goodness and your zeal for the salvation of these little souls of the country (who so often say your name with gratitude), that you will send someone appropriate to take my place (or if you judge that I should keep it), someone able to direct me and help me and above all capable of communicating in French, because at present there is no one of my sisters capable of that, and the major part of our children are Creoles.

It is quite probable that the house cannot sustain itself unless Providence does a miracle in its favor, but I think that a mother from France could do all here. Mother Eugenie has chosen the best subjects in each house for the new establishment. In a few days they will leave from here: 2 choir religious, 2 sisters and 3 little novices (who have been boarders), one carrying your name, consequently she is not the least dear to us because of that. Here we are six; the aged Sister Marguerite is among the number and the only French woman. I am very happy to have her. She is a saint, she loves much, and her delight is to speak of you, dear and worthy mother and of our dear Society.

Mother Eugénie is making all the arrangements before her departure. That is better because she knows much more than I do. I know nothing about government, money, expenses, etc., but above all about direction. Finally, dear Mother, I fear not having the spirit of our dear Society, so pray that the Heart of Jesus will give me the graces that I need.

October 25, 1825. Xavier Murphy was named new superior at Grand Coteau.

I wish to know, reverend mother, if you think that the little Irish woman (Marguerite Scollard) from whom I received a letter recently saying that she wishes to be a religious of the Sacred Heart, would be good for this country. I know that her family have had great confidence in me. Perhaps they will give her permission to come to join me. Tell me, dear mother, in your answer. At present I hope that you will give me the consolation of writing to me often, because it will certainly be sweet to receive advice from a <u>mother of the heart and soul</u>.

I prefer that your letters and the other objects that are designated for this house be directed to my address because they will arrive more <u>quickly</u> and more <u>surely</u> from New Orleans, with which we have many and frequent connections.

We recently had a visit from the Bishop [Dubourg]; he gave the cross to two of our sisters, Carmelite [Landry] (the former Ursuline) and Mary Layton, the first novice received in America. The two remain with me. They are excellent subjects suitable for several things but not at all for teaching and that is the most essential thing here.

It is more than a month that your nephew has been with us and he is very well.[169] The Bishop said to me about him: "See Father D. who was so eager to join you in America." And what a delight! What a pleasure! To see one of your family among us. He gives us all the news of our dear Society. The other day, speaking of yourself, dear, dear mother, he said: "Ah! My aunt has spoiled you, Mother Xavier." He is right, because if I could remain with you, dear mother, I would be too happy in this life and would be well in the other, and this privation is for all who left you for this country. They cannot await Mother Barat here, but God alone without any

---

169 Louis Dusaussoy (1794-1873), son of Sophie's sister Marie Louise, joined the Jesuits when they were restored in France in 1814, left them in 1822, came to America in 1825, and returned to France in 1829. He later returned for a short time and was chaplain of the house in New York in 1856, before once again returning to France.

other support, and what happiness to be entirely his, but for that it is necessary, it seems to me, that I expand myself a little more, but my heart had to tell you so that, in effect, you can hold the secret.

In a few days your nephew will leave to rejoin the bishop, who thinks a great deal of him. Every night he gives instructions to our children, who are eager to surround him afterwards. He is obliged to tell them "Enough."

[On the outside]
Many, many more things to offer to all my mothers and sisters. Ask them to pray for my needs, also my dear Fathers <u>Varin</u>, <u>Perreau</u>, and Barat. Dear mother, since I lack light for myself I must be even more blind for others. Make up for my negligence. I hand over to you this house and the <u>young saplings</u>. Be our <u>mediatrice</u> with the Heart of Jesus (who can have a similar role). On my knees like my <u>great patron</u>, I ask your prayers and your blessing. Think sometimes of your devoted child in *Cor Jesu,*

Xavier

To No. 3 Madame
Madame Barat Superior General
of the Religious of the Sacred Heart
Hotel de Biron
Rue Varennes No. 45
Paris

My children let me breathe, because one is taken by the hand and another by the vest. They have a charming simplicity. During our little vacation he gave us a retreat. I went to confession to him as in Europe. I often said, <u>no, never</u>. I wrote on that occasion to my <u>dear star</u> because it would be sorrow for me if he were ill. I hope that the Heart of Jesus will keep him for us.

1826

Xavier Murphy to Madeleine Sophie Barat[170]

Grand Coteau, April 19, 1826

Truly, dear and beloved mother general, you have put me to a test that I think our divine spouse does not require of me, by leaving me nearly 3 years without receiving a letter from a mother to whom I feel that I am every day more and more attached; for to the degree that I penetrate into the Heart of Jesus, I find that the bonds that attach us tighten, and I feel my gratitude grow for <u>her</u> who was the first cause of my happiness.

I had the consolation of writing to you last October. In this letter I laid out to you all my fears for the responsibility that you have judged it suitable to confer on me. You nevertheless knew that as soon as Mother Duchesne told me according to your nomination, I laid aside all my fears and resistances and I yielded right away to your orders. From that time on, what can I tell you? If I could speak to you heart to heart, I would no doubt have many things to tell you, but the difficulty that I have to express myself in French does not permit it. It seems to me that if I were on the little footstool in your room, I could tell you in Creole French all my little issues, but that will only be in eternity that your poor Xavier will taste that consolation.

Since the departure of Mother Eugenie everything here remains as before. We have the same number of children and hope to have several for the spring. I do not know why I am so loved by the parents, but they know that their children at present do not have the means to advance. They are generally Creoles and I must speak poor French with them and in the parlor, but it is the Heart of

---

170 Copy, *Lettres de la Basse Louisiane,* pp. 50-53. GASSH.

Jesus who draws them, as he has promised, these young plants, and who disposes them in my favor.

I have two aspirants here who ask their Mother Barat to send them their crosses. They want to write to you, but I just must send my packet by post to New Orleans so it can be turned over to a good priest who is willing to take charge of it, and who wants very much to see you. He is French and will give you all the details of our little Society in the New World, since he has seen our 3 houses.

Our foundress [Mrs. Smith] has left this place to go live in another state, where she wants to found a convent. She spent three weeks with us before her departure, and upon leaving us, she kissed the altar step, saying: "Dear house, it is here that I leave my heart." But I can only bless the Lord to have her no longer. She took all her goods, which were considerable. I always have the hope that she will found here a house for our fathers.[171]

I often think, dear mother, of a promise you made to me in our last private conversation: "When you are over there," you told me, "let me know what I can do to give pleasure." So, dear mother, here it is: give this little house a subject of your choice, and also please give me news of you more often and of those of our dear Society. I am concerned about my dear Father de MacCarthy, for even though "I have forgotten my people and my father's house,"[172] for him I will never forget it. Tell him please something about me; especially ask him to write to me. That is the only consolation that I can have in these vast deserts.

Give my respects to Fathers Varin, Barat, and Perreau. Get them to pray for me, but especially you, dear and venerated mother, ask the Heart of Jesus to give me all the graces I need to fulfill my charge worthily, to follow my holy rule exactly and to become a

---

171 That is, the Jesuits. They would not arrive in Grand Coteau until 1837, the year after Xavier's death, thanks to the accumulation of bricks she had assembled for the chapel.
172 Ps 45:10.

spouse worthy of my noble destination. Tears fall from my eyes. I am imagining myself at your side.

Goodbye, dear mother. Your blessing to the one who is all yours *in Corde Jesu*.

Xavier

Madeleine Sophie Barat to Xavier Murphy[173]

To Mother Xavier Murphy
Opelousas, Louisiana   Paris, February 6, 1826

I received your letter, my very dear daughter, that Mr. Fournier brought us with great care. It tells me of the approaching departure of Mother Eugenie and her companions and of your resignation and courageous acceptance of the cross laid on you. In spite of its weight, I have no doubt that the Heart of Jesus, for whom you accept it, will help you carry it and even soften it by the unction of his grace; no matter how it comes, always have confidence. God cannot abandon a soul who throws herself into his arms with love. Do what you can on your part, and leave the rest to God, who will not leave you.

The one thing necessary, dear daughter, is to remain in peace. Draw near to Jesus Christ by frequent prayer especially in the problems and difficulties over external affairs for which you are in need of counsel. Turn too to Mothers Eugenie and Duchesne for advice as needed.

I know well that you are in need of help, and I am trying to see what can be done to send you someone to help with the classes and

---

[173] French autograph GASSH. In spite of other evidence of frequent letters from Madeleine Sophie to Xavier, this is the only one that has survived. Xavier's letter acknowledged by Sophie here is probably that of October 16, 1825. Before Xavier received this, she would already have written that of April 18, 1826, above.

for the French; but in spite of my wish to help you as promptly as possible, it cannot be before the end of the year, and this means you will have almost another year to wait. However, if I find an opportunity before then, of course I will take it. So ask that the Heart of Jesus arrange everything for his glory and that we may soon send you help.

Yesterday I gave news about you at general recreation; each one expressed in her eyes affection and veneration for you—Mother de Marbeuf especially. What a sacrifice the Lord demands in taking you so far away from us, that I cannot get used to, and to console myself I often say that I am going to visit you before I leave this long and sad exile of life. So far no one has heard me, and everyone seems to be against it; but if this desire is according to the will of God, he will change their hearts or give me a possible way to carry out the project that would be so enjoyable.

In the meantime, my dear daughter, do not let us waste a moment, but grow holy. Life goes on at such a pace, and even in our virtue, what a lack our sovereign Judge will find! Let us be more generous and make the cross the only object of our desires.

Don't worry over your faults; self-love will disappear or at least weaken at the sight of your misery and the important duties that you have to fulfill. Forgetfulness of self will be the result and our God will be truly glorified by his little servant. You will gradually overcome your sensitivity. Jesus will help you and turn you toward his divine Heart, or toward the souls with whom you must now be occupied. So be full of confidence in him who can do all things with a humble and supple instrument, conscious only of her own weakness and nothingness.

I recommend myself to your prayers. You have mine since you became my dear daughter, and particularly at the moment that the Lord chose you to replace and represent him. Give my greetings to all your little family; tell them that I keep them in my heart and that they must pray for me.

Receive, dear daughter, the assurance of the devotion, tenderness, and affection with which I am all yours *in Corde Jesu.*

Barat

Xavier Murphy to Madeleine Sophie Barat[174]

Under the Auspices of
St. Peter of Alcantara
Grand Coteau Oct. 19, 1826

Finally dear and much loved mother general, I have the consolation to be able to write to you. The month of August past I had the honor to address you by the occasion of Abbé Graf, who promised to see all my dear mothers and sisters in Paris and to greet you in a most tender and agreeable manner. Without doubt he fulfilled this commission.

The same month I received your dear letter dated February 1826, which got here very promptly and which filled me with the greatest consolation. After I received what you sent with a little note from my dear star dated 1825, consequently that with my own address came first. During the month of May Providence sent a great affliction in the premature death of a young aspirant, an excellent subject and the only one here able to help me.[175] She was taken in the space of a few hours without any help of our holy religion; judge, dear mother, the sadness of my situation. Her hand was in mine, and she was dead a few moments before I was aware that she was no more. My first movement was to throw myself on my knees, saying: My God, I accept this cross and I offer it for the [benefit] of our dear Society in the new world.

---

174 French autograph. GASSH.
175 Mary Ann Summers, a coadjutrix sister who entered at Florissant in 1821 and went to Grand Coteau in 1822.

I wrote at once to Mother Eugenie asking her to write the circular to you, not having the strength at that moment, deprived then, not having the time, as I was obliged myself to fill the hole that death made in our little house, and having almost all summer an almost continual fever, but experiencing an inexpressible satisfaction in the midst of all my trials and a power completely supernatural.

In that way we reached the time of our prizes and our little vacation of 15 days. For the prizes I followed the rule as satisfactorily as circumstances permit, and during the absence of our children (who were then 16), we worked hard to make the house appropriate for the retreat and to have all in order. Each one did two days of retreat by turn, there being no way to have a general retreat. Finally all was ready to receive them; they returned with a pleasure which surprised and consoled me. All the parents were happy with the progress of their children and have shown me much gratitude. Since the vacation, eleven new children have come, so now there are 24 and I wouldn't be surprised if there will be 28 to 30 during this year; although the times are bad and the cotton crop is worse and worse each year. For me, I have only to say with the apostle, "One plants, another waters, and God gives the increase. So, for the future I rejoice in my weakness so that the power of Christ may be shown more and more."[176]

All our children are Creole so I am obliged to speak poor French with the parents. We are only two able to teach and the one who has the French class goes no further in grammar than adjectives and is not capable of sewing two lines together correctly. So judge, dear mother, our position and with what eagerness we await our nuns; in your <u>dear, dear</u> letter you said the end of the year for the arrival.

I hope to be strong enough to do everything for the children, but as soon as the heat comes, I fear what follows. At present I

---

176 1 Cor 3:7; 2 Cor 12:9.

have three classes each day, as well as writing and handiwork; and I am surveillante of all the studies except one.

Bishop Dubourg charged me to be always with the children, and indeed, I find it most agreeable. To avoid punishments, because when I am among them, a look suffices for those who are docile, innocent, and completely polite. We have 9 for First Communion at Easter and I recommend them to your prayers. I also have a postulant, one of our Creole orphans, 16 years old. She does not wish to return to the world and the other day her guardian gave permission that she remain here. At the first occasion I will send her to Mother Eugenie because I am not able to form a novice.

This year, with the agreement of Mother Duchesne, I bought a Negro woman and her two small children for $721.[177] I already paid $300 and next April I will be obliged to pay the rest. This month I only paid for the provisions for this year. Finally, dear and beloved mother, Providence has done marvels for your daughter and our house this year.

Because you already know that Mother Eugenie has taken all the money for the new house.

It seems that the location of this establishment [Grand Coteau] is so known for the combination of good air and good health that it will be more stable than that of Saint Michael, which had promised so much usefulness. In the month of August, they were obliged to send the children home without prizes because all were sick. And now, dear mother, a little about spirituality. I find myself often without time for the prayer of Rule. I try to make all my employments a prayer; however, I am anxious when it happens that I am not able to follow the Rule. For the others, I am glad that they have enough time for all the exercises prescribed by the Rule, in which I find all my glory that this is fulfilled. But for myself, I am often obliged to follow the counsel of St. Francis de Sales to make

---

177 According to the document, dated 7/10/1826, for $725, they were Philis age 24, Charles age 3, and a six-month old girl, purchased from Theodore Mudd. USCA.

often during the day short aspirations. I receive Communion every day except the day of confession, and here, dear Mother, I find the strength and the light that I need.

[*On the outside*:]
My heart says many things to Fathers Varin, Barat, and Perreau. I would like the 4 of them [including Father MacCarthy] to say a Mass for my intentions.

Farewell, dear and venerated mother. When I come to that word, tears fall from my eyes. Write to me often, for this is my greatest consolation. I write to Mother Duchesne twice a month to keep her informed of all that happens here. I am

Your devoted daughter *in Corde Jesu,*
Xavier

To Mother
Mother Barat, Superior General
of the Religious of the Sacred Heart
Hotel de Biron No. 43
Paris

I would like to know the decrees of the last council, and always the dear and interesting news of all my mothers and sisters in our dear Society. Say something to each one for your daughter. I do not have time to write to my good and dear Mother de Marbeuf with my pen, but my heart does its duty each day, and also to my dear star. His little note had all the effect that he wished it to have on me. Many greetings to him to whom I <u>owe all my happiness</u> for this life and I hope also for the other.

1827

Xavier Murphy to Madeleine Sophie Barat[178]

S.S.C.J.M.   Grand Coteau February 27, 1827

Without doubt, reverend and beloved mother general, I am the last of your daughters who has congratulated you on the recent cause of your joy in seeing our dear Constitutions approved.[179] However, I dare to say that no one has felt the price of your zeal on the occasion nor shared your happiness in a livelier manner than your poor Xavier, but the occupations that increase daily and the difficulty I have to render my ideas in French deprive me of the sweet consolation, that of being able to converse often with the beloved and venerated mother of my spirit and my heart.

Your letter dated in August 1826 I received toward the end of the year (and how many times have I read it since). Your choice has succeeded according to my desires with regard to Mother [Louise] Dorival. No doubt, the Heart of Jesus directed you, for she is entirely the kind of person who suits this house. More than once, I was on the point of asking for this person, but the idea that it would be more perfect and more according to the deference I owe you prevented me.

I have yet to get news of her arrival,[180] for here we are with 30 children. In a few days, they will be 33, and since the beginning of this month, I have refused 6. Since October, the house has had an extraordinary élan in this area. It costs me much to say "no" to these little souls so dear to the Heart of Jesus, but I have no means

---

178 French copy, C III 1 USA *Foundations Basse Louisiane* Box 1. "Lettres des Maisons de la Basse Louisiane. Grand Coteau, S. Michel, L'Assomption. 1825 à 1830." 1er volume. 2e partie. GASSH.
179 The Constitutions of the Society of the Sacred Heart were approved by papal decree on December 22, 1826, but the approbation was already known in August when Mother Barat issued the circular letter of convocation on August 10, 1826.
180 She would not arrive until September.

to teach them, because I am obliged to provide all the classes alone. Happily, the children who came recently are all older. I am obliged to correspond with their parents who are among the more important in the area: judges, generals, attorneys, etc., all Protestant and most of their children not baptized. Already several have received this sacrament, and I hope that all before they leave will share the same happiness. It seems that Saint Michael is destined to form the spouses of the Heart of Jesus[181] and this one, Christians, all for the same end A.M.D.G.

All is going well here. Our children are attached to the house and their parents are happy to let me do as I wish, though our finances were low last year, because of the purchase of a Negress and her children,[182] repairs done, etc. But in a month, the establishment will owe nothing to anyone. In all my difficulty, the treasure of the Heart of my spouse was my only resource, and what marvels he did for his unworthy but grateful spouse. We can certainly say that the finger of God is here. As soon as Mother Dorival arrives, we will send you an account of expenses with the present state of the house. I am not sufficiently updated to be able to do the accounts. I am very careful to keep Mother Duchesne apprised of what happens here. Her knowledge of English[183] is a great advantage, and gives me a facility in fulfilling our dear and holy rule. Happily, too, all the important letters are done in English. All the people situated here are either Americans or French who speak that language perfectly. It is a stroke of Providence for us, because the two Creoles who are with me are not capable of spelling two words correctly.[184]

I recently received the copy of your last circular, written before the convocation of our general council. I do not yet know the

---

181 The novitiate was at St Michael.
182 See details in the previous letter.
183 An ironic counterpart to Philippine's self-perception of inability in language.
184 The two choir religious with her at the time were Emily St-Cyr and Carmelite Landry. Two coadjutrix sisters, Marguerite Manteau and Mary Layton, completed the community with Xavier Murphy.

result, but like the Israelite captives, we must sigh, waiting for the news from Lyon.[185] The greatest problem I have now, and which truly weighs on me, is that nearly all our former boarders, with whom Mother Eugenie made such effort, are not faithful in the world. Most are established without confession and rarely go to church, though while they were with us, they were good and some even devout, but when they go home, all the seed we sowed is lost, at least for the moment. The families here are impious. Truly, dear mother, I am discouraged. To what end am I loved here, that the house is going well, etc. etc. if I do not have the consolation of winning souls to offer to the Heart of Jesus. Perhaps the fault is mine, for I know I lack the qualities that should adorn a spouse of the Heart of Jesus! Oh! If at this moment I could be on the little footstool next to you, how many things to say to the mother of my heart, for now I could make you understand me. But in every stage of my life, God has asked sacrifices of me. I think I am venting too much for a letter, but my heart had to say this. Truly, what can be hidden from you!

Your subjects here are very obedient and devoted. The youngest, a former boarder, who entered with us at the age of 14, will be old enough in a few months to make her profession. I have already written to Mother Duchesne on this subject. We are 5 in all. Old Marguerite is well, a model of perfection. Truly, dear mother, I am the most imperfect here. In spite of my daily communions, say this to my Star: with regard to him, believe me, dear mother, that two words written in his little note that you sent me were enough to encourage me and fill me with courage, etc. During the past year, we have had a peace and a charming tranquility. The departure of our good foundress greatly contributed to it. Perhaps Bishop Dubourg will have told you of the fracas that we experienced here three years ago with regard to her and a priest who badly directed

---

185 Ps 137. The general council was held in Paris in September 1826. It is not clear why she names Lyon.

the poor woman. But as our reverend foundress says: everything passes, everything changes, God alone! At present our chaplain is as peaceful and prudent as his predecessor was the contrary. The departure of Bishop Dubourg[186] was a great blow to our Society, to which he was very attached. Certainly he made his exit with all the finesse of an old Frenchman. Here are two sacrifices to make now: not having time to write to my dear Star and dear Mother Marbeuf, but the motto of a spouse of the Heart of Jesus is duty before inclination. As soon as Mother Dorival arrives, I will have this satisfaction. Meanwhile, please, dear and beloved mother, say to him and to her everything you would like about your daughter. My Star has had good reason to tell me that I would be in such or such circumstance situation. Everything he predicted about me has happened, and the memory and the reading of his counsels are my sole consolation, it is my compass in the arid desert of America.

(Here is a little supplement.) I have forgotten to tell you, dear reverend mother, about a conquest that the Heart of Jesus has made this year in our little house. An American (Protestant), 22 years old, entered [the Academy] for a year, not knowing much except an implacable hatred for our holy religion. She often said to her companions: "How I hate that name Catholic." In spite of that, her recollection and modesty in church were striking. Finally, she opened her heart to me, saying that she wanted to be baptized. After acquiring the consent of her family, the ceremony was done in our very little chapel on Pentecost. The chaplain was her godfather and your humble servant her godmother. She took the name Maria Xavier. On the happy day of our dear feast, she made her First Communion with the devotion of an angel. In the evening, putting her hand on the holy Gospel, she struck it with force and pronounced the words so loudly and in such an emphatic tone that the children noticed it, that she said emphatically: "This evening

---

[186] He resigned as bishop of Louisiana in 1826 and returned to France to become bishop of Montauban. At the time of this letter, he had probably visited the motherhouse in Paris.

I slapped the demon in the face." She is home now with the hope of making her mother Catholic. Recently I received a letter from her mother. In gratitude she proposes to send her little sister in the spring. This way, dear mother, you will have the consolation of gaining some souls to present to the Heart of Jesus. Since I began this letter, three more children are announced, but I fear to take more; we are so weak. They are even too much for two people. I have no news of your nephew. I have written to him three times, but it seems that the air of this country makes him forget the politeness of his nation. We are five here. Old Marguerite is the only Frenchwoman. Her health is good. She is a model of obedience, regularity, devotion, and attachment to the Society and her superiors. She speaks often of you, her dear mother, and gives to others such a desire to see you that they would be happy to leave right away to have that consolation, but that supreme happiness is reserved for a better life.

Your daughter *in Corde Jesu*
Xavier

I have just received a letter from Mother Duchesne who speaks of an establishment in Saint Louis. I hope that the house of Grand Coteau will do something for that work. In spite of all our difficulties the past year I find at this time the wherewithal to send to her $100. I [hope] very much to see that good mother. Her presence would be very useful to our houses in this state.

It seems impossible to end this letter, already too long for you. But I find almost all the words except <u>Farewell</u>. Nevertheless, I must say it, begging you, dear and much loved mother general, to ask the Heart of Jesus for the spirit of faith for everything needed here, and <u>faith</u> in Europe but the <u>spirit alone</u> for America: "a valiant heart [for which] nothing is impossible." So ask for this valiant heart for your daughter. It seems to me that you are all-powerful in the presence of this treasure. Ask it also of my dear Fathers Varin, Barat, and Perreau to whom I wish so many greetings, and also to all my dear mothers and sisters, Bigeu, de Gramont, de Marbeuf, de Charbonnel, etc. etc.

Farewell <u>dear, dear mother</u>. Receive the attachment, the gratitude, and the devotion of your daughter

in the Heart of Jesus
Xavier

Madeleine Sophie Barat to Eugenie Audé, excerpt[187]

October 5, 1827

See, daughter, if you can give someone of your least religious for Mother Xavier. Mother Dorival alone is little, and this house is worthy of your zeal and attachment; next year we will try to give you a little reinforcement again, if we can. Death takes away so many!

L. Dorival to MSB[188]

S.S.C.J.M.   Grand Coteau, October 19, 1827

Dearly loved Mother,
I had the intention to write to you as soon as I arrived at my destination, but here it is a month that I am in Opelousas and I have not yet written to my mother, because I waited from day to day for our trunks and boxes. I decided not to hold off any longer on a pleasure so dear to my heart, that of speaking heart to heart to my dear reverend mother. My last letter was from Baltimore, August 16th, the eve of our departure from that city. At six o'clock in the morning, we

---

187 French autograph. GASSH.
188 French copy, *Lettres de la Basse Louisiane* 1.2 pp. 64-72. GASSH.

embarked in a public coach, where we met an American colonel, who was going precisely to Saint Michael, that is, a few miles before. He rendered us many services during the month that we traveled in his company. After three days and three nights passed almost completely in the Alleghenies, we came to Wheeling. There was no steamboat, as we were hoping. The waters of the Ohio were too low. So we had to continue on the coach for five days, after which we arrived in Cincinnati, a very pleasant city because of its location on a beautiful river. We had to wait four days there for a steamboat. You can imagine, mother, that I was becoming worried, especially when I saw my funds diminishing and coming to an end.

That was when Bishop Fenwick asked Mother Dutour to take care of a young American, 19 years old, who had the idea of becoming a religious. She has a few talents, plays the piano pretty well, and seems to have good will to succeed. I think Mother Dutour, without having spoken to me, brought her to Saint Louis. The bishop had given her 15 dollars, or about 75 francs. That amount was not enough because of our staying in hotels. So it was necessary to pay ourselves some part of her travel expense. Then a steamboat brought all five of us to Louisville, where, after three days of waiting, another steamboat brought us to the mouth of the Ohio. That is where we left each other: Mothers Dutour, Xavier [Van Damme],[189] and the postulant, Margaret Short, accompanied by General Gaines, went to Saint Louis, where they arrived on the feast of the holy name of Mary, while Mother Piveteau and I had to wait another five days to go towards Saint Michael. The steamboat did not finish loading, or rather, the captain, until the 10th of September, when we began to travel on the beautiful Mississippi. On the 19th we debarked at Mother Eugenie's house, which is on the right bank of the river. They no longer expected us, having waited and been wrong for so long.

---

189   Xavier Van Damme, RSCJ (1794-1833), born in Belgium, came to America in 1827 and died at St. Michael in 1833.

My astonishment was great when I found there Father Dusaussoy, who does not know if he will stay in America, because he is very unhappy, or whether he will return to France. One sees that he is afraid of making us unhappy if he returns. He is heavy and well, though, and I hardly recognized him because he has put on so much weight. I gave him the letters I had for him. No news yet of the boxes. They should have come aboard with us from New York for New Orleans. I do not know when they will all arrive.

Mother Eugenie has a lovely house for America. The dormitories are vast and arranged with taste, about sixty students; right now only 50. 8-10 novices and I think five aspirants compose her community. The evening of my arrival, we left for Grand Coteau. Mother Piveteau was part of the group with the chaplain, Father Jeanjean, and a novice for my dear little house. But at the same time, a good sister was required by Mother Duchesne, so we are 6 in all for the community. I cannot describe for you dear Mother Xavier's pleasure. She could not say a word, she was so moved and surprised by our arrival. A few days later, Mother Eugenie returned home with Mother Piveteau, with whom she is very happy. For my part, I am very happy and I cannot thank enough Our Lord and his holy mother [rest of sentence continued on the bottom margin of the page:] for having finally sent me to this America, object of so many wishes. [Continued in text:] This house is very lovely, built in wood, very solid nevertheless; three dormitories elegantly decorated with fringes, a study hall, a refectory, a parlor, a very little chapel—that is all for the boarding school. The community has a tiny, tiny meeting room, which is the superior's writing room, for she sleeps in the attic with the two who are not in the dormitories—a refectory, a kitchen, and I forgot an infirmary, and a vestry next to the students' dormitory, besides a gallery that overlooks the garden, a delightful place after the oppressive heat of the day. We are still in the midst of summer, and now it is so hot during the day that one is tempted to want some extraordinary refreshment. Three or four days ago, a North wind that came up suddenly caused an icy wind for a day and a half. As for the interior of our house, dear mother, here is what it is.

Mother Xavier, who never stops expressing her happiness to have me with her, is superior, mistress general, and treasurer with respect to disbursements. She likes enough these activities that are hers, and makes local arrangements, to build, etc. She has told me several times: another professed religious named Carmelite [Landry] is in charge of everything inside the house, that is, the pantry and table, the students' and community vestry. There is no assistant named, but I find myself filling that place because of age as a professed. I am not designated to take it, but I find myself to be first in the house after Mother Xavier. There is a young aspirant of 21 years called Josephine who should receive the cross [of profession] in a few months,[190] a young novice of the same age called Stanislas [Aguillard],[191] who came with me from St Michael, who is good for manual work, and finally, good Sister Marguerite [Manteau]. So we are three professed of choir, one aspirant, and one novice, and Sister Marguerite.

I am in charge of the 2nd and 3rd French classes, handwriting, geography, and religious instruction, and do a class for the two young religious, so that I have enough to keep myself busy without being overworked. Mother Xavier does three times a day a kind of English class, and I am beginning to substitute when she is not free. I am as if obliged to learn that language immediately because of the necessity of making myself understood by the students, who barely know French.

However, one thing is troubling to me: if I did not think that it is according to your intentions; it is that we are so few that we

---

190 Emily St-Cyr, who had made first vows in Florissant in 1822 and come with Philippine Duchesne on her first visit. She made her profession at Grand Coteau on June 10, 1831.
191 Adelaide Stanislas Aguillard, RSCJ, born in Louisiana in 1806, entered at St. Michael in 1827 and made her first vows January 1, 1830 at Grand Coteau. She was professed there in 1839, and died during the yellow fever epidemic at St. Michael in 1855.

cannot say Office, nor are there conferences. Mother Xavier does not speak French easily enough. The class plan is changed because of English study. In the afternoon, there are only one and a half hours of needlework. The rest is class, and the walks take much of the students' time because exercise prevents frequent illnesses in this land, but not at Grand Coteau, the air is so pure. The spirit of the Society is much loved, but Mother Xavier says that too many of the little practices from France will not work with the Americans. It is a land where everyone breathes liberty. Nevertheless, there are many Protestants who give us their children because of the spirit of liberty and belief that we must give the impression of having, and by this means, many embrace the true faith. The children of this land are all charming. Our students are the best of America, where there are no titles of nobility. We have about thirty students now, all completely docile and fairly intelligent. In a short time, we will have more than forty. The parents are very happy at the arrival of a French teacher. I arrived at this dear house on October 22, a Saturday. You know, dear mother, that after God, I owe everything to Mary! ....

They expect brilliance in the education. We will also shortly acquire a [lay male] music teacher. Several of our students should learn it, as well as drawing. I expected something entirely different when I came to Opelousas, and I find that it is just as necessary here as in France to have religious who are strong in studies. So I will not lose a moment to improve myself, so as to be useful for this interesting work. Everything in this country is rich and elegant, so, dear mother, it will not be of any use to our school to have sent old things. They are only interested in things that are beautiful and new. I am also afraid that the import duty on our crates will be greater than the value of the contents. One can procure all kinds of things, but it takes a rather long time. It has to come from Baltimore or New Orleans. Something that surprised me is that there are no poor people in America. Everyone works and is respected by his neighbors, so every man has the air of a <u>gentleman</u>

of France. The liberty of government even influences the animals: steers, cows, horses, etc. graze in our vast prairies with no watcher or enclosure. They only have the brand of their owner, who goes to get them when he needs them. Cattle cost nothing for their food and are a great resource for milk. We have about twenty, as many steers as cows, calves, etc.

With regard to money, again it is different from France. Our five *francs* and five *sous* are equivalent to one dollar or one *piastre*, or to one *gourde* of this country. There are places in America where our five *francs* need 8 *sous* to be equivalent to the dollar. They divide this money in four parts called 25th or a quarter of a dollar, which can divide into 12 ½ called *escallings*, divided again in 6 ½ called *piscallions*.[192] The last is like one French *sou*, and they never use money any smaller. They give 6 *sous* for the same thing that would be 1 *sou* in Paris. You see from this, mother, that much more money is needed to procure what we need, and everything is like this, and the result is much greater use.

For my interior life, I speak to our good Master and to my confessor. Mother Xavier does not like to and cannot enter into these details. I am very happy and only want to advance in my holy calling to religious perfection. God and I! . . .

It is at your feet, that I place myself with the greatest happiness of my soul. Bless your poor daughter, who has so much happiness in being

your very obedient and grateful daughter *ICJ*
L. Dorival R.S.C.J.

---

192 The first of these two terms is clear in the manuscript, and is perhaps a confusion with the schilling? The second term is not clear. No such coin names seem to have existed.

Xavier Murphy to Bishop Rosati[193]

S.S.C.J.M.   Grand Coteau
Dec 27th [1827]

My Lord and father

    The recent pleasing intelligence of your Lordship's projected visit to G.C. has filled your daughters of the S. Heart with the most sensible consolation. Long & ardently have we sighed after this happiness to see our venerated father and cherished pastor amongst us. This indeed is the most acceptable newyears gift that the Heart of Jesus could bestow on his spouses.

    That your journey my Lord may be propitious and the results of your pastoral visits consoling to yourself and beneficial to your flock is the ardent prayer of your Lordship's

    Most respectfully attached daughter *in Corde Jesu*

                                                                       Xavier

1828

Louise Dorival to Madeleine Sophie Barat[194]

                               Grand Coteau January 14, 1828

Dear Reverend Mother,

    I received a little note from you the day before yesterday. As agreeable as it was to see the writing of my dear mother, so much was my heart troubled to know you are suffering, because of the death of dear Mother Camille.[195] Oh! How sorry I am for our Society! Mother Neline must be in confusion. Who will fill this void? Dear and tender mother, your daughters in America spend

---

193 English autograph. Rosati collection.
194 French copy. C III USA 1 *Foundations Basse Louisiane* Box 1. *Lettres de la Basse Louisiane*, Vol. 3, pp. 65-70.
195 Cecile Camille, RSCJ, born in Paris, entered the Society there in 1817 and was later superior in Bordeaux, where she died on October 4, 1827.

their recreations talking about everything that is dearest in this world, that is, our tender Mother Barat and our dear Society. Yes, we have no sweeter pastime than to transport ourselves into your presence and that of our mothers and sisters, and there to be witnesses as it were of what affects us that we would share with you. Mother, we are very aware that we are your children in the midst of the forest of the New World, as in the happy shelter that you inhabit. How we dread the affliction of another loss that we cannot even imagine yet, that of Mother Bigeu.[196] Oh, mother! I hope that our good Master will delay for a while the time of her reward for the good of our Society. How the illness of Mother Alexandrine also afflicts us. What a miserable life this is! I tell you that I feel more than ever the need to attach myself to Jesus alone.

I have already told you how happy I am with Mother Xavier. She is so good, so delicate, so desirous of the glory of God and the prosperity of the Society that I am truly too happy living with her. It is true, I ought to say it, mother, that I suffered when I reread your letter shortly after my arrival. She chose me as her assistant. I am so fearful, and with great reason from my incapacity of every kind, that I find well distributed those who should not get involved in the government of the house. But as you have said to me, dear mother, one must bend the shoulders under whatever responsibility that could be. I accept it all with confidence that Our Lord will help me. Up to now, I have nothing to do with the business of the house. Mother Xavier herself is treasurer. Certainly, God blesses her. This year she had to redo the whole house. She built a dormitory that cost more than 11,000 francs, and still she has a surplus.

The parents pay around 800 francs or 740 piastres. We have 35 students from the best families in the country, where, as I told you, they do not make the distinctions that they do in France. They are the children of military generals, of judges, and of property owners.

---

196 Josephine Bigeu, RSCJ, was assistant general in Paris. She in fact had died December 19, 1827. Louise's language is ambiguous. It is probable that she had heard only of Mother Bigeu's illness, not yet of her death.

What is troublesome is that they leave them too short a time in the boarding school. One year, two years, is a lot. If all the ones I have seen here had stayed, we would have about fifty. About a third of those we have now are Protestant. The parents say that they are forced to put them with us in spite of their different opinion on the article about religion. They only ask that they not be made to learn the catechism or church history. I had the consolation to see baptized at Christmas one of the children, 10 years old, who desired that favor ardently, to whose prayers the father acquiesced, giving her the permission to become a Christian. I think that at Easter we will have several again to admit to this sacrament. It is a particular thing how much religion occupies the young children of Protestants in this country, and what happiness for those of your daughters whom you employ in such an interesting work. What makes them decide to send them to us is our children's progress in writing.

The losses to our dear Society or those with which it is still menaced, make me fear that you will not be able for a long time to think about a foundation in Baltimore, where it seems that Bishop Marechal wants us. It is not easy to convey to you the zeal of several holy persons in America who want us to found a house in the region called <u>the East</u>, and nothing would be more advantageous than to be located in a place that would make our communications with Europe extremely easy, and would contribute to the conversion of so many souls! ...

Mother, I know well that your zeal would want to begin such an interesting work for the glory of the Heart of Jesus, but the money ... but the personnel .... I hope that Our Lord will remove the obstacles, and that the light of the Sacred Heart will soon shine in a country where they cultivate the sciences with particular enjoyment. We will do everything we can to make the project succeed. I think very differently now about America than when I knew it a little, or of that kind of savagery that I thought to find. There is a politeness that competes with Europeans.

We have here an excellent vegetable, these are soft potatoes, that is, sweet, but they can only be preserved in open air. They are much larger than our ordinary potatoes. Following local custom, our children eat very little in the evening: a little milk, a little boiled corn in broth—that is their supper. Never meat. With this regime, they do marvelously. Sometimes there are crepes, but salad is served very little on the tables, even though there are beautiful gardens. They use very little oil; everything is seasoned with fat, even on days of abstinence, because of the temperature, which is extremely hot. Even today, it is so hot that I am practically suffocating. This winter we had only 5 or 6 cold mornings. The birds called <u>Cardinals</u> are almost as common here as are the Pierrots in France. I never stop admiring them. In the summer there are many little birds. I saw them when I arrived here. They are very pretty. Our little house has a very happy exterior. It is white and green, big enough to house 50 students. Every Thursday we go out to picnic in the woods behind our house, where we walk in an immense prairie. That is where the name of our dear Mother Barat is pronounced and repeated with delight!

We have the consolation of receiving fairly often letters from Mother Duchesne, to whom Mother Xavier writes almost every week. Something that is very pleasant in this country is the way of building houses. Since most are in wood, after setting up the framework of the main rooms, they cover the roof in tiles that are also in wood, in such a way that the roof continues in front of the house. All our students take coffee every day; it is the local custom. Mother Xavier has enjoyed fairly good health since my arrival, and everyone compliments her on it. Before I came here, she had much more difficulty. From time to time, she suffers from colic. She also suffers from much weakness, to which the climate contributes. These days she was very tired, and she is subject to a little low fever. You can judge, mother, how we try to take care of her! . . . She says she has never been better. May God will to conserve her for a long time.

The desire of my heart would lead me to write to many of my mothers, but the cost of postage deters me, and besides, I have so little free time that I am forced to make the sacrifice. Mother Bigeu, who has so much right to my remembrance!... Mother Charbonnel... Mother Desmarquest... Mother de Gramont... Mother Ducis, Mother de Marbeuf, for whom I have made all her commissions. At least may these good mothers not forget me in their prayers, so I will not show myself to be unworthy if they claim me as their little sister. Xavier is not writing to you today, mother, since we are united in heart and spirit. That is also the sweet union that you love so much, and that I think will please you very much. Of this, I offer you the assurance of the most tender respect and the most affectionate devotion. All your daughters at Grand Coteau cherish you and are at your feet. Bless them. I am only too happy to say it in their name and mine *in Corde Jesu*

Dear mother,

Your most affectionate
And very obedient daughter
L. Dorival

Xavier Murphy to Bishop Rosati[197]

S.S.C.J.M.   Grand Coteau March 27th [1828]

I cannot my Lord and father let this post pass without thanking your Lordship for the esteemed favor of the 11th instant – Nothing could be more consoling or more truly congenial to my feelings than the intelligence it communicated. To be ensured the permanent possession of your venerated self has in itself alone something inexpressibly gratifying for your daughters of the S. Heart – but how is this blessing, enhanced by the nomination of

---

197 English autograph. Rosati collection.

your distinguished coadjutor.[198] Most sincerely do I congratulate your Lordship on this happy event – an event which predicts better days for poor Louisiana – Yes – father, union of mind and heart will consolidate religion in the Diocese and diffuse it permanently throughout the states.

Nothing of consequence has occurred here since your Lordship's departure. On the 25th every thought word and action of the day was directed for your intentions. I shall expect to hear from your venerated self how the <u>matter</u> terminated that was to have been discussed at N. Orleans during your absence. All here desire to be presented to your Lordship requesting your benediction & prayers. You know how much I stand in need of them myself and how entirely I am your devoted & gratefully attached daughter *in*

Corde Jesu Xavier

Xavier Murphy to Bishop Rosati[199]

S.S.C.J.M.   Grand Coteau
                        April 25th [1828]

I have my Lord and dear father just received a letter from *Mère* Duchesne announcing the permission *de Notre Supérieure Générale* for the <u>receiving of the Sisters of the Cross</u>.[200] I should like to know by the return of this opportunity your Lordship's determination on the subject and who the person is that you deem suitable for the Superiority. My reason for this, is, that unless Sr Carmelite be the person destined for Superior I will not give her up; she is too

---

198 It does not seem that Bishop Rosati got a coadjutor at this time. The following year, however, the two dioceses that had both been Rosati's responsibility were split. Leo Raymond De Neckere, C.M. was appointed bishop of New Orleans in August 1829, and perhaps it is this that she already knew.
199 English autograph. Rosati collection.
200 This was the assumption of responsibility for their school in LaFourche and their admission into the Society of the Sacred Heart for those who wished.

useful here, and in thus acting I am sanctioned by the advice of *Mère* Duchesne.

Father Rossi will give your Lordship all the local intelligence of this quarter. We have recently received a reinforcement of two novices from St Louis one of whom had the honor & consolation of getting the veil from your paternal hands.[201] The appearance of their conductress has had an unpleasant effect at Opelousas where the people amuse themselves at the expense of the Religious etc. etc. In the ensuing week I expect 9 children from Alexandria all Americans whom I trust we shall have the happiness of seeing baptized – What a consolation dear father and what a dignified noble employment etc. "To separate the precious from the vile" to form these tender susceptible plants and present them to the Heart of our Divine spouse? Your little god daughters are well & full of the pleasing hope of seeing their father next year, but they find the time terribly long – a whole year and why not sooner, they say.

I forget I am trespassing on your precious time. So shall finish by presenting your Lordship the respectful attachment of your flock old & young of G. Coteau. Our medallion[202] has requested the permission of writing for herself & companions who often mention the cherished name of Msgr [Bishop] *parmi elle(s)*.

Requesting your Benediction father and a continual remembrance of your daughters on the Holy Mount.

I remain your gratefully attached child

in Corde Jesu
Xavier

---

201 Eleanor(e) Gray, RSCJ, born in Ireland in 1808, entered at Florissant but made her first vows at Grand Coteau July 3, 1829. She was later superior in St. Louis, Buffalo, and St. Michael, and part of the founding group in St. John, New Brunswick in 1854, where she died in 1862.
202 The student with the highest leadership position in the school.

[On the side in another hand in French:]
1828 April 25 Mother Xavier G. Coteau

[no address]

Xavier Murphy to Bishop Rosati[203]

S.S.C.J.M.   Grand Coteau
May the 27 [1828]

    This letter will I trust salute your Lordship safely landed at *votre chère maison de prédilection* (where surrounded by your dear children you rejoice in your favorite solitude after the bustle and fatigue of your late tour).

    There is at this moment, in this quarter, a subject in question regarding your favorite house of G. Coteau and upon which I desire father, your <u>candid opinion</u> and <u>advice</u>. It appears that the inhabitants of Rapides & Opelousas wish conjointly to erect a handsome brick establishment for us at Opelousas to which place the unanimous preference is given on account of its healthy situation. Now father in the event of our acceptance of this proffered generosity I foresee many, many difficulties, privations & sacrifices to make. But if by our *dévoument* the Glory of God may be promoted and Religion extended, why, in such cases self must be forgotten or annihilated. I shall await your judicious decision with anxiety. In the meanwhile we are earnestly recommending the affair to the Father of light & counsel. Pray father unite with our community that the will of God alone may be done. I have written *Mère* Duchesne on the subject. I see no probability of the question being quickly decided here, but in the event of an application to

---

203 English autograph. Rosati collection.

me on the matter, I wish to be furnished with the decision and answer of my <u>Superiors</u>.

Father Rossi handed me your Lordship's letter for which I feel much indebted. That to our medallion existed the most lively gratitude amongst our children who all cry out "but when is it that our dear Bishop will come." In their name & that of our little community I thank your Lordship for the distinguished marks of parental kindness shown us. Be assured father they remain embalmed in the memory of each individual particularly in that of one whose pride & consolation it is to call you her <u>father prelate</u> & <u>friend</u>, and that is your Lordship's most respectfully attached daughter

in Corde Jesu
Xavier

Letter of Louise Dorival to Madeleine Sophie Barat[204]

Rec: to St Ant, de P.

S.S.C.J.M. Grand Coteau, June 16, 1828

Dear beloved reverend mother,

I see that I must renounce the consolation of seeing again one of your letters, which would give me so much happiness! But I fear that our eyes, already so fatigued, would suffer from it; thus, dear mother, rather than call for a few lines from your hand, I will have the joy of offering it to Our Lord. This sacrifice for the general good of our dear Society that is spreading and rising in an admirable manner!... Oh. what happiness I have to see the Sacred Heart of Jesus honored so specially in the capital of the Christian world![205] O, mother, your heart must feel a very sweet consolation!

---

204 French copy in notebook, *Lettres de la Basse Louisiane*, pp. 20-22. GASSH.
205 The first foundation of the Society in Rome began in March 1828 at the Trinità dei Monti.

Our children give consolation, about half (they are 37) Protestant, but they love the instructions on religion; there is always a harvest. We do not follow at all the plan of classes; we cannot, I have already told you! It seems that this house will become more considerable. The leaders of several districts or civil parishes speak of building for us an establishment in the town of Opelousas itself, from which we are three leagues distant; they have already chosen its location near a little hill. They think that we will have a multitude of advantages for leaving Grand Coteau, where our distance from the town makes commodities more expensive. The parents who come from afar have no hotels to receive them. The male teachers of the arts have no houses to lodge them, and we have just lost several students for lack of a piano teacher. At Opelousas we would have that. The gentlemen seem fervently occupied with this. They say that it is the thing to do, not only for the education of young people, but that this will be a building for the embellishment of their growing town. Think, dear mother, that nearly all the Protestants dream of this: to raise a house of the Sacred Heart! For it is the town that will give us everything, and without our having to get involved in subscriptions, a large brick house will be built, perhaps within two years, if you, dear mother, give your consent. Mother Xavier has written to Mother Duchesne, for everyone speaks of it as something that will happen.

I have truly sensible consolation to work in this vineyard, so precious to the Heart of Jesus in these far lands. From time to time my spirit and my heart call on my mother!... But I answer: in a little time we will see each other above![206] My health is a little changed right now. I was bled day before yesterday; I think that will go better. I only want to work well for the little time that I no doubt have to live...I am sending you my annuity certificate with regard to my pension. These are friends of the house who

---

206 Born in 1795, Louise Dorival died July 11, 1832, the first missionary from Europe to die in America, and the first to be buried in the Grand Coteau cemetery.

have given their name. If there must be other formalities, they will cost almost as much as the total sum. I hope they will not quibble about it over there. In effect, there is no stamped paper in America. Bless me, mother, and always count on my tender and respectful affection.

Your obedient daughter
L. Dorival r. of the S.H.
Assistant at Grand Coteau

P.S. Mother Eugenie has 63 students, and this establishment has real promise. Unfortunately, it has been threatened by flooding of the Mississippi, which has grown extraordinarily this year. The Heart of Jesus turned back that calamity!

As I had foreseen, here we must show the dormitories to parents, papas and mamas, uncles, etc. without which we would have no students. We will perhaps also have to let them attend the final prizes and to do a few little plays because here this means almost everything. We try to conform to the Decrees in everything else as far as possible.

I get along well with Mother Xavier. We have again begun to say Office, but I cannot continue; we have returned to saying it in speaking voice. The climate strains the throat. I am sometimes exhausted, but it is the first year. Perhaps I will become acclimatized. We breathe the purest air in Louisiana.

My respects to all my dear mothers and sisters. Our most pleasurable recreations are those in which we speak of our dear house in Paris and all the Society, and our house in Rome! ... All yours in C.J.

LD....

Xavier Murphy to Bishop Rosati[207]

S.S.C.J.M.   Grand Coteau November 7, 1828

Has my Lord and good father been surprised at his daughter not sooner replying to his esteemed favor of the 7 July. Indisposition was the first preventative and then finding that *Mère* Duchesne had put your Lordship in possession of all our movements induced me to defer this gratification, awaiting the decision of my superiors and the result of the subscriptions – the former being granted at the price of so many sacrifices & the later [*sic*] for the present appearing dormant together with Mrs. Smith's answer to your Lordship, which *Mère* D has just communicated, induces me to conclude that the wisest & most beneficial plan to be adopted is to <u>renounce the enterprise</u>.[208] For I doubt much if the good resulting from the change would ever counterbalance the sacrifices exposure and ostensibility [*sic*] we would incur by such an undertaking. Fortunately we are still free to act on every side of the question, for not having had your Lordship's permission for the change when waited upon by the Judge to sign the argument and after I received it seeing no urgent necessity to proclaim it, consequently leaves everything as yet entirely at our disposition. In addition to the above reasons, it appears that the parents & friends of the establishment unanimously prefer our present situation, arguing that the general good health & great progress *de nos élèves* are the best testimonies of the eligibility of the local (which to all strangers appears delicious).

    Indeed Rev. father, I do think that sweet Providence has visibly presided over the affair permitting & directing the whole for his great glory & the ultimate good of the institution. The more I reflect on the subject, the more I see its acceptance incompatible

---

207 English autograph. Rosati collection.
208 The proposed move of the institute from Grand Coteau to Opelousas.

with our present situation. Admit only in the respect to subjects - where find them? And such an engagement with the public would make a sufficient number of well formed subjects indispensable – as to leaving this house exist (in the event of the change) it would be entirely useless. The local here admits of no mediocrity nor have we had for 3 years an *élève* of G.C. why then leave a house useless which should necessarily be kept up (and that only to look at it) according to your Lordship's desire. I wrote last summer to Mrs. Smith enclosing the paragraph on the Gazette respecting the change to this letter. She has not replied. I did not mention anything of the Jesuits thinking that you, father, could more prudently discuss this matter & prepare her mind for its adoption. *Enfin, bon père*, to conclude this subject I must tell you that during the entire process of the cause, I endeavoured to keep my mind entirely free whatever may be the event & the refusal and permission of my superiors were both equally agreeable to my feelings.

Your Lordship must now permit me to dwell a little on the heartfelt pleasure I experienced on hearing from your valued self the consoling prospects now opening for Religion in the Missouri, above all the amicable termination of the Church of St Louis. Providence father is an ample fund to draw on & never disappoints those who place all their stock in its charge. The flourishing state of the Seminary, etc. etc. <u>all all</u> afforded me delight & filled me with courage & gratitude. But the fate of your distinguished Son and future hope was more than sufficient to counterbalance my pleasure and mingled a bitter portion in this passing cup of Joy. From your Lordship's letter of September (to Fr. Rosti),[209] I suppose him no more and here can only say in your own words, "God be blessed" *fiat fiat*.

---

209 John Rosti, C.M., was born in Milan, ordained by Bishop Dubourg in 1821, and served for several years as pastor at Opelousas. He left Louisiana for Missouri in 1836 and died at The Barrens in 1839. Not to be confused with Flavius Rossi, mentioned in the next paragraph, a secular priest also in the same regions in those years.

Do you remember father that whilst at your knees in the little chapel of G.C. I told you that I feared the contentment of Mother Dorival was too much to last. Well then, it appears she desires to change houses. This is no small trial for me but I shall try & submit. "The arm of the Lord is not shortened." What the event may be you will in all probability know ere long. For the rest, all goes on as you left us. The pensioners are 40, several of whom are to be baptized. If you father think it prudent, the ceremony shall be deferred until your promised visit, a moment that all here (old & young) look forward to with anticipated delight. During our recent vacation we had a retreat of 5 days. Fr. Rosti preached once a day & I had the consolation of seeing the sisters derive much benefit & courage from his discourses. He suits us admirably here. Fr. Rossi continues embellishing his Church some months since he was on the wing of departure for a transatlantic flight. He appeared really <u>home sick</u>. I induced him earnestly to visit you at the Seminary, thinking it would dissipate his thoughts. He now seems to have abandoned his rash project & determined not to quit his post. The Gouche [?] establishment it appears flourishes. I saw by Mother Duchesne's letter that your Lordship had consecrated the Church at S^ت Charles & that *notre maison* had commenced. A.M.D.G. under the fostering auspices of our venerated & beloved prelate, on whose time I have, I fear, trespassed.

[On the outside:]

215

The Right Rev^د Joseph Rosati
St. Mary's Seminary
Perry County
Missouri

[On the bottom, in another hand in French:}
1828 Nov. 7 Mother Xavier Opelousas

[On both outside flaps:]
Pray father write me & waft us your Benediction. Your last was received with much consolation by your daughters (even *nos élèves*) felt proud at being included. The little Americans tell the newcomers that indeed the Bishop is a <u>very good man</u> & has a beautiful ring on his finger etc., etc. I recommend these interesting plants, community & house to your Lordship's prayers. During this octave I have particularly remembered you and yours above all that you, dear father, may <u>not yet</u> increase the number & enhance the triumphs of the blessed, for the consolation of your children & the general good of Religion etc. etc.

Your devoted attached daughter
In Corde Jesu   Xavier R. du S.C.

1829

Xavier Murphy to Madeleine Sophie Barat[210]

Grand Coteau, February 22, 1829

Your letter, dear and much loved mother general, reached me six weeks after its date (and what beautiful New Year greetings). Thus you see that your correspondence reaches us directly, much more quickly than by way of the other houses, because although we know that our Constitutions and our Office books are in America, we are deprived of the delight of seeing them.

Although I have been very pleased to have your approbation for the move of our establishment of Grand Coteau to Opelousas, it seems that the obstacles on the side of Mrs. Smith joined to the disapproval of our bishop have finished that business for the present. Mrs. Smith, the foundress of this house, in the case of a change will reclaim <u>all her donation</u> and would put other religious

---
210 French autograph. GASSH.

in our place, besides the lack of stability for our houses in this area. The more prudent thing is to hold onto the <u>certain</u> rather than the <u>uncertain</u>, since thanks to the divine Heart of Jesus, we are <u>on top</u> of our affairs. Our debts for the improvement recently completed are paid as well as the current expenses of the house. At this moment there remains $600, that is, 3000 francs for our provisions for the year, which makes (...) per month. But (to New Orleans) for the rest. Mother Dorival will send it to you from last March, but not in great detail because we have found that our expenses for this house do not require all the articles mentioned in the printed domestic sheet. However, dear mother, if you judge it proper, we will send in the future the articles <u>left blank</u>. Let me know <u>particularly</u> your intention on this point.

I have just received sad news from Mother Duchesne—it seems that the funds are very low, since she tells me that in St Louis they lack the necessities, they have only 6 boarders, and at St Ferdinand there are only 12. A short time before the arrival of your <u>precious</u> letter I sent her for her needs $150, that is to say 750 francs. By the last courier I received a letter from Mother Eugenie that told me that you want Mother Duchesne, Mother Dutour and me to meet at St Michael to consult together[211]; she added that her hopes are not yet realized, her school is not growing, and for the first time she told me a touching word about the house. With me she keeps the most profound discretion concerning her affairs. As soon as I learn of the arrival of Mother Duchesne at St Michael I will leave and in this season I will arrive in <u>two days</u> by the magic means of the <u>steamboat</u>. I will be well replaced here by the <u>good</u> and <u>very useful</u> Mother Dorival, who presently conducts herself <u>marvelously</u> and seems very content and very happy. For myself, I have a

---

211 By this time, there was a need to have the superiors of the three houses, Grand Coteau, St. Michael, and LaFourche, come to an agreement regarding courses of study in the three schools. Madeleine Sophie directed Philippine to convoke this meeting. Philippine first tried to get them to come to St. Louis. Failing that, she set out in November and did not arrive in Louisiana until the end of that month.

thousand thanksgivings to the lovable Heart of my Spouse, and to you also dear <u>venerable</u> and reverend mother, for having sent this useful religious, and capable of making the Heart of Jesus loved. Please do not change her. Perhaps in other houses she would not be so happy nor so useful. She is a <u>pleasure</u> for me here as well as one who does what must be done. Everything makes her happy here.

As I am satisfied with your decision concerning <u>the rooms, clothing</u>, etc., etc. I perceive that M. Dorival has an inclination to do it here rather than S^ت Michael (certainly for the good). My ideas on the subject were completely opposed, since I saw no good result for that infraction of the Rule, seeing that the children lose much time and unconsciously acquire a taste for theatrical representations. In short, that in a small community, things like this are a cause of great <u>dissipation</u> and of much work to make the necessary arrangements for the reception of outsiders. Consequently, our religious exercises are disrupted and finally the parents often are discontented with the sharing of their children. When justice presides in the distribution of prizes, for the three years that I am here at the head, I have done all in my power to end the custom and I have the consolation to see that the parents are all happy enough with <u>our</u> distribution rather than <u>theirs</u>.

Pardon me, dear mother, I have much more to say on the subject, but I do not find other time to express <u>my ideas to you</u>. Oh, how happy I would be if I were able to make my thoughts flow clearly and distinctly to you, <u>dear and tender mother</u> from whom I would wish to keep nothing hidden concerned with (...)[212] I wrote to my <u>dear star</u>. If he is near you he can give you without doubt a little of my interior that, alas, is not very brilliant. Physical strength often is lacking to me, but what a consolation to say from my heart that: "my life is no longer mine, but that of J.C."[213] Ah! Three special moments that I unite myself with our <u>dear, dear</u>

---

212 Illegible word, possibly *démesuréments,* excesses.
213 Gal 2:19.

Society, but I am talking too much. My heart is full of gratitude, etc. and it is necessary to immolate even those thoughts that are too agreeable to nature, and I continue as a brave soldier to <u>do everything against nature</u>, until the end.

All our sisters are doing well; we are 9 and our children about 40. I had the consolation of seeing 2 baptized on the Feast of the Purification. Their Protestant fathers asked that their children be raised in our faith and that I be their godmother. They took the name of <u>Xavier</u>. At present we have three more who want the same happiness and I hope they will receive the permission of their parents. For the rest, everything is going well here. The parents leave us all authority over their children. We are encouraged by their visits. Finally control is entirely ours. We are obliged to show them the dormitory. It seems that this arrangement brings praise for the house. Elsewhere, our little community, etc. is totally separate. Recently, I have had an outside staircase made that prevents others from entering the interior. Finally, I will try to conform in all that our situation allows to our Rule. At the time of the visit of our dear Mother Duchesne, she will tell you how everything is here – such a consolation for us to receive this good mother, your <u>representative</u> in this hemisphere. She returned with me from St Michael, where I found her, following your orders. I planned to write you from there if I found a dictionary. It is penance to have to search for words.

God knows if you are able to understand this letter.

[On the outside:]
All our sisters greet you with respect. They are aware of the wishes you have formed for them. You assuredly have their prayers, above all the elderly Sister Marguerite who becomes holier every day. Her health is very good and her devotion to the whole Society.

Finally. I must stop, and that is the most difficult. Here I am at your feet, <u>venerated</u> mother, begging your blessing on your Xavier and on the house you have confided to her, above all our dear children who speak the name of Mother Barat with veneration and love. They are yours by every title. Have you decided to send me the religious I requested in my last letter of November 1st?[214] Again I repeat that I can take care of all the expenses of the trip, etc. Dear mother, farewell. Read my heart and you will see how much I am completely your devoted daughter in the Heart of Jesus, in time and eternity. Finally I am your Xavier R. du S. C.

P.S. Much love to my star. Fathers Varin, Perreau, and Barat, without forgetting my mothers, sisters and my dear Mother de Marbeuf. United with devotion.

[Postmark:]
Opelousas, Louisiana, Feb 25
<u>New York</u>
Mother
Mother Barat Superior General
of the Religious of the Sacred Heart
Rue Varennes N°. 41
Faubourg S^t. Germain
In *Paris*

[Along the side of the first page:]
I have just received the letter of <u>affiliation</u>. What a balm for our hearts. Our very active link with this group larger than ever at the time of their persecution. Mother Dorival will tell you of the deplorable state of our religion here at present, and the lack of workers in the field of the Gospel. I am wearing your <u>pelerine</u>. It is for me like a <u>shield</u> that surrounds me and communicates wisdom to me. Your veil is fine. Please send me another. Your daughter,
Mother Xavier

---

214 A letter from Xavier dated November 1 has not survived, but the request for more religious is frequent.

Louise Dorival to Madeleine Sophie Barat[215]

S.S.C.J.M.   Grand Coteau, February 22, 1829

Reverend and much loved Mother,

   I cannot express to you the consolation that I experienced last December 13 in receiving one of your letters that I desired so ardently. I read and reread it; that reading increased my courage. Saint Francis Xavier, my favorite saint, whom you propose to me as model, gave me a new push to make me run my holy course with joy and fervor. Yes, dear mother, I have had more desire than ever to do in this new world everything that depends on me, aided by grace, to make the kingdom of God increase. Nothing is more proper to stir up zeal than to see up close how little God is known, his religion neglected, holy worship abandoned! . . . . There are so few priests in this part of Louisiana, and in general they are so little eloquent, however zealous, that the Methodists succeed considerably over the Catholics; and as they see this very well to their advantage, they get the best <u>preachers</u> of their sect and attract many Americans, who look especially for learning in the discourses. The spirit of error and impiety is being propagated; in a state of America not far from ours (Ohio) a man claimed to be Jesus Christ, and in his extravagance he charged his brother to ask Congress for 50,000 francs to secure his title as descendant of David. The journalist who reports this fact adds that it is shocking and foolishness; nevertheless, several people are following this crazy man! A <u>preacher</u> in a discourse on Jesus Christ compared him to an American general against whom a conspiracy was raised. This scandalized some and pleased others.

   We always have from thirty-five to forty students, most of them Protestants. Nevertheless, some time ago the father of one of them

---

215 French copy GASSH, C III USA 1. *Foundations Basse Louisiane* Box 1. *Lettres de la Basse Louisiane.* Vol. 3, 1827-1830. (Green hard cover) 95-101.

wrote to <u>Madame the Abbess of Grand Coteau</u> to ask that his daughter, 9 years old, be baptized and instructed in the Catholic religion, even though he is Presbyterian. Another general asked the same thing for his daughter in spite of his particular opinions, and in effect, these two baptisms took place on February 2. These children seemed so happy that several whose parents did not give permission to enjoy the same benefit, were completely saddened. Only four of our Catholics made First Communion on Easter, and many more will be confirmed at the next visit of the bishop, which will undoubtedly be toward the month of May. In general, the children of this area are docile and not lacking in spirit. Our classes in English and in French go alongside; it is absolutely necessary to know the two languages, so much so that we are obliged every day to take an hour away from work for instruction in English. We no longer follow the plan of classes. The children stay so little time and the parents are so demanding that we have to give at the beginning what in France would only be given a little more advanced. All the work is done on a piece of <u>slate board</u>, and even from time to time handwriting. This way, we save a considerable amount of paper and pens. The parents never stop praising the letters that are sent to them every month by their children, and a little design that I show to several during recreation charms both parents and children. In this I admire divine Providence that uses the least thing to attach these Americans and Creoles to a house where God is honored.

There is no longer question now of another house in Opelousas. I tell you, dear mother, that I am very happy about it. We enjoy in Grand Coteau a peace and solitude that you value. We do, too, and certainly no other place would suit our establishment better. May God be blessed in everything! Nevertheless, we have not given up the hope of using the same means (a subscription) to build later a house in brick next to the one we now live in, which is in wood. This is all the more necessary because in one part of the roof, there are little openings through which, in strong rains, which are fairly frequent, the water finds a way to flood us. I have spent several nights moving beds from one side of the dormitory to keep them from dampness. The workers who have been consulted about this say that to fix it we must completely redo the roof, and they add that the house is not worth such a great expense. As for the rooms, I will follow your intentions to the letter, that is, the Constitutions. I find that the best thing to do, and the way to draw down more blessings from heaven on our houses.

We await soon the visit of Mother Duchesne. I will be very happy to meet her. Mother Xavier will go to St Michael as soon as she is sent for. I fear her absence because I am apprehensive about the responsibility, finding myself all of a sudden at the head of the house. Besides, most of the parents of our students are American and do not understand French. I still have difficulty understanding and speaking English, so I will be at a little disadvantage, but with God's help, I will do what I can so that everything goes well in the boarding school, and then I hope that it will only be for a few days that I am charged with it. I have such a fear that someday this burden will be placed on me, that I never cease praying to our good Master not to let it happen. I feel ever more that I need to be guided, without which the work of God would undoubtedly suffer from my ignorance and inexperience, especially in temporal affairs, where I do not understand much.

The gold watch of Bishop Dubourg has arrived here from Baltimore, where I left it waiting. Mother Xavier will take it to Father Jeanjean as you recommended to me.[216] I am very much in harmony with my superior, by the grace of God. Nevertheless,

---

216 Madeleine Sophie to Eugenie Audé, February 1, 1829: "When our religious left for America, I entrusted to Mother Dorival a gold watch that the Bishop of Montauban [Dubourg] entrusted to us to deliver to one of your neighbors. He gave explicit instructions. The note was with the watch. It seems that our travelers have lost it. I have therefore written again to the bishop to get new documents. I send them to you just as his Excellency gave them to me again. Try, dear daughter, to comply and to turn over this object as soon as you can. If Mother Dorival has not given you this watch, write to her to tell you where it is."

it often seems to me that many little things (not very essential) that she thinks cannot be done here could be done anyway, but I do not torment her with my ideas. I conform to hers, after having laid out for her what I would think best. We still have the same chaplain. We have confession regularly, every eight days, and we have Holy Mass every day. Each of us is so busy with the children or for the children that we have no time for <u>scruples</u>. This is a great grace from God; nevertheless, if it should happen, or if there were need for another confessor, it would be truly most unfortunate, because in our area there is only one priest, Father Rosti, who is suitable for religious souls, since he is himself a Lazarist religious. We hope, dear mother, that you will hear favorably Mother Xavier's most recent request, that you send us one or two religious for this house. If one could teach music, we would no doubt have a larger number of students. It is so difficult to see the Methodists compete with us and perhaps take them away from us because of "accomplishments." Music teachers do not want to come to Grand Coteau except at double the price, which the parents are not willing to pay, and there are so few teachers around here that we would have to have one attached; otherwise, they are too occupied in town to come to us. – When you want to send us anything, letters, or packages, please simply put our address; it will arrive directly. By another way, it takes much longer to reach us.

    I am going to enclose a little note about expenses and the receipts of the semester. Mother Xavier does the accounts herself and enjoys this little survey, thinking that she cannot do any better. For the rest, the house is doing well and has no debts, and has an advance for provisions. God blesses us by taking away worry about earthly things. I thank him every day for having sent me into this charming solitude where I am beginning <u>a little</u> to see him alone. This is my rendering of conscience, dear mother, that I send to your maternal care, begging you to ask our good Master that I may finally be worthy both of the Society of his divine Heart and of the tender mother who deigned to accept me....It is in this divine Heart that I will always be, dearly beloved mother,

> Your grateful and very obedient daughter,
> L. Dorival, R.S.C.J.

Louise Dorival to Madeleine Sophie Barat[217]

> Grand Coteau, March 3, 1829

Dear and beloved Mother,
How much gratitude I owe you for your truly maternal goodness with which you encourage me through your letters to fulfill worthily the mission with which I have the happiness to be entrusted. I received on February 22 your answer dated September 11, and I thank you with all my heart. You must be as tender and sensitive as you are for your dear American daughters, to write to the last of all, and with an effusion of ardent charity. I see well, reverend mother, that God has supplied what is lacking here of spiritual help, for your letters, which have always made the greatest impression on me, stir me up a thousand times more to attempt to render me worthy of a mother who knows so well how to instill the practice of perfection. Oh! Undoubtedly, I did not desire enough the sacrifice that Our Lord has given me the grace to offer him, in order to work more efficaciously toward perfection, that is, conformed in everything to the Heart of Jesus; and I have the sweet confidence that his divine assistance will help me all the way to the end in this great enterprise.

Since you are so patient as not to tire of my poor missives, I will profit with all my heart from your loving invitation; so, since I wrote to you last week, today I will take advantage of an occasion to tell you again something of our dear America, which pleases me

---

217 French copy, *Lettres de la Basse Louisiane 1827-1830*. Pp. 79-84. GASSH C III USA Foundation Basse-Louisiane, Box 2.

more every day, and about our little house that I know interests you actively, as you want me to do. In return, what joy there is in Grand Coteau when it is question of news from our incomparable Mother Barat!

We have an unusual climate: in the same day, we often experience the 4 seasons. Winter was so mild this year that it was not necessary to light the stove. Nevertheless, since Christmas almost regularly there is one very cold day and the next day is extremely hot. The main food of the country is beef and pork. For our house it is the same except that rarely someone gives us a pig. Vegetables are not as abundant as in France; we have little salad, much cabbage, a few carrots, potatoes in winter, and in summer a kind of sugared apple, called <u>sweet potato</u>. The children like it very much, and it is a great resource for *goûter* that they often do with one of these boiled potatoes as big as about 2 fists. They eat a very light supper, according to American custom. We follow this, too, and it is very healthy. Our children are never sick. This supper consists of a kind of very heavy cereal made with water or a little fat. The corn flour is the one used for this. Our children are happy with a cup of milk and hardly a little piece of bread. Or otherwise, it is one potato and always with milk or tea, or even refined syrup that they call here molasses. In the morning, they always take for breakfast coffee or milk. Doing this regularly is advantageous both for the health of our students and for the budget. The parents never stop praising it and admiring how much their children profit. It seems that Mother Eugenie cannot follow this economical plan, which her Creoles perhaps do not follow like our Americans; so that she is obliged to serve suppers like those in France. Our little community eats like the boarding school, except when the wheat flour diminishes, we eat corn bread, which is eaten everywhere, as much by the Negroes as by the animals that have to be fed in winter. In good season, the prairie suffices for their maintenance.

At this time we have ten cows who give milk, but not as abundantly as in Europe, nor is it as good, but nevertheless it is essential because we take milk morning and evening. Without this help, we would be bereft. This year there has been an increase in calves, so that with the help of God, we can hope always to have this resource. Dear Sister Marguerite has a chicken yard of about 50 birds, with hope of increase. She cares for these little creatures with an affection that often amuses us. Besides, this dear sister, who is about 60 years old, leads a life that is very edifying.[218] She wants to write to you on this occasion, and truly, dear reverend mother, if you could address two or three lines to her, she would be filled with joy. She is well, but I always fear that she will be taken from us too soon. She is a blessing for the house. She sees to morning prayer for 6 or 8 Americans who barely understand French, and all our students revere her. Our cowherd sister comes from St Michael. She is nearly 6 feet tall and proportionately strong, and very desirous of serving God.[219] Her mother is at St Michael. This family has merited by its devotion and probity to be called by the inhabitants of LaFourche, Great good God, in such a way that sometimes they call this sister Great good God. But Mother Eugenie has given her the name of Cecile. She is very good and very exact. She made her first vows on December 27 last year, with the approval of Mother Duchesne, since her two years of novitiate had finished. At this time we have as cook a little sister who came from St Ferdinand as an orphan.[220] Ordinarily, a Negress does the kitchen during the summer, because the heat is too intense for the whites to do it all the time without running a risk to their health. Since we have been obliged to send away our Negress, who was not happy with us,[221] Mother Xavier will see about getting another. Our Negro is all we need for the

---

218 Marguerite Manteau, RSCJ, was born in 1779, so about fifty at this time. She did not die until 1845.
219 This is Cecile Josephine Boudreau, RSCJ (1793-1847). Her mother, Mrs. Sophie Boudreau, had entered the Society at St. Michael, and died as a coadjutrix aspirant a few months after this, in December 1829.
220 Possibly Clemence Pillet, who came from St. Ferdinand in 1827 and left the Society in 1831.
221 This is possibly Phyllis, acquired in 1823 with children, about whom there is no further information.

commissions. He goes on horseback twice a week to Opelousas Village to look for meat. Everyone says there are few Negroes like him. He is very faithful and does all his duties like a Christian.[222] This was a very long account, since mother wanted to ask me.

In spite of the fact that there is no longer question of our moving to Opelousas, this does not mean, dear mother, that we do not need one or two religious for Grand Coteau. Because we are not numerous enough, regularity suffers on account of our work. Often we are obliged to let go some of our exercises in order to be there enough with the students. With a few more, we would be more regular. And if one knew music, we would attract children, and we would not have to hire teachers here at immense expense. Mother Xavier has sent you recently how we would need the religious that you will be willing to send, mature persons, professed, and disposed to die to self at every moment, to see nothing but God alone, in a word, who live in the spirit of faith.

We have had very pretty material for our clothing; it is a kind of veil that is of very good price. We would need one or two pieces of black veiling for veils. Ours are worn out and we will soon get some in crepe, because there is nothing else.

What pain the sad state of health of Mother Neline has caused me and Mother Xavier, and how we ask our good master not to take her from us so soon, even though it is ever his good pleasure. O mother, what a heart you have! It is rightly called the victim of our Society! If only it were given to me to take away so much pain that weighs it down unceasingly! But what am I saying? This divine Heart of Jesus has filled with the favors of his cross those who have the happiness to appreciate it. May I be in the end among this number! . . .

All your American daughters are at your feet and ask your maternal blessing. Mother Xavier will write to you soon. It is in the divine hearts that I will be always with a tender respect,

---

222 This is Frank Hawkins. His wife Jenny Eaglin arrived in December of that year.

> My beloved mother, your very grateful
> and obedient daughter.
> L. Dorival.

Louise Dorival to Madeleine Sophie Barat[223]

Grand Coteau, June 5, 1829

Beloved Mother,

I think you will already have received a letter that I had the pleasure of writing to you last March. I gave you some details about our charming little house of Grand Coteau. I think the simplicity of this refuge of peace would be to your liking. How many times when taking the evening air after a burning heat, Mother Xavier and I carry our thoughts and our heart toward our dear Mother Barat! . . . How you would like this little gallery where we take recreation during the summer! Oh no, this isolation from the world, this calm, this tranquility is not for sale! . . . How can I ever thank you enough, reverend mother, for having deigned to choose me for dear America. I know well that God, knowing my weak character, had me find here something entirely different than I expected, for I thought I would not find in this dear country anything but sacrifices of all kinds, and on the contrary, this house offers me all kinds of pleasures. One especially that is very precious to me is to see the haste with which our young people want to become Catholic. I have been more than once touched during Holy Week, when our children make their retreat for First Communion. A young American of 14 or 15 years, whose parents refuse permission, very desirous of becoming Catholic, could not assist at the ceremonies without collapsing in tears that the ardor of her desires made her shed. Another in the same case proposed that when she is free, she will embrace our holy religion.

---

223 GASSH. French copy; green hardback notebook, pp. 86-91.

We hope that Bishop Rosati, whom we expect these days, will secretly baptize the first. The other has recently left. A third, raised in strict Protestantism (that is what the parents call it), who entered the boarding school about 15 days ago, has nevertheless just asked and obtained permission to be baptized. I am in inexpressible astonishment to see the manner in which God acts in these young souls, to whom we say nothing to influence them, since our prospectus says that explicitly, and it is after this assurance that parents of different opinions confide their children to us. You see, dear mother, what consolation your daughters must taste!

The day after Easter 4 of our children made their First Communion and 4 renewed it. We hope that one of these last will become a Religious of the Sacred Heart. She left the boarding school 4 years ago, and came to spend her Easter here. She seems to have decided to become a religious. She is 18 years old, has a good appearance, has a facility for study, and is especially good for needlework. She is an American, has a great deal of devotion, and it seems that her family will weakly oppose her plan. I have delayed hope that this plan will succeed, but I fear that it will not last.[224]

During the month of May, the Blessed Virgin[225] completed our 40th student, so it seems that we will soon reach 50 and beyond. Many are making promises and should come these days, so that our house is too small. We can house 50 by crowding very much, but it would be impossible to place any more. So it is now question of interesting the inhabitants, by whom we are seen very well, to make a subscription to build us a brick house next to ours, so as to render service to a greater number of children. It seems that several people are already well disposed to contribute to this building, which is indispensable for us. Before going public with it, Mother Xavier is waiting for the consent of Mother Duchesne and Bishop Rosati. It seems to me that you will approve an action that will improve our

---

224 No student in the student records at this time entered the Society of the Sacred Heart.
225 May is the month traditionally dedicated to her.

work, since it is no longer question of going to the town, about which I am very happy. I believe that you will have received a long time ago the letter of Mother Xavier who sent in detail the reasons that have made us desist from the project of moving our establishment.[226] Everyone admires the situation of our house more; its total separation particularly pleases the Americans, and us.

We have at last found a music teacher and already 7 children have begun. In a few days, several others will also begin. That means a doubling of tasks; I have the consolation of writing to you during the surveillance. We have to take on the expense of a piano; it will cost $300, that is, about 1500 F. Happily the money is already there. The classics books that we have received from Mr. Rasand are also paid for. At the moment, Mother Xavier is setting aside all she can to pay for the voyage of the two religious that she hopes you will be willing to send to Grand Coteau, for Grand Coteau.

We are very busy because of the two languages that we are obliged to teach equally, which doubles our classes and we are only 5 to do it, the 6th of our religious being completely employed with the pantry and economic management of the house. We only have three [coadjutrix] sisters, which means that our young choir religious help in the dormitories between classes. We wash the laundry of almost all the children. It is true that we have some Negresses to help, but they cannot do it in our interior areas. They are not likely to take enough interest.

Please, dear mother, take under special consideration our children of Grand Coteau and send them reinforcement. It is so essential to conserve the spirit of our dear Society to receive some religious that are well formed in France! If they are very devoted, they will only find consolation here, but truly, one has to set oneself aside completely, if one wants to be happy far from personal and spiritual help where we live. But Jesus is there and we have souls to save. What more do we need?

---

226 Xavier's letter of February 22.

We have neither Office nor exposition of the Blessed Sacrament during the day. We are too few. So mother, please increase our little community. We will willingly pay all the expenses of the voyage.

We have learned of the death of our very Holy Father the Pope Leo XII. What loss for the Church and for our Society! Is Mother Neline better? We are so happy when we have some news from France! A few lines give much pleasure.

Bless me, dear mother, as well as all your daughters of America, so far from their mother. It is very consoling to know that she offers us to the Heart of Jesus with her lucky daughters of Europe. As for me, my happiness will be to be always with the most respectful devotion, *in Corde Jesu*,

Reverend mother,
You very grateful
And very submissive daughter,
L. Dorival

Supplement to this letter

Of June 15, 1829

Dear Reverend Mother,

I am only sending my letter of the 5th today. Bishop Rosati has just written that he must postpone the visit to us that he had hoped to make until next year. He must go in August to Baltimore for a council or synod that will take place in that city, and that he hopes will do much good for religion. He is sending us the election of our Holy Father the Pope [Pius] VIII. I have just learned that Mother Van Damme is at St Michel, that Mother Dutour has 40 boarders [at LaFourche], and that St Michel is ever prospering. It is our dear bishop who gives us this news.

To give you an idea, dear reverend mother, of what the Americans do on the subject of the religious, here is what has just arrived to Mother Xavier. A lady of the first families of the area, when she withdrew her daughter from our house, wanted to show her gratitude in a delicate way, as she said. This she did by putting on Mother Xavier's finger a gold ring that contained hair from the father of the young person. We laughed quite a bit at this gift; to refuse it would have been offensive in the eyes of this lady. So accepting it to please her, Mother Xavier asks your permission to keep it. Of course, she does not wear it and never will. As soon as the lady left, she put this ring with some other little objects.

L. Dorival

Xavier Murphy to Bishop Rosati[227]

S.S.C.J.M.   Grand Coteau June 15, 1829

If my Lord and dear father, anything could have compensated for our recent disappointment, your amicable letter of the 5th instant just come to hand assuredly would. I shall not trespass on your Lordship's precious time by a detailed description of the general dissatisfaction felt by your flock at G.C. Suffer it to say that it has proved to demonstration that fruition is not our portion here below. Immediately on the receipt of the sad letter the medallion and ribbons were simply distributed without crowns, etc. for I really had not spirits to place them on their disappointed heads.[228]

I write these few hurried lines for this day's mail thinking they may yet salute you in our state. There is now question of the necessity of enlarging the Institution by the addition of a brick building adjoining this by the means of a subscription. I have already spoken to Mr. Louaillier on the subject but could come to no fixed point until after your visit when I propose discussing this and several other imperative affairs with my good father & Bishop, but *fiat*

---

227 English autograph. Rosati collection.
228 Bishop Rosati was expected to preside at the awarding of prizes at the end of the school year. Medallions and ribbons were symbols of student leadership; crowns were usually bestowed on graduates.

fiat. Mr. L recommends my addressing Genl. Jackson on the subject (having a niece of the President's in our pension whose father is a friend of mine induces Mr. L to engage this planning). Therefore my Lord, I request your immediate decision on the practibility [*sic*] of both these questions, upon neither of which can I or shall I determine until fully sanctioned by Your Lordship's approbation. That of last year on an almost similar occasion proved so propitious for the general good of the establishment and so accordant with my own feelings that I must deem it a <u>heresy</u> to act without your entire concurrence. Yes father, our delicious solitude has charms & advantages peculiarly advantageous to the labors, peace of mind and interior spirit of the spouses of the Heart of Jesus.

As I suppose your Lordship will go direct to St Louis, pray communicate the above mentioned plans to *Mère* Duchesne from whom I have not heard for nearly 3 months, a silence unusual on her part. It also appears that our letters have been opened. This is amazing us. I have been accustomed to think aloud with this *bonne mère* in all my letters. I have also to solicit your permission for Sr Gray's making her first vows on the approaching feast of the S. Heart.[229] As the time is so near I suppose I am to construe your tacit answer. She promises fair to be an excellent religious & useful subject. She remembers with gratitude that you, father, & one of your priests have been the means of her entering the Society.[230]

Until the receipt of your most <u>esteemed communicative</u> letter I had no intimation of the arrival of *Mères* Van Damme and Detchemendy, nor of the nomination of our Holy father, nor of the final sweep of the now free sons of Erin.[231] The inviting words

---

229 Eleanor(e) (Josephine) Gray (1808-1862) had entered the Society in Florissant two year earlier. She was later superior in Saint Louis, Buffalo, and Saint Michael, and one of the foundresses in Saint John, New Brunswick in 1854.

230 Eleanor(e) Gray, RSCJ, would make her first vows at Grand Coteau on July 3, 1829. She had come to the novitiate in Florissant at the special recommendation of Bishop Rosati.

231 This refers to the Roman Catholic Emancipation Act on April 13, 1829, repealing the Irish penal laws against Catholics, in place since 1672.

of the prophet psalm 44: *Audi filia et vade*,[232] which I have endeavoured to reduce to practice in this country of my adoption causes this intelligence to convey less joy to my heart than the assurance you give of our once more possessing Fathers De Neckere[233] & [De] La Croix with the additional pleasure of having your own valued self (in the bargain), our own head bishop. Apropos, father, as this letter is addressed to you in <u>entire confidence</u>, in the event of your approving of our building here and that Father [De] La Croix soon returns, try & give him to us here. You know how devout he is & how calculated for inspecting workmen, etc. The auspicious omen which the synod gives for the general good of Religion, as well as the success which evidently attends all your undertakings, my Lord, fills me with hope & new courage, that all may be crowned with a happy conclusion, is & shall be the daily prayer of all your daughters there. I have positively recommended the sisters to direct all their communions, etc. for this momentous affair. A letter from Mrs. Overton on board the steamboat informed me of her *rencontre* with you. She added that they find "our Bishop & priest most agreeable gentlemen." I expected to have announced you, father, by showing the <u>elegant ring</u> (set with Genl. Overton's hair) that his Lady put on my finger, when taking out her daughter. As soon as she got to the gate I had to strip my finger of this ill suited finery.

But I must cease chatting with your Lordship on whose time I have too long intruded, By assuring you of the present regret, entire esteem, and sincere affection of your own attached little flock of G. Coteau, whom I have the honor of placing at their father's feet, requesting his Benediction & prayers. Your most

---

232 Listen, daughter, and go. Ps 45 (44):11.
233 Leo De Neckere, C.M., born in West Flanders in 1800, was one of Dubourg's recruits to the American mission in 1817. He joined the Lazarists at St. Mary's of the Barrens in 1820 and was ordained in 1822. Named first bishop of New Orleans, August 4, 1829, he was only consecrated June 24, 1830, because he had been back in Europe recovering his health. This letter is written between the two events. He died of yellow fever in New Orleans in 1833.

Respectfully attached daughter *in Corde Jesu*
Xavier

[On the outside:]
The Right Revd Dr Rosati
Bishop of
St Louis etc.

[On one side, in another hand in French:]
1829 June 15 Mother Xavier Grand Coteau
Received July 15

Louise Dorival to Madeleine Sophie Barat[234]

Grand Coteau, August 14, 1829

Dear Reverend Mother,

How good you are to think sometimes of your poor <u>Louisianans</u> and to encourage them with your precious letters! The last one I received was dated in March and arrived a few days ago. I was so consoled that it would be difficult to explain it. I always experience a kind of inner renewal each time you address a few words to me. You know well, mother, that you are my only director; in America, one cannot expect to have a priest as director. They are too rare, and then, there is no choice. Confession is all there is, and happy are we when we can procure a chaplain. The divine heart has given us this grace. We have a good Italian ecclesiastic who says Holy Mass for us every day and hears our confessions every week,[235] but what a difference between him and <u>those</u> I knew in France! Nevertheless, I feel that Our Lord himself makes up for what we lack in spiritual help, and I see well that God alone is worth more than all his creatures, no matter how holy they are.

---

234 French copy in notebook, *Lettres de la Basse Louisiane*, pp. 91-97. GASSH.
235 Probably John Rosti, C.M.

Nothing equals the happiness I taste in this dear Louisiana, where there is so much good to do, unfortunately very few workers. The Protestant sect of Methodists, very widespread here, put all their efforts into making <u>converts</u>, and sadly we know that they succeed enough in their enterprise. We have in our area a woman who is totally preoccupied with her sect and who works ceaselessly to make proselytes. If it were possible to her, we would not have a single student. The name <u>Catholic</u> is a horror to her and even that of the <u>Church</u>. Lately she has made efforts, happily unsuccessful, to find women who would be willing to take charge of building a house of education alongside ours, to prevent our boarding school from growing. This same woman, who has established one in the neighboring state to ours, sees sadly that it does not prosper very much. We hope that our good Master will continue to protect the house of his divine Heart, and that he will not permit error to prevail over the truth.

Our students, as you know, reverend mother, have surpassed the number of 40, and it seems they will go on increasing, so that our house is too small and we will definitely have to enlarge it. Since in this country everything is done by subscription, we intend to use it to help us in this enterprise that will become indispensable if we do not want to refuse children, and I swear to you, mother, that I would be deeply chagrined if we had to. These poor souls, what would become of them?

I do not think I told you that last year in August, lightning hit our lightning rod and caused an extraordinary commotion in the whole house. One of our young people was so stunned by this event that she said afterwards that she shook herself to see if she was still alive because she thought she was dead. It is very fortunate that we have this physical preservative, no doubt joined to divine protection, for several gentlemen who were in the parlor then assured us that without the lightning rod, the house would have been destroyed.

June 26, feast of the Sacred Heart, we tried to celebrate the best way possible. Two of our young Americans were baptized, as well as an old Negress who works here.[236] On July 2, an Irish novice named Josephine Gray made her first vows with great fervor. She is only 22 years old, well composed, and very useful especially for English. I think she will be a good religious.

Around July 22, for your feast wishes, we acquired a good old Negro who will be baptized tomorrow and married to the old Negress whom I had just mentioned.[237] He says he does not want to go <u>with the devil in hell</u>, but rather <u>with God</u>. He listens to the instructions on religion with an attention and a pleasure that is very consoling for us who are the witnesses. We have another Negro who is like the <u>Mr. Bullard</u> of Grand Coteau. He is very faithful and receives the sacraments on the big feasts.[238] We are renting a 4th black person for the laundry, without which we could not manage. Here we do the laundry of almost every student.

God has protected us this year in a very special manner: in the environs of Opelousas, smallpox, measles, etc. have ravaged, and not one of our children or sisters or Negroes were attacked. Everyone here enjoys good health, and it has become like a proverb, that one must come to Grand Coteau to be well. Nevertheless, dear Mother Xavier has often had fever this summer, and I have been very troubled for a week because of three rather strong attacks that really weakened her a month ago. Fortunately, we have a good doctor, and above it all Our Lord, who I hope will not abandon his work. If Mother Xavier were to leave us, it is morally impossible that the establishment would subsist with the reputation it has acquired among the Americans. We have half the boarding school of strangers who arrive without understanding a word of

---

236 This is Melite.
237 Melite had been acquired some time before 1829. The house journal records the acquisition of Martin and his baptism and their marriage on August 15.
238 Probably Frank Hawkins, acquired in 1823. In December 1829, his wife Jenny and two sons would join him, acquired by Xavier Murphy to reunite the family.

French. The parents require correspondence that is very exact and very frequent, in English. As a result, without someone like her, it is feared that poor Grand Coteau would decline. At the end, *fiat*!

Nevertheless, these poor young Americans are so interesting that it is to be hoped that they could always find at the Sacred Heart a shelter against infidelity, at least during the time of their education. Have everyone pray for her, dear mother, so that she can still work for a long time in the Lord's vineyard and edify us by her fervor and her love for our dear Society. As for me, I am acclimated and am very well. May I use my strength in a useful way for the glory of the Sacred Heart of our good Master![239]

You will probably learn with pleasure that every year for May 1, feast of Mother Duchesne,[240] we send her from here a quantity of clothing of our students, who consider themselves lucky to do this charity for the little Indians. This package is of such dimensions that Mother Duchesne only calls it the big package. Each time, she seems very happy with it. She finds there the means to clothe everyone. Even the sacristy gets its part. She noted to us that she would not have any expenses for clothing because of this.[241]

If you could, dear mother, send us by our dear sisters who should come to join us in this dear Louisiana, the collection of works of plantade,[242] or hymns for church (I do not know if that is the title, but almost), that would give us great pleasure and would be very useful for us to solemnize our great feasts. Several of our students are learning the music, waiting until they are sure enough to accompany us on the piano. The teacher sees to it willingly. Already the little pieces that Mother Vidaud had the generosity to

---

239 Louise would die four years before Xavier, in 1832, the first of the French missionaries to die in America.
240 The feast of St. Philip, whom she celebrated as her patron saint.
241 On June 30, 1830, Philippine wrote a thank you letter for such a package, maybe this one, to a Grand Coteau student named Felicia Chrétien. French autograph USCA.
242 Probably meaning the sacred music of Charles-Henri Plantade (1764-1839), but the word is not capitalized in the copied letter.

copy for us have served this end. May she receive again my thanks, with the request to continue to send us something beautiful, especially the hymns the way they sing them in Paris. It is so pleasing to us to draw near in every way to the dear cradle of the Society.

This year, mother, has been bad in many ways. The waters lowered at the time when it was least expected. The yearly provisions cost triple because they had to come by alternate routes, and just as flour was lacking in many parts of Europe, we suffered from a scarcity double that of last year. Besides, the harvest was missed because of continual rains that we have had and that it seems are not yet over. In spite of all that, thanks be to God we are not in debt, and we are in a position to pay the voyage of our two sisters. We are already waiting for them impatiently. We are always happy in America to see our dear compatriots, especially when they come for such noble reasons; and then, mother, I am convinced that it is necessary to speak about France in your houses of the New World, if you want to preserve the spirit of the Sacred Heart, which is only understood with difficulty in these regions. In addition, what joy would we not have to learn your news from the mouth of your daughters who have left you so recently. Oh! Mother, this life is a time of sacrifices and of continual sacrifices, but God is there. It is the consolation of the soul in its exile.

I am at your feet, beloved mother, bless your poor child who is so little capable of fulfilling the designs of God by herself. Bless her and all this little house that is wholly devoted to you *in corde Jesu*. But above all, your Louise, who owes you her happiness, and who will always be yours,

Your very submissive and
grateful daughter
L. Dorival

Xavier Murphy to Madeleine Sophie Barat[243]

S.S.C.J.M. Recommended to the star of the sea, Mary our good mother.

Grand Coteau, August 15, 1829

Your precious letter of March 9, dear and much loved mother general, that of Mother de Marbeuf with the journal of our motherhouse, all reached me and filled me with delicious consolation so I was able to say to you with the apostle, "All is yours, you are Jesus Christ's and Jesus Christ is God's."[244] It remains to us to wish that our present Pontiff will be as willing to protect us as his illustrious predecessor.[245] What a loss for our Society, but God is everlasting.

The arrival of our Office book and our Constitutions fills me with strength and gratitude to see our holy rules imprinted for me. This is a special blessing, [since I am] always afraid that I will not read the writing well. And in effect I rather feel at present that the Holy Spirit instills in me the meaning, because I have not understand each word well.

But dear mother, I have so many things to cover in this letter that I am forced to be quiet about my thoughts, opening my heart, etc. etc.

I leave the news of the (...) to Mother Dorival but she is not (....) Finally I send you the address of our banker for the amount marked in the order that accompanies this letter. I recommend to you the greatest economy because we will be indebted for a long time to the gentleman friend of our house of Grand Coteau who has authorized me to draw on his friend in Paris, and pay attention, dear mother, that he accords me this permission only in <u>favor</u> of our house <u>here</u> which he desires very much to see flourish.

---

243 French autograph. GASSH.
244 1 Cor 3:21-23.
245 Pius VIII (1761-1830) became pope on March 31, 1829. His predecessor, Leo XII, had died on February 10, 1829.

In the trousseau of our sisters, a winter shawl is useless; the climate is too hot to be able to use it. I ask that a large number of bonnets be brought; we do not have the time to make them here; a piece of veiling for us and also for our sisters. It cannot be found in this country and the crepe is not sufficiently religious and too expensive. I beg you, dear mother, do not send anything old. The shipping is too expensive to be worth it. No classic books because thanks be to God we are well furnished, but we are very poor in books of devotion, especially retreats and meditations. I think Father Barat will gift us with some. I know how much he loves the Louisiana mission. Finally since it is a question of perpetuating the work of the Sacred Heart in Grand Coteau among the living temples of the Holy Spirit[246] (the 2 new religious), I think that the sacristy at this moment is going without ciborium and ostensorium, which annoys me, but justice is the only theological virtue in this country. Send me please, dear mother, a <u>veil</u> and a <u>pelerine</u> of yours; the previous one is worn out. In spite of myself, I am happy to see these dear sisters among us and when I am no longer, I will at least have the consolation that the spirit of the Society is preserved in the little house of Grand Coteau, and believe me, dear mother, that it is the religious from France who alone can consolidate this precious work in America. The subjects from this country enter young and for lack of education as children, they rarely attain that <u>tact</u> that forms the *je ne sais quoi* of our charism.

Judge then what ought to be the qualities of those who wish to join us; consequently they are <u>conquered</u> by the <u>pious</u> <u>emblem</u> of our Society, which will be for them a continual guard against the temptations that human nature gives birth to in one so far from her dear motherland. But the Holy Spirit will tell our mother how he has already formed persons proper to help the last and the least of her daughters, <u>that is to say</u>, your poor Xavier, who from day to day feels more and more the grace of her noble vocation and the

---

246 1 Cor 3:16.

inestimable favor of having been chosen as spouse of the Heart of Jesus – Oh! Yes, dear mother, that thought alone occupies all my thoughts at the foot of the altar.

In my last letter I spoke of our reunion at St Michael as a positive thing, but the impossibility of Mother Duchesne to come down obliges us to wait until next spring, so it appears that Mother Eugenie and I will be obliged to go to meet her in St Louis, because it seems to me completely useless to meet without good Mother Duchesne, because if Mother Eugenie has one opinion, Mother Dutour another, and I arrive with a third, which ought to predominate – because you know well, dear mother, that women are women <u>everywhere</u>!

You can be sure that I am well disposed to send to good Mother Duchesne all that is in my power, having much expense this year with regard to the travel of our sisters, of the purchase of a piano, the enormous price of flour and other provisions, because all of this was needed this year. I have just sent her the dowry of a novice (sent here by her) and who made her vows the last Feast of the Sacred Heart in our chapel, that is 2,000 francs [Eleanor Gray]. The aspirant is Irish with an angelic perfection and the most useful of our sisters here, except for old Marguerite [Manteau] who always edifies us.

The health of the good and very useful Mother Dorival is excellent. She is everything for me here; with a little management for her character all goes well. She is more educated than I, her strength is the class, she is not up for external affairs; with the children she does marvels, fortunately because my health is not good. Almost continual fevers weaken me very much, but for the good of the house it is necessary to suffer, and a spouse of the Heart of Jesus ought to be a spouse of blood – the more my body is feeble, the more my spirit is tranquil and resigned. Pray, dear mother, that God gives me the strength to be completely given for his glory. The thing that burdens me the most is the correspondence of the house – it is absolutely necessary in English as the Americans predominate in the boarding school and their parents demand letters continually. Otherwise they are very content and we are free to do what we judge appropriate without interference at all and the greatest esteem. Several among our children have had the happiness of being baptized and several await that grace.

I must end this letter, alas, because I need to put an address for New Orleans. I find all the words easy except <u>farewell</u>. You know, dear mother, how I love you and esteem you and that I am entirely your daughter devoted in the adorable hearts of Jesus and Mary, at your knees awaiting your blessing. Xavier, R. of the S. Heart

P.S. I think that you will send our sisters via New Orleans – it is much less expensive, and the religious are less exposed than when they travel through all the United States. In the event that they stop with Mother Eugenie, it is necessary to pay attention to see that their baggage is <u>deposited</u> in New Orleans <u>with our agent, Messrs. Kennedy and Duchamp, No. 50, rue Toulouse</u> – in this way we will have it in eight days and with less expense because the communications with St Michael are very difficult and very expensive. (...)[247] X.

P.S. The copy of the letter enclosed will reach you two weeks later with the receipts and expenses of the last 6 months – in a letter of Mother Dorival in which you will also find the interesting details of our little house. I think that we will have our sisters for the new year. I recommend all our needs with a tender remembrance to Mother du ...[248] as treasurer general.

---

[247] Three uncertain words, possibly meaning, "See the case of the watch" (as example of difficult communication). See letter of February 22, 1829.
[248] The name is not clear, and does not correspond to the general treasurer at the time, who was Catherine de Charbonnel. It appears on the manuscript that *du C* was written first, then the ink scratched off.

Xavier Murphy to Madeleine Sophie Barat[249]

S.S.C.J.M.   Grand Coteau October 19, 1829

    Finally, dear and much loved mother, here I am entirely content. I thank you over and over. Mother Dorival will give you all the details of her arrival at Grand Coteau and of the visit of Mother Eugenie and of Mother Piveteau, etc. The same day as their arrival, in the morning I was sitting down to write you in a very sad way, but impossible to continue my letter, a *je ne sais quoi* rendered me incapable. I complained to Our Lord, asking him why he took from me the power to speak heart-to-heart with my Mother Barat, but by evening the answer was very clear: because I have all that I need from <u>my mother</u>. Believe me, dear mother, that I have not yet received your letter, nor that of my dear star, nor that of Mothers Bigeu and de Marbeuf. Mother Dorival left all these treasures at St Michel and Mother Eugenie has so much to do that as much as she (…) her return, she forgot to send these precious letters. God permitted it, I think, but you know, dear mother, I am so accustomed to doing all against nature since my time in this country that at present I scarcely feel the struggle; my character is entirely subdued. Listen then, please, if I have no need of faith and of the spirit of sacrifice; Mother Eugenie has taken, in order to send to Mother Duchesne, a coadjutrix sister whom we've had here since the foundation of this house [Mary Layton] and who is very helpful, and this is what good Mother D. said in her last letter: "You now have a good helper. What will you say if we take another from you (Mother Carmelite) to be superior of the Sisters of the Cross? I have written to our mother with this proposition. If you find any obstacles about this on your side it is a great good to procure a little peace."

---

249 French autograph. GASSH.

Oh, very dear mother, all that I have to say on the subject is that the person in question is the most useful in the house, the only one able to help me with external business; she is the assistant, treasurer, manages the clothing of the children and of the community, of a mature age, etc. etc. finally all that I need. But God replies that I think of myself when it is a matter of his glory. If he requires this sacrifice of me, *fiat, fiat*. However, if this house is deprived of religious when we have so few, I will not be able to continue to help the house of St Louis as I did this year. I will be obliged to have recourse to enslaved who are extremely expensive here and extremely difficult to manage. You will find inside a little note with all the expenses of this year, that is to say, for the <u>building</u>, <u>repairs</u>, and <u>those sent</u> to Mother Duchesne; and note, dear mother, that we are not in debt to anyone. At present we are obliged to enlarge our little house. We are making a 3rd dormitory. A propos of that, even though we live in a palace of the Sacred Heart, Mother Dorival says that you would be very pleased with our little dormitory, and above all our pretty gallery with the beautiful moon that you love so much. Mother Duchesne spoke to me of our vow of stability. I await your dear letter so as to make it <u>according to your orders</u>, and certainly it will be with all my heart and all my soul that I bind myself more and more to this dear Society that is my joy and my glory. What delicious feelings I experience in reading of our approbation and the letter of our father protector. I have not yet received the decrees, nor your dear pelerine.

As you are loving toward your Xavier who loves you more and more in the Sacred Heart of our spouse, as soon as I have the joy of receiving your letter and that of my star, etc, I will have the sweet satisfaction of writing to you all, while waiting (...) for this precious remembrance of his goodness.

We have finished our scholastic year with glory; the contentment of the parents was complete and the attachment of our children is so great for the house that none want to go home. All

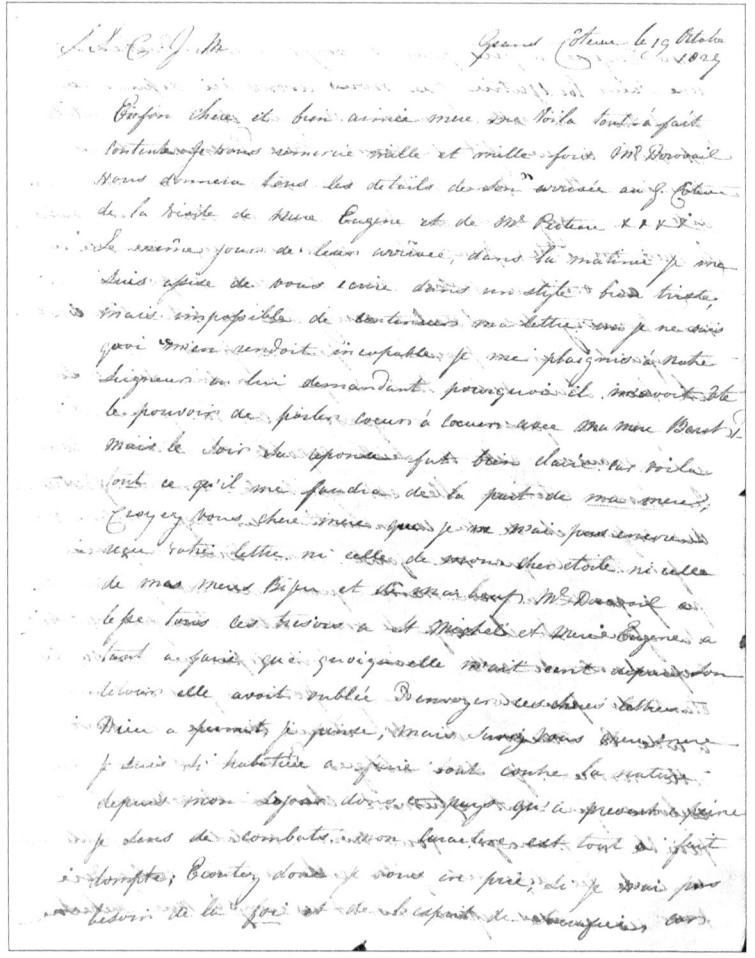

Xavier Murphy to Madeleine Sophie Barat, October 19, 1829.

returned after vacation. Several Americans were baptized during the year, thus you, dear mother, perceive with reward, that the finger of God was here, because certainly it is he alone who has done all this for us; to him alone honor and glory.

[On the outside:]
I close this letter with great difficulty; my hand trembles because of the fever that I experience continually. I feel more strength of

soul than of body; my spirit is almost always tranquil. It seems to me more that the more imperfect I am, the more God loves me. I don't have any taste for prayer; <u>naked faith</u> is my only support. God gives me a great attraction for poverty because it is

[On the other side of the outside:]
four months that I carried the shoes of our children with a delicious joy; at other times I had much difficulty in doing that. It seems to me, dear mother, I am at your feet as a little footstool. But sometimes I knock at your door, saying a <u>little louder</u> that this transatlantic daughter is away from you too long, but that your mother you always have, poor me; rarely, dear mother, do I leave you. The end of your letters is too much for a heart that is entirely yours always and forever in the Heart of Jesus.

Xavier Murphy

1830

Xavier Murphy to Madeleine Sophie Barat[250]

S.S.C.J.M.   Grand Coteau, January 20, 1830

I have so many things to tell you, dear and much loved mother general, that I have just said a prayer, very short but very fervent, for the Spirit to direct my pen and infuse my words.

Mother Duchesne just left us after a visit of three weeks, during which we arranged the financial accounts and catalogues that are included here. Tell me if you want me to do the same every year. Mother Duchesne was not happy with the cloister that she did not find sufficiently strict, because of the prairie that is in front of the house. I have changed the dimensions and the arrangement; I have asked Mother Dorival to explain to you. While awaiting your

---
250 French autograph. GASSH.

decision, Mother Duchesne has allowed the boarders to continue to walk there but not the community. She also found it bad that I have not made English the predominant language in the house. I do not know why this holy Mother holds to that language in which I speak with all our children, carry on correspondence and keep the accounts, but our sisters being French or Creole, I speak with them habitually in their language. Besides for our rules and usages, French is much better and I would fear making any innovation in our practices.

I have received the letter from Mother Ducis with your little word, dear mother, which gave me so much pleasure. I have paid Father de la Croix the 1,000 francs for the trip of Mother Lavy, and Mr. Borgna 430 francs, my part for the things sent to St Louis; as for the 3,000 francs that you have received from Mr. Davillier, I ask you, mother, that after the purchases that we have requested, you keep the surplus for the needs that we will have for our building that now will be at our expense, since it was stopped by Mother Duchesne. It will be more prudent only to enlarge *this house* with a chapel and a dormitory rather than to build an entire building by subscription, having neither priest nor reliable persons to oversee the work done here. Because if we had accepted the offer of the city of Opelousas, we would enter a house all clear [of debt] and we would not have to fear any claim on our property here. A completely different situation. We will be responsible in case the subscriptions are lacking. Besides, the isolation of our situation displeases Mother Duchesne, who thinks that only the children of the very rich can get here, since the expense of travel is so great and consequently the boarding school will never amount to much. This situation has deprived us for a long time of the possibility of being useful to the houses of Missouri. There is no doubt that if I had kept in an account all the money I have sent to St Louis, we would be at present able to erect a beautiful building independently from the public. I assure you, Mother, that it is truly an enigma for me, that after having seen the success that our Society has had in Louisiana, our houses in Missouri constantly meet so many obstacles. I believe that Mother Duchesne is too good; she accepts all kinds of candidates, deprived of all means, weighed down besides with work that maintenance of the Jesuit Fathers gives, etc. etc.

For the rest, I assume that our mothers recently arrived have already brought you up-to-date. As for me, I promised Mother Eugenie before leaving her to ask you to send a <u>visitator from your side, and between the two of us we will cover the costs of the trip</u>. Besides, as I have told you everything, I think that Mother Eugenie herself needs an assistant and I made to her and to Mother Duchesne the observation that since she has decided that the house of St Michael is the general noviceship, it is necessary that the novices see the way of the Society; and since Mother Eugenie (who certainly has done marvels) in the future will not be able to do it all, and often because of her many occupations the young novices are alone. If someone delegated for the visit of our houses can be installed at St Michael as assistant I think that that house will flourish.

As to our house at LaFourche, I believe that it will be the most stable house. It will furnish vocations for the Society; all our sisters from Louisiana being from that area (the only area in the country that has kept the faith), Mother De Tour [*sic*] is delighted with her house and its people. She seems to be the only superior here spoiled by the good God, and such a holy soul, such virtue, etc. etc.

As to your daughters of Grand Coteau, Providence has deprived us of the possibility of having postulants, the majority of our children being Protestants and all rich. It seems that according to the Gospel, the kingdom of heaven is not with them. All the young novices who are at St Michael were educated for free in the boarding school, and their parents are flattered to see them in such a beautiful house – in proof, there are 5 sister aspirants or novices and 3 boarders from the same family at this moment in the house of St Michael.[251] Tell me please <u>without fail</u> in your next letter if I say too much to you, but it seems that God gives me more openness of heart with you, mother general, than to anyone else, because as much as I venerate and greatly esteem Mother Duchesne, I am not completely at ease with her as she is in charge, as she is exhausted by mortifications and frustrations. It even seems that the religious up there are poorly formed, without any education, often lacking in this regard, and this applies to the boarding students also. In truth it seems to me that if I were in St Louis I would soon die with discouragement and frustration to see us so despised. Finally, since I have told you all, mother, this seems to me the cause.

The new religious are the children of the poor of the countryside, or the Irish, raised in the day school, who speak a jargon common in their region, which is in no way the English of the Americans. It is not surprising that the parents are without faith, without religion, and those who have no taste for the Gospel maxim: "Blessed are the poor," do not give us their children, but prefer to send them to the Methodist schools. Nevertheless, it is certain that the character of our Society <u>as it is in France</u> or even <u>as it is in Louisiana</u> is completely appropriate to the American character. So, dear mother, since it is under <u>your auspices</u> that our Society is colonized in this hemisphere, it is necessary to consolidate this work, perhaps the most useful and most glorious of your administration, from time to time to make the sacrifice of religious from France capable of carrying on our spirit. Then in the next century, America will be the most <u>beautiful diamond in your crown</u>.

I have almost forgotten to ask your permission that our children continue to walk in the prairie, since that is the only pleasure that our narrow location offers, and which attracts the parents to put their children here, in spite of the privation of masters [teachers of fine arts] because they are delighted to see the space that our

---

251 Six of the Lévêque sisters entered the Society: Maria in 1825, Seraphine and Louisa in 1826, Amelie and Evelina in 1828, and Lisa in 1830. Seraphine left in 1842; the others remained for life.

children enjoy. For the community, I keep them from going there, awaiting your decision. As for the woods, Mother Duchesne said that since you have given that permission at St Michael, and since our house is very near, for the sake of uniformity, we can__

[On the outside:]
__continue to enjoy them, and besides, our house touches them, as if we were in the woods themselves. For the rest, Mother Dorival will explain in more detail, in a letter that will reach you soon.

But in spite of myself, I must leave you. How short the time is when the heart speaks. And how hard it is to find <u>this word Farewell</u>. So accept, dear and beloved mother, this word <u>so hard</u>, and receive the expression of the most generous devotion, the most fervent attachment, and the complete esteem of your daughter

In Corde Jesu, Xavier R. du S.C.

Give my remembrances to all our mothers and sisters, especially to my <u>dear star</u> and Fathers Varin, Barat, and Perreau. Your Xavier.

[Address:]
New York

                        Mother
          Mother Barat Superior General
        of the Religious of the Sacred Heart
             Rue de Varennes No. 41
                    In Paris

[Postmarks:]
Opelousas, Louisiana Jan 26

Paid 50
Mar 23 1830
Mar 25 1830

Louise Dorival to Madeleine Sophie Barat[252]

S.S.C.J.M.   St. An. P.   Grand Coteau, January 28, 1830

My dearly beloved Mother,

Even though you undoubtedly received a few days ago news of your little house of Grand Coteau, nevertheless, Mother Xavier has given me the pleasant opportunity of writing to you myself, because she wants me to explain to you to what she only made allusion in the letter on the subject of cloister.

Our house is situated in an immense prairie, of which the greater part is ours; behind and in front is a large forest that we have never completely explored, even though it is also the property of the Sacred Heart. Nothing is more pleasant nor better for health than these two walking areas. We have the consolation of seeing that all of our students are well. This is one of the reasons that they confide them to us despite the distance and the bad roads. Until now, we have enjoyed these advantages peacefully and consider ourselves according to rule, since we have absolutely no one in the neighborhood, and consequently we are in perfect solitude. Nevertheless, Mother Duchesne, who spent three weeks here, tells us that to be according to rule on this point, we need your permission, reverend mother, to walk through that area that is not closed in by any cloister, and while awaiting your decision, we would do well to deprive ourselves of going into the prairie. That is what we are doing and what we will continue to do, and we allow our children to go with only the mistress who watches over them. For this is the only pleasant aspect offered by our location, which is too small for them to take their recreations. Beside, Mother, we are always (...) of certain limits of this beautiful walking area in which we have never set foot in spite of the extent of terrain that belongs to us. This area could be compared to the garden of the

---

[252] French autograph. The manuscript is very difficult to read. GASSH.

Hotel Biron. I know well that if we could have a cloister made, this would be better, but mother, it would cost us something like 10,000 francs to do it only in wood, and we would not be able for a long time to carry such an expense, while it seems there is question of a subscription for a building that is absolutely necessary for our house. So we have to deal with this.

You know, mother, all that Mother Xavier sent to France to help you in sending us reinforcement, and that now her treasury needs to be filled to pay for necessary works. To keep going, our establishment needs repairs and augmentations. Another reason that I must explain and that makes us ask this permission is that the woods, while pleasant for walking, are only so during the day, and the excessive heat in this region only allows going out after sunset. So the prairie is the best place to get some air, and if we deprive our children of this pleasure, they will no longer have access to our part, as I told you above. I think, dear mother, that I have said enough to you on this subject, and if you give us this exception that we think is necessary for the good of this little house, it will be with heartfelt gratitude. As well, be sure of our perfect submission in every possible case. Oh mother! It is so sweet to have to lay out these doubts and perplexities to a heart as maternal as yours! How happy I am that it is you, our foundress and mother, true mother, who has given me my mission in this new world where from time to time, I especially feel the immense difference from our hemisphere. This does not prevent me from being happy to the bottom of my soul through the assurance I have that God called me here, and of the good there is to do, but that will be done slowly, for lack of zealous and eloquent priests to spread the faith.

I must confide to you, dear mother (for it is only to you that I open my heart) how disappointed I was to get to know Mother Duchesne. I thought to find in her a means of renewing myself in the spirit of my state, and to increase the good of our house, but, mother, even though this is so holy a person, I felt constantly toward her an opposition of heart that I was careful to hide, but which hindered me very much during her whole stay here. Oh! What a difference from our mothers in France! Without certainly comparing her with you, dear reverend mother, who have holiness but also that amiability that gains you confidence. How I was mistaken to think I would find in her another Mother Bigeu. I admit to you that I was troubled to see that despite her eminent virtue, she is far from the approachability of our mothers. I do not mean to say that she was hard, oh no, but it is a style that doesn't fit me at all, and I feel a more lively gratitude toward you, dear mother, who has sent me precisely where I can be best, even though I am prepared to suffer much here. This holy Mother Duchesne is very old and very broken. She seems not to remember exactly things she had said before. She seems not to approve what would contribute to the enlargement of our houses, yet she wants to see them prosper. I think the fatigue she has endured has contributed to weakening her very much. I respect her as a saint but I cannot prevent myself from being glad that I am not obliged to live with her. I am confirmed more than ever in the resolution not to ask anyone but you, dear mother, about decisions that have to be made. My heart is ill at ease since the little visit of Mother Duchesne here, and I saw that Mother Xavier seemed constrained with her, which made me suffer more. Besides, the eve of her arrival here, I coughed up blood all day for the first time in my life, and I was burdened by it, thinking that I would become consumptive, but it seems to have been only a discharge from the chest caused by a bad cold. I was bled and since eight days ago, I am well.[253]

During three or four weeks that Mother Xavier spent at Saint Michael, O mother, how I suffered! ... for I assure you that I am in no way fit for government, especially in charge. It was time for her to return, for it was then that I became ill. I know that Mother Duchesne wants her for Saint Louis, but now, mother, Grand Coteau would fall, since it is the Americans who sustain

---

253 Indeed, she would die of consumption less than three years later.

it by sending their children, because Mother Xavier speaks their language and writes it perfectly. I had to tell you all this, mother; my heart unloads into yours that is so good, and it feels lighter, and will begin again to try to be less unworthy of the happiness of belonging to such a mother!...

A good and beautiful piano has just arrived here from New York. It has a superb sound. We are awaiting every day Mother Lavy, who is still in Saint Louis, but whom Mother Duchesne has finally promised to send us soon. Several of our children are waiting. As for us, it is already late to have this dear companion, too.[254] You will find here, dear mother, the second annual catalog; the first went off eight days ago.

As for postulants, we have none; the only one who presented herself and about whom I told you last year was prevented by her family. That is how it ordinarily happens in this country when people are wealthy. Several of our children here still show the desire to embrace our holy state but when they return to their families, it is over. Spiritual resources are completely lacking to them, even if they do not completely forget their religion.

I must end a conversation that is so pleasing to me. Mother Xavier missed you in her last letter dated the same month. Everything she thinks about the state of our Society in these faraway regions, I see things the same way, mother, I will say no more on that subject...My whole desire is that the spirit will be preserved the same as in France. This is the only consolation that I can experience so far from my mothers and especially from you, dear reverend mother. I have ever greater esteem for Mother Xavier. She is a soul of faith. I follow her tenderly. United in Our Lord; otherwise I find myself in an isolation of soul that makes me suffer sometimes but it is what I expected, and I fear, too, that my infidelities contribute to it. Pray a little, dear mother, for your poor Dorival who feels all her weakness and only trusts in the mercy

---

254 She arrived sometime in the next two months.

of the divine Heart. For I must admit that I do nothing or nearly nothing for the glory of our good Master. I do not see these souls turned toward God with ardor. Oh! How painful it is! Mother, and to think that it is doubtless by my fault, but God is so good, this is my only resource.

Please accept, dear mother, the assurance of my tender respect (...) as that of my lively gratitude. Your very submissive daughter. L. Dorival r.S.C.J.

[On side of p. 1:]
Respectful and affectionate remembrance especially to my dear Mother de Marbeuf. Please also, mother, recommend me to the prayers of our sisters and the fervent novitiate. I need them.

[On the envelope:]

Mother
Mother Barat Superior General
of the Religious of the Sacred Heart of Jesus
Rue de Varennes N°41 St Germain
Paris   France

[Upside down :]
For Father Varin

[Postmarks :]
Opelousas Louisiana Feb. 4
April 20 1830
April 22 1830
Overseas via L Havre
Paid 25

Xavier Murphy to Bishop Rosati[255]

S.S.C.J.M.   Grand Coteau February 19, 1830
[*In another hand in French:*] M. Xavier received April 21

Among all the congratulations my Lord and dear father that you may receive on your safe arrival in your Diocese, and the happy termination of your recent occupation, I hope your Lordship will believe none more warm or sincere than those now presented to you by your daughters of the Sacred Heart at Grand Coteau.

I have just read the circular (addressed to Father Rosti) announcing the final nomination of your distinguished Son[256] and whilst we join in thanksgiving to the kind Distributor of all good & perfect things, and in self-congratulation on this auspicious event, yet I must confess to you father that we experience a mixture of regret on reflecting that perhaps we may never more enjoy the consolation of seeing you amongst us. The entire satisfaction conferred on us by your paternal visit of 1828 filled every heart here with entire confidence & grateful affectionate veneration, and the no small delight I have myself individually experienced on learning from every quarter that your Lordship was pleased with his visit to G. Coteau makes me now sensibly feel "that there is no pleasure without pain." May I at least dear father hope that you will continue to hold us in the light of your great children and that in consigning us to the future care of your Son you will still reserve the claim of primogeniture in our regard.

As the pleasure of this life consists in hoping, I now calculate that as your Lordship must necessarily descend for the consecration [of Bishop De Neckere] you may perhaps favor & console us here by a <u>visit</u>. This you may remember we have a double claim to expect having being [*sic*] cheated of this satisfaction last year. I

---

255 English autograph. Rosati collection.
256 Leo Raymond De Neckere was named Bishop of New Orleans in August 1829, but not consecrated until June 1830.

have been also thinking that if our new prelate would determine to pass a few of the summer months in the delicious solitude of G. Coteau the presbytery could be arranged for his reception. I would most gladly defray the expenses of reparation etc. etc. I do believe father that an occasional residence in the Western District would be of ultimate advantage to Catholicity, which calls aloud for amelioration. In a recent visit made by Father Rossi to Rapides several of the inhabitants there offered to subscribe for the erection of a Church and in Franklin many advantageous offers have also being [*sic*] made of a similar nature. In both these quarters Americans preponderate. Unfortunately the Methodists try to proselytize but I can glean from the better informed Americans (who present their children here) that they find the Methodists in general profess a vulgar jargon and too illiterate ideas to effect any ascendency over the people. The Methodist establishment formed near Natchez about 2 [*number not clear*] years since, decidedly to counteract this is now on the decline & the parents from that quarter still sometimes bring their children here. At this moment and for the same ends a similar Institution is now forming at Lafayette. At Opelousas they have attempted but could not succeed. So much on the chapter of our wants.

I must now relate you father a little history of my movements during your absence. The end of November I received a letter from Mother Duchesne announcing her arrival at St Michael and requesting my immediate presence there. Accordingly I arrived and saw with no small degree of satisfaction the wonders effected there by Mother Eugenie. I had also the pleasure of finding *le bien bon* Father De La Croix from whom I heard particularly of your Lordship. Mother Duchesne returned with me to pass the feast of Christmas. After she returned for St Michael with the intention of immediately going to St Louis. She did not appear to admire our situation which she found too isolatatical [*sic*] & solitary. For my part it appeared after my short journey to possess still more attractives on this score for the retreat and peace here are delicious. But I am trespassing on your Lordship's precious time & so running on that I cannot even stop to change my pen which prompts me to assure you venerated father of the entire submission and respectful attachment of your daughters & children. *Apropos* the amiable & promising Miss D. Archinard [*name uncertain*] terminated her earthly career last November. Pray for her. She had no consoling assistance at that awful moment __ sad reflection. One of our novices made her first vows whilst Mother Duchesne was with us.[257] Our children are over 40, generally Americans. I have entirely relinquished the plan of building by subscription but mean to enlarge on our own finances. I only await the answer of Madam Smith of whom I proposed buying her late dwelling house to add to ours. Should she refuse ceding it, we must build a brick addition. I expect a subject from St Louis, who left France to become musician here for our pensioners,[258] we could not obtain a master. I have just got a handsome piano from New York.

Enfin my Lord & father I am your devotedly attached
daughter
in Corde Jesu Xavier

[*On the outside*:]

25

[*Postmark*:]
Donaldson V.L. Feb 28
[*in another hand in French*:] received April 14[259]

---

257 Adelaide Stanislas Aguillard, RSCJ, a native of Louisiana, had entered at St. Michael in 1827 but made her first vows January 1, 1830 at Grand Coteau, while Philippine was visiting after the meeting of the three superiors at St. Michael.
258 Felicity Lavy-Brun, who arrived within the next few months.
259 This contradicts the note at the beginning of the letter in the same hand, which appears to give an arrival date of April 21.

The Right Rev^d. Dr Rosati
St Mary's Seminary
Perry County
Missouri

[*On one end*:]
Father Rosti is well & is the happiest man I do believe existing. The appointment of our <u>Prelate</u> has so charmed him that for the first time, since any acquaintance, I heard him declare a wish to be <u>hospitable</u> in doing honor to receive <u>such a guest</u>.
    Father Rossi is now in New Orleans. Pray for your loquacious daughter. X

[*On the other end*:]
Will Y. Lordship please to present us to G [?] Dencker for whose health & future success we most fervently petition our Divine spouse. In all our communions etc. etc. he shall have an intention. <u>Now</u> he is obliged to pray for us.

Xavier Murphy to Bishop Rosati[260]

S.S.C.J.M.   Grand Coteau May 11, 1830

    I had the honor of addressing your Lordship a very long letter in February last. This therefore shall be a very short one merely to remind our good father that his daughters here are anticipating the consolation & happiness of seeing your Lordship. As an inducement there are three of our children who in the American style say "<u>tell the Bishop he must come to be my godfather</u>." In effect three have just obtained permission from their parents to be baptized. Come then gratify these tender plants who in unison with all the

---

260 English autograph. Rosati collection.

other inmates of G. Coteau desire with the utmost ardor to see their good father and venerated prelate amongst them.

Your respectfully attached daughter
in Corde Jesu
Xavier R. du S. Cœur

P.S. Excuse this scroll
Father Rosti awaits for it
     X

Xavier Murphy to Charles de la Croix[261]

Grand Coteau, June 3, 1830
St. Michael

To Rev. C. de la Croix

I was indeed, dear and valued friend, charmed to hear from Bishop Rosati that the foundation of your church had been celebrated in due ceremony, etc. that its progress and sweep may be commensurate with your zeal and my wishes are and shall be the ardent prayers of your daughters of G. Coteau. In return I shall request yours in our behalf, in a few days we shall find ourselves in a similar situation with you. You may remember that in my last letter I mentioned we had not then received the answer of Mrs. Smith. Since it has arrived, but her terms were so high and the house so ill suited for our present wants that we have finally decided to enlarge in brick. The plan is now preparing to be contracted on and $5000 are secured in bank to meet the payments. Our funds you are aware are <u>vested</u> in Providence. As soon as the contract shall be accepted all the [terms] of the building payments etc. will be adjusted by three agents appointed for the business, that is Governor Dupre,

---

261 English autograph. GASSH.

the elder M. Louaillier and Hypolite Chretien all of whom have signed the notes payable in Bank.

Now for this circumstantial detail of our movements here I shall in return expect to hear yours. You can read this for Mere Eugenie to whom I shall also address a little note on business and as I have nothing secret for you I shall mention my request, namely if she could cede me Mother Van Damme. The Americans form the majority of our children. My health <u>is so bad</u> and our English teacher so weak for the class that I feel for the credit of the house in want of assistance. Should Mere Eugenie assent to my request it would be well to profit of the steam boat of Opelousas that is still running but will soon stop, having no more freight to bring or take. On Sunday 4 of our children were baptized with the ample permission of their parents who granted the favor in gratitude for the improvement of their children (they are to be Catholics) our number is now 45, all that we can conveniently accommodate. I last evening drew for you the Thrones[262] [in a tirage] and shall salute them in your name and behalf. Methinks I could tell ever so much more but time presses hard here and your workmen now occupy you entirely, but pray find a little moment to inquire after your friends in the desart [*sic*] who all venerate and often speak of their good Father de la Croix. Apropos Mother Lavy wrote you, she says you are not polite. That is, you are too <u>American</u> and forget etiquette. Recommend me and mine to the Sacred Hearts of Jesus and Mary in which I am your entirely devoted and attached friend

                Xavier R. du S.C.

[*On the envelope*:]

[*Postmark*:] Opelousas, Louisiana

---

[262] One of the nine ranks of angels, according to medieval theologians.

Brangier Office
Rev. Ch. De La Croix
S Michel

Xavier Murphy to Madeleine Sophie Barat[263]

| S.C.J.M. | Under the auspices of the Novena of the S.H. and of St. A. of Padua | Grand Coteau June 12, 1830 |

Alas! Dear and much loved mother general, you are still suffering and we are still sad. Oh! One truly very sad since the last letter of Mother Ducis. I seem to see you continually in your painful situation, and add to that cross your concerns and solicitude for this numerous flock with which God has charged you for his glory. Your perfection and our happiness and consolation.

Since I received the letter from Mother Ducis, I have been busy planning the building so long projected, which you have already sanctioned, and now so necessary since there is no more room for the children. The house will not be finished for a year. It will cost 7500 piastres, that is, 37,500 francs. 4,000 piastres are borrowed at the bank for a time, under the responsibility of the most distinguished people in the region. The bank notes are payable for six years with a mediocre interest. The sum is large but Providence will help us and the parents ask for this improvement. I have acquitted all the debts. All the provisions for this year are already paid for and I have at present 400 piastres on deposit for the building. What we owe now is about 1500 piastres, and the children are continually increasing with the revenue from the music that yields 600 piastres this year. So, dear mother, be at peace and even sure that the S. Heart will provide the funds for us. I am sure, and I think at the same time, that good Mother Duchesne will not be happy with this expenditures, which prevents us from sending her help, because last year with all that I sent either to Paris or St Louis or elsewhere, the total was 2,000 piastres. Dear mother, bless with us the Heart of Jesus, who disposes everyone as well as possible in our favor.

One of the gentlemen, a friend of our house, wrote to me one of these days these four lines that I am sending you, marked +. They are so happy with our establishment at present that there is question of establishing a state college [secondary school] in our neighborhood. In spite of the great resistance to the Jesuits here, nevertheless they are saying that they must have a corps like these ladies to raise their boys, for see when they need help, they get it from the Society.

On Pentecost, we had four of our children baptized with complete consent of their parents. One of them told me in his American style: "Madame, if I could belong to a religion, it would certainly be yours. It seems as if I am already. But infuse your principles in my children." The box announced by Mother Ducis has not yet arrived. We will be very happy to have it to decorate our chapel, which is in our new building. Now we are so constrained for space that we are deprived of having exposition on feast days except Sundays. Judge, dear mother, what a privation it is for your daughters in the desert of America, to be deprived of the only object worthy of their attention.

The letters sent to you last year were not carried by a missionary but by a gentleman from Opelousas. Soon Mr. Borgna, brother of the priest who is in New Orleans, will send you a large packet. The letter of my dearly loved Mother de Marbeuf, dated to June 1829, reached me a few days ago, and the relics it announces rather arrived 9 months ago. It seems that all the letters addressed to Father Borgna have the same outcome. Therefore, dear mother, for the house of Opelousas please send what you want to send us by means of Mr. Davillier. My health is so weak and my tasks so many that I recently asked Mother Eugenie to send me Mother

Van Damme for English. Maybe she will not consent. In this case, may the will of God be done. Amen.

Dear reverend mother, my heart is filled with most lively gratitude for your maternal goodness in choosing Mother Lavy for our house of Grand Coteau. She is a precious person, especially for relationships. I have never met anyone who fits better with me. She edifies us by her virtue, etc. and is an honor to good Mother Desmarquest. Would you please, dear mother, name her along with another professed here (a Creole without means but with a good heart) for my councilors. Then I will be <u>according to the rule</u>, having an assistant and two councilors, these last two to balance the authority of ___,[264] who you know well has a tendency to dominate—no room for an opening of heart with my mother Barat. Patience. In eternity we will see it, when this will be the delicious moment for the mother and her daughter. But in these days of grace and blessing, think more than usual of your children of America who love you, who venerate you, and who have all their delight and their glory in belonging to you. Oh! If during our octave, seated on your little stool, my heart can express to you all that I feel...! A tender and filial remembrance for my dear star, Fathers Varin, Peroot [Perreau], and Barat. I would like to have news of Father Dusaussoy, if his health has improved, etc. Also of Mothers de Gramont, de Marbeuf, Charbonnel, Desmarquest. At the end of the present semester, I will have the pleasure of addressing a letter to good Mother Ducis.

Dear and venerated mother, give us your blessing and receive the assurance of our solicitude and very fervent prayer for your complete healing, with the devotion and attachment of your daughters of G. Coteau, especially of your Xavier who loves you and venerates you in the Heart of Jesus, the <u>link</u> who binds us from one end of the world to another.

---

264 Written thus in the French autograph. Both knew to whom she referred without naming her.

Xavier

[*On the outside: four postmarks, three undated, one:*]
August 1830

Overseas via Le Havre
   By way of New York
    Mother
  Mother Barat Superior General
  of the Religious of the S. Heart
   in Paris Rue Varennes No. 41

[*Two paragraphs by L. Dorival. First four lines are details about whether her pension has arrived. Then:*]
Your little house of Grand Coteau is going well. Our dear Mother Lavy seems happy, and we are very much so to have her; her talents will be of great usefulness to attract young people, who through this way will hear someone speaking about God and their salvation. I am well, though always a little suffering, but I see that the climate contributes to this. It takes nothing from my happiness; on the contrary, it seems to give me a little trace of uniformity with our good Master. Goodbye, dear mother; my heart is all yours in that of Jesus, with the most tender and respectful sentiments. Your very obedient daughter,

          L. Dorival r.S.C.J.

[*Continues on the other side of the address:*}
 A little word, beloved mother, from your poor daughter who from time to time feels in a very vivid way how great is the distance that separates us here—but what have I said? Do I not find my special Mother Barat in the Heart of Jesus? Oh! Yes, and that is my place of repose and consolation. How anxious I am about your health, dear mother. Is that foot healed yet? How my heart suffers from this uncertainty! All your daughters have made supplication

to heaven for your prompt healing. Mother Xavier is sending you the account of the building that is about to begin. 37,500 francs is a considerable sum; nevertheless, everything is not so expensive here that we can at least have this chapel and dormitory of which we have indispensable need. It is also true that in many circumstances they will give a piaster or five francs as they give one franc in our dear France.

Xavier Murphy to Madeleine Sophie Barat[265]

S.S.C.J.M.   Grand Coteau, August 23, 1830

Dear Mother,

Hardly had the wound to our hearts last month of the death of one of our young Americans begun to heal, when our good Master demanded another sacrifice still more painful, by waking us at 5:45 in the morning. Our dear Sister Frances Roche, coadjutrix novice of one year.[266] She was a young Irish girl, 18 years old, whom Mother Duchesne received in St. Louis and sent to us when Mother Lavy came down to Louisiana 5 months ago. She continually edified the whole community. Always busy to fulfill the least things enjoined by obedience, she knew how to accompany the exterior works of Martha with the recollection of Mary. Gentle, obliging, fervent, she was ripe for heaven. Her most ardent desires were to bind herself to Our Lord by the sacred bonds of the vows. How many times she expressed this wish of her heart! It was so vehement that Mother Xavier, with the advice of the confessor, allowed her to make her vows in secret on the feast of the Sacred

---

265 French autograph GASSH. Signed by Xavier Murphy but apparently written by someone else, who twice alludes to her in third person.
266 Lucille Frances Roche died August 16, 1830. A medical expert to whom the following symptoms were described suggested a rare bacterial meningitis causing blood clots that suddenly burst. There is no record of the death the previous month of the young American; she was a student; see next letter.

Heart. However, even more, she wanted to make them irrevocably, and when she was struck with the illness that would take her away from us, she testified from the first days how happy she would be for that favor in case of death. Without doubt, that was the intention of our mother, but it seems that Our Lord received her desires and held her to account for them. On the 12th of this month, this sister, who up to then had strong health, complained of a violent headache. She was very red, and went to bed after bathing her legs, which brought some comfort. The next day she was very well. But on the vigil of the Assumption, when she rose at the usual hour, she vomited spontaneously with a little bile. We put her to bed in the infirmary. The doctor was called. He assured us that since she had evacuated everything, it would be all right. There was a cause to this illness: it was eliminated. She was bled. She felt well, and we were led to believe that soon she would return to be with us. Nevertheless, she went to confession in her bed. The fever that at the beginning was not excessive became bilious. But the assurance of two doctors that there were not the least symptoms was reassuring. She remained in profound sleep until nine o'clock in the morning. Then she was given something to drink. She made an extraordinary effort with coughing, and at that moment, she broke an artery and gave forth a quantity of blood through her nose and mouth. The doctor arrived quickly. At the sight of the color of the blood, he declared what had happened and said it was the end. The priest was called immediately. He administered Extreme Unction. She had already confessed the evening before, but she seemed too well then to give her Viaticum. She could not receive it [now] because of the large amount of blood. The chaplain recited the prayers for the dying with the whole community, and it was only at the end of the Passion according to St John with these words, "he gave over his spirit," that this innocent soul rendered her spirit into the hands of her dying savior. Up to 8 or 9 minutes before her death, she tried to pronounce the sacred names of Jesus, Mary, and Joseph, that Mother Xavier suggested to her. This poor mother, despite her extreme sensitivity, which is worse than ever, assisted her to her last breath with maternal tenderness. Nothing was lacking for this dear soul, whether spiritual or corporal help. There was the same today as when she took the veil. Her tender devotion towards the Blessed Virgin was remarkable; after Jesus, Mary was everything to her. Each day she said a certain number of Ave Marias to obtain a good death. Her modesty was angelic. When her confessor was asked if he found her changed during her illness, he said he had never seen anything like it. He believed that she was presented before the tribunal of God in her baptismal innocence. Nevertheless, we recommend her ardently to your prayers, dear mother, and to those of everyone in our dear Society.

Receive the assurance of our respectful greetings *in Corde Jesu*
Xavier

Sister Frances Roche
Novice, died
At Grand Coteau
August 23, 1830 [*date of letter, not her death*]

Louise Dorival to MSB[267] (partially excerpted)

S.S.C.J.M.   St A. de P.   Grand Coteau, August 31, 1830

My Beloved Mother,

It has been more than a year since your daughters in Grand Coteau have received some little word from your hand. How long it seems! ... At such a distance from a dear mother, the sacrifice is even more painful. We do not know if your foot is finally healed. The length of this sprain raises many worries. When will we learn that you are completely healed? This is what most holds the interest

---

267 French autograph, GASSH.

of your poor Americans...You will see, mother, from the attached page, that our good Master has visited us with the cross. The little American was baptized here at the Sacred Heart last year, and if she had returned to her parents, she would have become Methodist like them. She was anointed before her death, and I tell you that in the midst of our sorrow, we blessed God for having removed her from the dangers of error and the perversity of the world....The death of our young and fervent Frances Roche leaves us with no more than eleven in this house; we are very sad about these happenings that come almost with no interval. The little one [the student] died July 26, but Our Lord willed it; we must submit and adore his decrees.

Poor Mother Xavier astonishes me by her constancy. Her physique that is so delicate made me fear that she would be overwhelmed by so many frequent blows, but I have seen with gratitude that her faith has raised her above natural sensitivity and that this generous soul is capable of the greatest sacrifices. Her example confounds me, I who am not capable of suffering from even the lightest contradictions without feeling them even physically. I must tell you in confidence, dear and tender mother, that my poor heart is in great pain at the sight of its lack of virtue that it experiences now more than ever. I tell you of its miseries for my own confusion and so that you will always be informed about what concerns her who from afar and from near has promised you complete confidence.

I ardently desired the arrival of dear Mother Lavy, when all would go better. Indeed, a large number of children are learning music. It is good revenue, but I find her character susceptible, and I am not the only one, to the point that I am not sure of having an understanding with her about the classes, for fear of offending her, as has happened two or three times. Nor can I communicate easily with Mother Xavier any longer, because she approves everything she says and does, no doubt to make life easier and prevent disagreement. This way, I suffer because several things are not the way I think they should be, but I dare not say anything so as not to cause trouble, so I feel the tension that I have never expressed and it leaves me, in spite of myself, depressed. Besides, I see that I am of little use here, and I am persuaded that in France I worked more directly for the glory of God. Here there is not much instruction to do, and one must wait without seeing any fruit, for lack of priests to develop later these germs of religion. I always have this need to teach that made me so long for America and I can no longer satisfy it. That does not make me regret having come oh! no, mother, but I am confiding to you my intimate thoughts. You are the only one to receive them, after the Hearts of Jesus and Mary. My health is declining visibly. Since last December, I coughed blood twice rather abundantly. For eight days, a pain in the chest remained, and a tiring cough. Mother Xavier thought with me that perhaps a stay of several moths at St Michael would bring improvement. The doctor says that the advantages of the trip would probably have that effect, so that it appears that she will make that proposal to Mother Eugenie, to send me to spend the winter with her, where it is even milder than here. On the other hand, dear mother, I desire what seems to be neither health nor illness in life, but rather death, because I am so disappointed to see that I am advancing so little in the way of perfection, that I want to have the heart and the esteem of my superior.

[*Omitted here is a long discussion of her personal doubts about herself and her status in the community.*]

I am sending you the receipt for my <u>pension</u>, in case you want to collect it. I do not know if anyone collected it last year; I will write to Mr. LeBeau.

We are experiencing this year a suffocating heat. We have had as many as 46 students; at the moment, they are only 43. Our building is underway. In October they will place the first bricks. It is really hoped that it will be easily paid for. This will be 8,000 piastres, and Mother Xavier already has an advance of more than

1300. As for the construction, it is not very well done; mother understands nothing about how to do it well, but what is easy to see is that she is not in debt.

Give your blessing, dear mother, to your poor Dorival. If I go to St Michael, I will write to you as soon as possible. Your very affectionate and very submissive daughter, L. Dorival r.S.C.J.

[*On the side of page 1:*]
By a letter of last January, Mother Ducis told us of a carton containing sacristy objects. We do not yet have any news of it.

[*On the outside:*]
[*Stamps*]   [*Address:*]
                                    Madame
Opelousas, Lousiana Sept 4   Madame Barat Superior
Paid   of the Religious of the Sacred Heart
26 OCTO 1830   rue de Varennes No. 41 faubg St G
28 Octobre 1830   Paris   France

[*In another hand :*]
Papers for the secretariat

Xavier Murphy to Madeleine Sophie Barat[268]

                       Recommended to St. A. of P.
S.S.C.J.M.   Grand Coteau October 16, 1830

As your daughters here, dear and beloved mother general, are distressed at hearing of your critical situation, perhaps this is enough to say on the subject out of prudence. *O altitudo*! We have already shared the joy of your improvement and the convalescence

---

268 French autograph. GASSH.

of dear Mother de Gramont. It seems a century since I have received a letter from you, tender mother general, but I know that you have anxieties about your colony here. I hasten to tell you that your little house of Grand Coteau is doing well. It has no debts <u>at all</u>, the building is on schedule, the first two payments have been made and the third is ready on time, and we have not touched the bank notes deposited by our friends for our use in this way. Thus, dear mother, bless the Heart of Jesus who smooths out all kinds of things for the last and most imperfect of your daughters. During the past summer, I was obliged to send home several of our children, not having room and fearing the heat that is excessive here. You already know of the loss of one of our students and one of our sisters. The death of the first was not followed by any consequences for the house. All the parents shared our sorrow but did not remove their children. The building will be finished next June. In one of the letters of Mother Lavy (for the novitiate), you will find what I wrote in English to be placed with the first brick.

Pardon, reverend mother, the style of this letter, but I am pressured by the situation. It is my hour of prayer that I am taking for an opening of heart with you. I have so many things to tell you that weigh on my spirit. Oh! If it were possible, I would prefer to be with you on a little footstool for half a day. How my heart would be content. But *fiat*. Since the arrival of Mother Lavy here, Mother Dorival seems completely unhappy. I think in the last letter of August she brought you up to date on her business. Just after the letter was posted, she got it into her head that she would be better off in every way at St Michael, and that her health, which is indeed suffering (because of her imagination) would be restored there. So I arranged everything for her departure. She left here last month with all our regrets. Now I have just a letter from her and one from Mother Eugenie saying that Mother Dorival will be here in a few days, finding herself bored at St Michael and sighing after the house of Grand Coteau alone.

As for me, I do not understand at all their arrangements, but I am happy at her return. It also seems that she has visited Mother Dutour with the hope of speaking to her about the sad situation in which that mother finds herself [at LaFourche]. Mother Eugenie just wrote to me asking my opinion about the decision that Mother Dutour must take, with 100,000 francs of debt and no resources. I said that I think it would be better to give up on her enterprise, since she cannot count on the help of France at such a critical time, and that it would be very hard to make new wounds (by our colony here) on your heart that is bleeding <u>at this time</u>. It seems that there is too much traveling back and forth from LaFourche to St Michael. I know that some ecclesiastics have made remarks about the issue with respect to cloister. Maybe it is necessary; I do not know anymore. The distribution of prizes was public at St Michael this year, even though it was decided at our <u>last meeting</u> that this would not take place. I refused that permission here to the most important of our parents, saying that it is not our custom. Where is the uniformity that should distinguish us as the Society of the Sacred Heart, and a union that should be our <u>shield</u>, our <u>strength</u>, and our <u>defense</u>. I attribute all the difficulties that have happened at LaFourche to the lack of union between Mothers Eugenie and Dutour, and I see now (with pain) that the advice of Mother Duchesne counts for nothing among her daughters here. So it is necessary, dear mother, that you decide something about a visitator, etc., to study our current situation in this country. It seems that I am not at all constrained in private conversation with you. If I am going too far, you, mother, will have to tell me. So I will surely follow the plan that you gave me. Mother Lavy is well and very useful here (music is sure revenue for the house). She seems happy because of her great sensitivity. I have managed as well as possible but I think she will not be so happy after the return of Mother Dorival.

It is astonishing that the two people are so opposed to one another. Pray for us all and for our children. Several of them have abjured Protestantism with the consent of their parents. An Episcopalian gentlemen presented his daughter and said: "Mother, my daughter has too much spirit not to be raised Catholic. Please raise her in <u>your religion</u>." Several will make their First Communion next Easter, so, dear and tender mother, be consoled in your heavy suffering, considering that you are the means chosen by the Heart of Jesus to introduce these precious souls to his sanctuary. Oh. What will be your reward? What will be your crown awaiting that beautiful day? Dear and worthy mother, receive the assurances of all the <u>respect</u>, <u>veneration</u>, and attachment of your daughters of the Sacred Heart.

Especially of your poor, weak child
In Corde Jesu
Xavier

Be my interpreter to all my mothers, my dear star, Fathers Varin, Barat, and Perreau.
Ask their prayers for your daughter
X

[*On the outside:*]

Mother
Mother Barat Superior General
In Paris

Xavier Murphy to Bishop Rosati[269]

S.S.C.J.M.   Grand Coteau Dec 30th, 1830

Will you dearly Beloved father & bishop (for so I must ever call & consider you) accept in the language of the season the wishes that

---

269 English autograph. Rosati collection.

your daughters of G.C. form for your preservation, your success, and your happiness for the ensuing and every succeeding year.

    I have long desired to have a *tête à tête* with your Lordship for methinks I have quite a budget to disclose. Your dear letter of August by our sisters filled me with such consolation and I have blessed & blessed a thousand times over the prime Distributor of events for having peculiarly seconded all your enterprises for His glory. May you go on and prosper thereby showing that all obstacles will eventually cede to the meek and humble of heart. The description of the new Church quite pleased us and the resources are so stable that nothing unpleasant can occur for the ways and the means of defraying its expenditure. I have also, father, the consolation of telling you that all goes on in this your <u>favorite house</u>. To God alone be glory our building progresses it will form an handsome addition of 50 feet in length and 53 in width including the gallery on the south to correspond with the present. Payments have been already made and the 2 next to be called for are ready. Our children continue as you saw them and we had several baptisms this year. A recent mission that Fr. Rossi made in the parish of Rapides has filled us with consolation and delightful hope all our children there persevere and the parents allow the little brothers and sisters to be christened to please our *élèves*. Some of the most distinguished persons there write to me that Fr. Rossi has captivated them by his liberal manners and conclude by regretting that he cannot address them in English.

    The establishment formed by the Methodists at Natchez <u>to rival</u> ours declines. Those of Opelousas and Lafayette finished their career so that Grand Coteau now remains the solitary queen of the Western forests. Finally, father, the citizens of Opelousas demand a college on the plan of our Institution. A few days since the proposals for its erection, etc., etc., were brought me to communicate to our bishop, who will of course fully acquaint you of his determination on the subject.²⁷⁰ Should the affair be concluded it will be of essential utility in this section of the union and tend to put down the zeal and too successful labors of the Methodists who gain ground on account of the language. Our dear Prelate does not appear disposed to visit our province. We anxiously expected him all the fall but were cruelly disappointed. Mother Dorival who made an excursion to St Michel with the project of remaining there (I suppose for variety) told me that she found him extremely feeble. Indeed I was not surprised for he has had so many unpleasant and truly painful events to contend against just on his *entrée* among us that I fear their effects & consequences for his sensibility.

Our little oratory on the recent feast was really *un bijoux*. We lately received from Paris a set of beautiful candlesticks, cross, *ostensoir* & *S^t. Ciboire*,²⁷¹ all new & of exquisite workmanship. The flowers presented for the feast of St. F. Xavier [December 3] finished the decoration. Our children were all devotion for the little Jesus, as they say, and how consoling in effect to present at this adorable infant's feet the little ones for whom he became little. How great is this mystery of love and how calculated to inspire <u>confidence</u>, <u>love</u> & *dévoument*. Well may we exclaim, "O Lord if we love thee not after all thou hast done for us what will become of the glory of thy name."

Sisters Short and Shannon appear pleased with their change.²⁷² The former has changed much to her advantage. Mother Dorival after a few weeks stay on the river returned again to her solitude. I saw her departure from here with anxious pain but submitted to the will of God who arranges all for the better. Mother Lavy

---

270 Leo Raymond De Neckere was then bishop of New Orleans, from his consecration on June 24, 1830 until his death of yellow fever in 1833.
271 An *ostensorium* is a sacred vessel with a stand in which a host could be displayed (also called a monstrance); a *ciborium* is a closed container to hold consecrated hosts.
272 Margaret Mary (Madeleine) Short, RSCJ, was born in New York in 1807 and had just made first vows in Florissant. She was professed in 1842 at St. Michael, then lived at Manhattanville, and died at Kenwood in 1870. Mary Shannon, born 1810, had also just made first vows at Florissant. She left the Society in 1831.

has several pupils. We have now two pianos. All the rest of the community are pretty much as you saw them, all impressed with veneration and respectful gratitude before your Lordship's paternal affection and goodness. We all (....) you in the light of our <u>great father</u> who in blessing us [with] his Son, still remembers that we are his adopted daughters, indeed our memento is always made in the <u>plural</u> for I think it would be an act of injustice to pronounce it other times. My paper tells me that I have chatted rather too much, perhaps for your time but I am sure not for the interest you feel in all our concerns.

We should be all most happy to receive your Benediction father, particularly one who glories in signing herself your devoted daughter

in *Corde Jesu* Xavier R. de S.C.

[*On the cover*:]
The Right Rev^d Dr Rosati
St Louis
Missouri

[*On the side of the cover*:] Fr. Rosti's health improves. He goes on the same old pace. Our children often enquire when will our own Bishop "come to see us" for so they style you father, your fine ring is still held in tradition amongst them.   X

[*On the bottom in another hand in French*:]
1830 Dec^e 30 Mother Xavier – Grand Coteau, received February 8

1831

Madeleine Sophie Barat to Eugenie de Gramont, June 4, 1831 (Excerpt)[273]

Here is my plan, if you think it will work, that Mother de Kersaint will speak to the bishop of New York when she passes through, and she will see with his excellency if there is a way to found this house [New York]. She should take his advice, his instructions, as she continues her route and arrives to dear Mother Duchesne. She will tell her everything she has gathered, and will see with her about when it could begin. For this foundation, we will need Mother Eugenie Audé. I do not see anyone else at the moment. Mother Xavier Murphy would perhaps have been preferable, but I think we must leave a head in Louisiana. If we lose our wonderful Philippine, who will govern these six houses? I am going to try as much as I can, at the next general council, to have named an assistant general for this region, because each house is too independent, which does not work well, and I see only Mother Xavier capable of filling this responsibility, since our dear Philippine can scarcely travel.

Louise Dorival to Madeleine Sophie Barat[274]

S.S.C.J.M.   2. S. etc.   Grand Coteau, November 12, 1831

Dearly loved Mother,

In my last letter I had to deliver a sensitive blow to your maternal heart by telling you of our fears about Mother DuTour's

---

273 French autograph, excerpt, letters of Madeleine Sophie Barat. GASSH.
274 Fremch autograph. The letter was written by Louise Dorival, who signs it at the end. Xavier writes on the front a short note that this will be Mother Dorival's last letter. She died July 11, 1832.

hydropsie[275]; and I should have hastened to take away your worries, which I would have done with all my heart if I had been capable; but here it is three months that I have been held by a fever that sometimes leaves me for one or two days or more, then comes back for several days following. It weakens me and makes me able to do nothing (or almost nothing) with the children. Yes, mother, our dearly beloved Sister DuTour, after having received Extreme Unction on the feast of Saint Matthew, was at first normal, but the next day had a crisis that we thought would carry her away. Happily, she has been given back to us, and from that time her swelling has steadily diminished, so that at the beginning of classes, she was well enough to take charge of a 4th class and a sewing course, and thanks to our good Master, her health gets better every day. When our physician saw the danger of her illness, he proposed using the most active remedy and the one most common among the Americans, mercury. But it was not given in full force, and we are persuaded that it was the grace of Extreme Unction that saved our dear Mother DuTour, who wishes for me to offer you the assurance of her completely filial tenderness. Your poor Dorival also took mercury more happily. Calamel [?] but it did not cut the fever as was hoped, and now everyone is condemned to spend the winter in a state of languor, weakness, and uselessness, because along with it, having my chest attacked, I cannot teach classes, at least for long times because of the throat and the heaviness that seldom leaves me. I have had to have Mother Lavy take charge of my class, which she has done since vacation. But mother, I must tell you in secret to my dear superior, that this person is so bored and tired in this house that she says herself that she can no longer live here. Everyone hears her say it, and I can assure you, mother, that no one has been treated with more attention. My poor M. EG.[276]

---

275 Helene Dutour, who had been removed as superior of LaFourche and was now in residence at Grand Coteau. Hydropsy is edema due to excessive fluid retention.

276 The meaning is not clear. The letters are possibly M.G., perhaps mother general, to whom she is writing.

knew she was difficult, but it seems that the more concessions she is given, the more she demands. Lately she has fallen into some sort of crisis as extreme and ill advised as painful for the spouses of the Heart of Jesus, and in these sad moments, she asked with all her strength to be sent away from here. After this Mother X carefully reduced the number for music, not being able to count on the amount of time this person will be here. Our hearts suffer to see one of us in a difficulty that no one can take from her. It is even more unfortunate that the purchase was made of 3 pianos that may remain unused.

The new building that we call <u>Academy</u> is finished. It cost 10,000 piastres. 7,000 is paid, so only 3,000 are left, payable in two years. Those are the terms. God has so favored us that at present mother has her money before the deadline, the terms fulfilled. She also hopes that you will give us permission for a church. The children are increasing, and for lack of teachers we must limit them to 70. Although everyone knows it, if at present we do not go to 100, we have the room for it, but see, good mother, how few we are for such a flock. 14 in all, and subtract from that my present uselessness, I do nothing. Unfortunately Mother Lavy, who is unhappy, will perhaps leave. Since we have only 4 sisters included in the 14, the teachers do the dormitory in their free time. Mother X replaces me for penmanship when my turn comes, and in my new surveillances, so that with the classes and her correspondence, she is completely overworked. Without seeing for yourself, it is difficult to understand the burden that causes the need to teach in two languages with equal perfection. This doubles all the classes, and necessitates doubling all the teachers. Mother, if you could send us one or two religious with the spirit of the Society, who are willing to find some privations for nature, more perhaps in America than in Europe. Our house that has a burst of extraordinary reputation because of the new building is in well-established order. Through the care of the one at our head, our boarding school requires that our mother general take Grand Coteau into consideration and support it by some reinforcement of the work that is so interesting for our Society. As for resources that this letter requests, you know, mother, that what you permit us to take and use does not return to us. It is impossible to send from here by the same way as originally, because these gentlemen would be too *au courant* about the amount of money that circulates. If one pays my little fee, I think that 1200 francs could help at least for a trip. Mother X has asked for people from Mother Duchesne, who answered just today that she cannot accede to our wishes or our needs. We have a young postulant 16 years old whom we are keeping to help us in the vestry, where she succeeds very well. Without that, we would already have sent her to St Michael for novitiate. Please mother, accede to our requests if possible for you, and we will be more regular and happier. Office has not been said since illness has caused the others to replace them. There are not enough voices to sustain it. Every time I have the consolation of writing to you I think that it might be the last time, because I keep getting weaker.

I am at your feet asking your blessing for myself and for all your dear family of Grand Coteau. Dear good mother, believe in all my respectful wishes with all my heart,

L. Dorival r.s.c.j.

[*On the outside*:]
In July we had the hope that your foot would be cured at the end of a month; how the certitude of that happy event filled us with joy.

A word about the Methodists: they are a sect in the country who are scorned by all the Protestants, and who declare themselves openly against the Catholics, and especially against our house. Already 4 Methodist establishments having fallen recently, it matters little, they try another with the title in concurrence with Grand Coteau. A preacher said the other day in talking about our glorious denomination, of the Sacred Heart of Jesus: what profanation that mortal servants should appropriate such an august name. He was indignant in his Methodist zeal. The mother of one of our students addressed a Methodist to have a silver cup made for her daughter. He asked where she was in school—at Grand Coteau—"Madam, I would never work for the convent." Everyone who knew it laughed. It is fortunate that none of our students see in Catholics this kind of hostility. That is what makes them love our holy religion.

I am sorry to end. The health of dear Mother X. is excellent. She needs it because she cannot otherwise sustain the burden that she has, as I have told you.

Your American daughter very happy in her vocation. L.D.

Mother
Mother Barat
Etc., etc.

[*Perpendicular to the address*:]
Mother Dorival
At Grand Coteau
November 12, 1831

[*In Xavier's hand*:]
I fear, dear and tender mother, that this is the last letter you will receive from dear Mother Dorival. She has been attacked by consumption and is going gently. She is making extraordinary efforts to get well but the die is cast. Pray for her and for your daughter who feels how sweet it is to suffer for Jesus, our spouse. Completely yours in C.J.

Xavier R. of S.C.

1832

Xavier Murphy to Bishop Rosati[277]

S.S.C.J.M.   Grand Coteau April 15, 1832

Just as I seated myself to reply to your Lordship's welcome letter handed me by our sisters, I was called to receive a present from generous Father Rossi and what present - define no less than the portrait of your venerated & much loved self. Yes indeed the <u>old</u> & I may well add the always remembered <u>friend</u> of G. Coteau you cannot dearest father & bishop conceive the pleasure I derived from the perusal of your parental letter, and the pure joy I experienced on hearing the progress that Religion makes under your fostering auspices. I have only to regret that our communications are so rare on my part; time alone prevents me from addressing you as I feel my heart on my fingers and when indulging a *tête à tête* with our <u>great</u> father & our valued friend. As the *père* Van de Velde[278] will put your Lordship *au fait* at all our improvements plans and movements here, I shall only tell you that since my arrival in this country I have not experienced a more poignant sorrow than at this moment. *Voilà* the cause. The parish of Rapides which I call my pride & my glory has after offering the most advantageous allurements secured a clergyman Presbyterian of the new sect (Cumberland), Mr. Ogden who has literally captivated all the people. He visited here with introductory letters from the principal persons of the District and appeared so pleased with the plan of our Institution that he has sent for his daughter (who is in Kentucky) to place her here.

---

277 English autograph. Rosati collection.
278 Jean Olivier Van de Velde, SJ (1795-1855) came from Belgium in 1817, entered the Society of Jesus, and was ordained at Georgetown in 1827. He was at this time a professor at St. Louis University, and later its president, then bishop of Chicago and Natchez.

Nothing will console on the chapter of this person but his conversion which I hope to <u>obtain</u> and our bishop to <u>effect</u>. Bishop De Neckere promised me to visit that quarter of his Diocese. He was much desired and they even spoke of forming a Church etc. etc. You of course heard of the fate of the Fourche & that we possess all the subjects. This was an unpleasant affair but circumstances seemed to require the proceedings. The health of Mother Dorival is declining fast. They pronounced a heart complaint. All the rest are pretty much as you knew them. Our pensioners give general satisfaction. Several have been christened and four or more are now candidates all with parental permission. Indeed dearest father of all the inmates of your <u>favorite house</u> your Xavier is the one who gains least and I can well say "When I was exulted I was troubled exceedingly." I feel more & more the charge of others & my total incapacity for direction. You may remember my telling you how much this occupation cost me and how badly I discharged it. The sisters from St Louis appear content. Sister Stiggers [Stegar][279] pleases me & I trust she will make a good tho' not a brilliant subject. She begs to be presented to y^r Lordship. Mère Dutour edifies all by her amiability, resignation & truly religious comportment. She is simply mistress of the 3rd class & first course of Instruction. You may suppose what <u>acts</u> she had to make on seeing subjects' baggage etc. arrive in her presence. Yet not a complaint. But I perceive when I begin to chat with Y^r Lordship I forget that actually they are waiting for this scroll. Will you then dear & venerated father allow me to lay at your feet all my charge <u>old</u> & <u>young</u> demanding for them your Benediction and a part in your prayers & remembrances, above all for one who shall ever feel full of gratitude & respectful attachment for her great father and beloved Prelate. Your daughter *in C.J.*

Xavier *R. du S.C.*

---

279 Anna Stegar, RSCJ (1815-1885) entered the Society in Florissant in 1830, came as a novice to Grand Coteau in 1832, and made first vows there in 1834. She was not finally professed until 1854. Cf. Callan PD pp. 509-511. 517.

I opened this letter to tell you father that there is question of removing Father Rosti from us. This I am sure you will <u>not permit</u>. No person can be better aware of the treasure we possess in this priest and if the house of G.C. be proverbial for <u>order</u>, peace and charity he is the cause. Do then use your influence with the Superior. Tell how much the good of this Community depends on possessing a man who appears to have been created for his present station. All my confidence is in you dear Bishop don't disappoint your

Xavier

[*on the outside*:]
        The Right Revd Dr Rosati
        Rev. *Père* Van de Velde   St Louis

[*outside edge, in another hand in French*:]
1832 April 15 Mother Xavier S.C. Grand Coteau
Received May 15

Xavier Murphy to Bishop Rosati[280]

S.S.C.J.M.   Grand Coteau April 30, 1832

    How true it is my Lord that at this moment I feel you are a father and friend, for I have but just perused a letter from *Mère* Duchesne where she marks that your Lordship desires I should send Mothers Bazire and Cloney. Well then I frankly tell you that the state of this house absolutely requires both. Mother Bazire is the only one capable of replacing Mother Dorival with regard to the pensioners and the later [*sic*] declines like a candle that will softly but quickly extinguish of itself. Mother Cloney is now mistress of a class (the 5th) composed of 9 Americans all of whom

---

280 English autograph. Rosati collection.

have entered since our reunion [with LaFourche] for until that event I refused accepting children as soon as the reinforcement was announced in the papers. The parents now every day present pupils. Add to this that Mother Cloney having in a measure lost all she professed (of useful) in her language. I have commenced to form her for a suppliant at a future period as I hope to have the sweet consolation of one day taking my exit and closing my pilgrimage. *Voici* dear father my reasons which I submit not only to your judgment but also to your heart that teems with such parental feelings for this house of your fostering predilection. A few lines from your Lordship on this subject will be gratefully received by your devotedly attached daughter in C.J.

Xavier *R. du S.C.*

[*On the cover*:]
P.S. Father Jeanjean informed me of his determination of deposing with your Lordship a procuration of Mother St Cyr. I have since his letter addressed Mother Duchesne on the subject, but I now perceive she requires some other formalities from which I beg leave to be exempted, the difficulty here being great to obtain the legal signatures. Pray tell her so. X

25

[*postmark*:]
May 20

The Right Revd Dr Rosati
Missouri   St Louis

[*At the top, in another hand in French*:]
1832 April 20 Mother Xavier Grand Coteau
Received June 14

Xavier Murphy to Henriette Ducis[281]

S.S.C.J.M.   Grand Coteau, May 2, 1832

Your letter of February 17, dear Mother Ducis, arrived in April, so you see that when you write directly, your letters arrive quickly. You did well to close the pension account of Mother Dorival. It is an advantage sometimes to know how to lose something. You can keep the 1200 francs with the 1234-70 due through Mother Eugenie, who told me herself that she will not pay it (as I told you). But recently she wrote to me that our mother wanted her to send her the money herself. That is fine with me to have the sum in our hands for the needs of our house of Grand Coteau.

I was somewhat astonished that you said nothing to me about the church, so I am forced to construe your letter as giving permission, having put it off until the last minute. For as a last resort, we would have to stop everything this month, or wait until another year, which would not be good in view of the increase in our children and of our religious. Undoubtedly you know, dear mother, that we carry the greater part of the debts of LaFourche. Thus we can now receive the children.

On that subject, pass this little line to our mother general. Already Mother Duchesne is asking for religious from LaFourche, Mother Bazire and an American whom I cannot give up [Regina Cloney]. Mother Dorival's health makes her incapable of action, and I only have Mother Bazire to take her place with the children. Thus with your support and approbation, I will not give her. Anyway, it is not your will nor according to your ideas about it. Nevertheless, the public has learned from the gazette about our increasing numbers. The public will undoubtedly find such a change so fast a little odd. Your daughter,

                                                                    Xavier

---

281 GASSH. French autograph.

We have certainly shared the sorrow and the loss that the Society has just had of good Mother de Vareaux.[282] How these blows must be painful for our mother who has to support all our setbacks. This way we can regard her rightly as the expiatory victim for the (...) that she has formed, and which extends into another hemisphere. Dear mother, I think I have found a way to send circulars or any other package that you would like to send us. It is by means of the gentleman who gives you this packet. Please put with the letters a piece of veil for choir religious. Add one of our mother's veils for my use. You said there was one in your last packet but you forgot.

We have 7 children for baptism. The Americans are beginning to allow us the power to imbue our principles in their children. Several are children of the first rank, very interesting and attracted to virtue. They listen to the instruction with an avidity and a respect that shows that their heart is formed for righteousness.

Soon you will have news of us from Father Jeanjean, and also from a lady to whom I am confiding letters for rue de Varennes. The health of my dear Mother de Marbeuf, and I hope of dear Mother de Gramont, fills me with consolation. Give my greetings to all my mothers and sisters. Your letters are for us a source of delight. Continue, dear Mother Ducis, to give us these proofs of your friendship and your attachment.

Your very affectionate and very grateful daughter closely united in C. J.

Xavier R. du S.C.

Mother Dorival is reaching the end of her pilgrimage. Pray for her.

[*On the envelope:*]
Mother Ducis
Rue de Varennes no. 41

---

282 Louise de Varax (so in death notice) was born in Lyon 1802 and died in Paris 1832.

Xavier Murphy, obituary of Louise Dorival to Philippine Duchesne[283]

S.C.J.M.   Grand Coteau, July 11/12, 1832

My very Reverend Mother,

In these days of mourning and sadness, when the hand of God seems to weigh heavily, it has also asked of us a great sacrifice in calling to himself our dear Mother Dorival. He attended her with so many graces, as is expected from his goodness, that our hearts, however filled with bitterness, bless him, adore him, and see in his decrees the will of a Father full of love for his much loved daughter.

This faithful and happy spouse of the Heart of Jesus, our very dear Mother Louise Dorival, was born in Paris May 20, 1795, of esteemed parents whom she lost at a tender age; but left an orphan, she was not abandoned by the one who feeds the birds of heaven and makes the flowers bloom in the deserts. Jealous of the purity and innocence of this privileged soul, from the age of nine years, he kept her distant from the world that only breathes corruption; and in the shadow of his sanctuary, he kept these so fragile and so beautiful virtues in all their freshness. Received as a boarder by the religious of Saint Maur, at the age of sixteen she took the habit of that order and lived there until 1819 when, feeling called to a more austere life, she entered the Carmelites. But since that was not where God wanted her, she remained only a year, at the end of which she was admitted to the novitiate of the Sacred Heart in Paris, under Mother Deshayes in July 1820. Her superiors, seeing in her the virtues and talents appropriate for a foundation, chose her with Mother Bigeu for that of Bordeaux, where she made her first vows June 7, 1822, and final vows June 22, 1823. That favor,

---

283 French autograph. GASSH. There are two identical French copies of this letter, one dated July 12 and the other, in a different hand, July 13. On the last lines of the earlier one there are blots in various places, perhaps tears.

so rarely given [to make final vows after only one year], was the praise of her virtue and compensated a little for the silence that we are obliged to keep on the first years of her religious life, about which we have no details.

When the Religious of Saint Vincent[284] united with us, our dear Mother Dorival was sent to them to spread the spirit of the Society and to direct the classes under Mother Catherine [de Charbonnel]. There, animated by devotion and ever-growing zeal, she heard the voice of God that called her to the Missions of America, and by that attraction, then the most powerful stimulus for her virtue, he stirred up great sacrifices and generous efforts, for which he rewarded her. Called to Paris, where she made her vow of stability in 1827, she left the next day for that beloved America, object of all her desires.

She arrived in Grand Coteau as assistant in that house, and her zeal that knew no limits always surpassed her strength in the exercise of her employments. Her devotion and her kindness made her beloved by the children, the parents, and the community. Her profound and lively faith, her exactitude with all the rules, her zeal to have them observed and to establish union, her prudence, her religious spirit, her charity, her tender devotion to the Holy Virgin and to Saint Francis Xavier, her respect for all the ordinances of the Church, her excessive delicacy about issues of purity, her union with God; these are some of the virtues that shone forth most brilliantly in her whose loss we justly deplore. But this beautiful soul, under the veil of humility, hid many others!

A year after her arrival in Grand Coteau, her superior was dangerously ill; she secretly offered herself as victim in her place. The Lord accepted her sacrifice; Mother Xavier recovered, but from that time, Mother Dorival felt the first signs of consumption that silently undermined her and finally led her to the grave.

---

284 Probably the Sisters of Notre Dame, a small local community in Bordeaux led by Mme Vincent, incorporated into the Society in 1825. They had given hospitality to Philippine Duchesne and companions on their way to America.

The affliction of her sufferings did not stop her zeal, which she exercised until the last moment, to our great edification. Fifteen days before her death, however, she was forced to remain in bed and gave us the example of inalterable patience, the virtue that she continually asked us to ask of the Lord for her, feeling that her great suffering exposed her to a lack of it. Always united to Jesus on the cross, she loved it when we spoke of him ceaselessly and of his holy mother. The name alone made her smile in the greatest of her pain. When she could no longer meditate, she was happy when one of her sisters did it in her place or in her presence. Full of gratitude, gentleness, and zeal for her infirmarian, she exhorted her to virtue, to love for regularity and the Rule, and was deeply interested in her perfection.

On the feast of the Sacred Heart, she received Extreme Unction and a plenary indulgence, and from that day on, she grew visibly worse, but she would not consent to our praying for her healing. The will of God was everything to her. A few days later, Mass was said in her room and she received holy Viaticum, the indulgence *in articulo mortis*, which purified her and prepared her for the formidable passage whose moment was approaching for her. The next day at about 6 in the morning, her agony began. She was often heard to say: "My Jesus! I am nothing. I have nothing but my life, but I give it to you! Oh! How sweet it is to die in the Sacred Heart! Nothing can hurt me." When her superior exhorted her to patience, she answered: "Yes, for love of Jesus." As if to say a final goodbye to our mother general, she cited one of her recommendations. When someone asked her to whom she was leaving her cross? She answered: "I have nothing but my life; I offer it to Our Lord." Then, to Mother Xavier, who expressed her sorrow at losing her: "You have always been a tender mother to me; no, I will not forget you. God will console you."

A few moments later she completely lost consciousness, then suddenly cried out: "I am leaving," and gave over her soul in the peace of the Lord, about 9 in the morning, July 11, 1832.

We earnestly recommend her to your prayers, in order that he who judges even virtues and is the God of all purity have mercy on her soon, if she has not already obtained it.
[*On the July 12 letter only*:]
I am with respect *in Corde Jesu,*
Dear Mother,
Your obedient daughter,

Xavier Sup— [*in her own writing on the July 12 letter*]

Helene Dutour to Madeleine Sophie Barat[285]

S.C.J.M.   Grand Coteau October 11, 1832

My very Reverend Mother Barat,

I believe it is my duty as member of the Society to manifest to you the need there is for you to send us one of the older mothers from France to visit our houses, especially in lower Louisiana. What is happening is that the religious who came from France are suffering here. It is not only the difference of spirit that they find with our houses of Europe. There is not the same way of teaching, either. I cannot tell you here all the details of this difference but it is great and real on these two points.

I told you, dear mother, in March of this year, 1832, that the house and land at LaFourche still belongs to me legally, and that according to the Constitutions and the Decrees, I will not cede them to anyone until you have indicated to me what is your will. I beg you to answer immediately with what you want me to do in this regard. Mother Eugenie is pressuring me for Mother Xavier to give it to the bishop. Neither of them wants one of our houses there. The bishop, whom I asked what he thinks for himself, answered

---

285 French autograph. GASSH.

that he would find it convenient to enter a house that is ready, but when he considers before God, it is completely the same whether it is we or he who occupies it, providing, he said several times, that religion benefits. To me, it is the same. He put up 7500 francs for the building and the debts, which we would return to him if we came back. (I can say that I received 750 francs.) Separately from that, what we would give him if we cede the establishment to him is more than 40,000 francs. There is immense good to do there. The bishop is so convinced that he wrote to me when he was at LaFourche: "I am so convinced that your house is according to the order of God that I will do everything I can to sustain it." He told me another time that if we leave, he will put other religious there. But Mother Eugenie and Father de la Croix have such confidence in him that he is persuaded to put his seminary there.

Another thing that it is good for you to know is that the debts of LaFourche, which have been greatly exaggerated, have been paid in part by the bishop's money. I think he has put in 3,000 francs. Since the two mothers do not want this house, they will be happy that what the bishop advanced will be to his advantage. I hope that God has made you aware in some way of the true reason for the closing of this poor house that had such an attraction for me because it was all for the [social] class without resources and for the poor. Please answer me without delay. To make me give an answer before I get your answer, Mother Xavier says that if it remains empty for a year, the one who gave the land could take it back and profit at the expense of religion, from the houses and repairs that have been made, but there is still the protector of this business.

[*On the edges of the paper*:]
Mother Xavier absolutely wants me to give her today a power of attorney, so that, if I do not want to take it on myself to turn over the house, she can do it herself. I will do it, but by specifying that she cannot act in virtue of that act until after February 15, 1833,

when the year will have run out. Please answer me, for love of the Immaculate Conception.

...less here and there, and I am resolved to wait for your answer before doing anything. Do not put me off, please, reverend mother. I only have time to assure you of my deepest respect and the attachment of my heart in that of Our Lord, where I have the honor to be your obedient daughter h duTour.

The whole community is well. You will already have learned of the death of holy Mother Dorival, which happened three months ago today.

Xavier Murphy to Bishop Rosati[286]

S.S.C.J.M.   Grand Coteau Nov 3rd, 1832

The first impulse that my heart instinctively feels during the leisure of our vacation is to dedicate a few moments to you my lord and D^r father. Indeed it would be impossible for me to express what I experienced on hearing from your distinguished son[287] and my own dear Bishop (in our recent *tête à tête*) all the good that you have & daily are effecting in your favored Diocese. Go on and prosper, continue to diffuse the riches of the Gospel and by your Godlike manners captivate all hearts & surmount all difficulties. This dearest father is the unceasing prayer of one who glories to hear of your success etc. etc. Your cherished son has just left us after a visit of 6 weeks during which he was our chaplain, confessor etc.etc. His time was usefully employed. He gave scientific lectures to the sisters, Religious lectures to our American boarders, controversial ones at Opelousas, administered Baptism to 10

---

286 English autograph. Rosati collection.
287 Presumably Bishop De Neckere, now bishop of New Orleans.

adults here, made a first Communion, gave Confirmation, distributed the prizes, gave a retreat and received the first vows of two choir sisters,[288] *enfin* diffused consolation, peace & fervour, and left us embalmed with his devoted zeal and enlightened Piety. The people of Opelousas venerate his name and boast of his profound erudition.

They are speaking and in fact commenced a subscription for a Catholic Church at Alexandria. All our children of that parish persevere in our faith and diffuse a favorable idea of our holy Religion, so much so that the inhabitants recently refused cooperating with a Presbyterian minister for the erection of a temple, saying that they preferred the Religion of Grand Coteau (as they term it). The majority of our boarders are from that section, also Natchitoches and Wasichota.[289] But *a propos* when will you come and see your once so cherished spot. You will find everything here changed, except the veneration & attachment of your daughters and these are proof to time and circumstances. We have got your portrait in our little parlour. How many filial expressive glances did I not see, our dear Prelate, cast on it. Methinks at times he seemed to converse and feel animated, whilst gazing on the venerated bust.

We have just commenced a plain frame house at the end of the garden for a summer residence for our bishop. It is called the cottage of G. Coteau; a temporary sojourn in this quarter will be of efficient utility to catholicity in this our Western section. The Methodists & Presbyterians (Cumberland) are becoming numerous and not one American clergyman to combat or counteract this doctrine on plans. It is only at the foot of the sanctuary that we can bemoan the poverty of our Diocese in regard to talented clergymen. You ought to share with us.

---

288 One was Louise Prosper Prud-hon, who therefore must have come in 1831 as a novice; see allusions in letters of February 2 and 24. The other is not known.
289 Probably Ouachita, a town about 160 miles north, beyond Alexandria and Natchitoches.

I was most happy to hear that Mrs. Smith had decided on living with the Sisters of Charity. This step I deem the completion of her happiness. I have just addressed her a long letter. I am now confined to my bed by a sore leg and feel much difficulty in writing, but my desire to address your Lordship a few lines could not be overcome, and your parental indulgence will overlook all the defects in writing composition etc. etc.

I have been so completely americanised that for some time back I nearly forgot that I ever had any claim on the Emerald Isle. But on hearing from the Bishop of all the noble dignified acts of J Mullanphy & of his cooperating with you in all your undertakings for A.M.D.G. my national pride felt awakened and I exclaimed oh! I cannot forget that I am Irish when I have <u>such</u> a <u>man</u> to claim as my countryman.[290] You have also dear father the sons of Loyola[291] and what powerful auxiliaries for your Godlike mission. Poor Louisiana! You have nothing save hope and anticipation. Your cane & cotton are flourishing, your cattle are in prime condition but the noblest growth of your fertile soil the masterpiece of the Creator are bereft of the solid means of attaining true & lasting happiness.

Do then dearest father pity our wants & by our prayers and unceasing desires hasten the <u>end</u> of the <u>captivity</u> of our ignorance etc. etc. Your devoted daughter *in C.J.*

Xavier

[*On the outside*:]
Father Rosti's health is a little improved, but his constitution is vitally impaired. He just continues the old plan & may well be termed the hermit of G. Coteau.

X

---

290 John Mullanphy, Irish-born, was a wealthy patron of the Church in St. Louis, having already by this time subsidized the founding of the Society's City House in 1828 with an orphanage, and a hospital with the Sisters of Charity.
291 The Jesuits had arrived in St. Louis and were setting up a farm in Florissant, not far from the Society's house at St. Ferdinand there.

[*Postmark*:]
Nov 7   25

The Right Revd Dr Rosati
St Louis
Missouri

[*At the top in another hand in French*:]
1832 Nov ² 3⁰ (corrected to ²) Mother Xavier Opelousas

1833 ——————————————————————

Xavier Murphy to Henriette Ducis[292]

Recommended to Mary our Good Mother
S.S.C.J.M.   Grand Coteau, February 2, 1833

[Here?] dear Mother Ducis, you will find the receipts and the expenses of the past semester. You will see that our expenses are the same as our receipts. Why? Because our improvements and even our needs are according to our finances. As a result, we are free from debt, thanks be to God. So much for business.

Now I must tell you that my heart is distressed when I see that I and our house are forgotten by yours, for it is now a year since we have received a letter from our mother. I am even ignorant of her situation or whatever residence. No one at the head of our Society writes to us. Even you, dear mother, seem to have forgotten your duty. Nevertheless, we love you very much and are worried, having no news of you except through the public newspapers that we do not have here. So think of the fear your American children have for those in France. In spite of this cloud, we are working as well as

---

292 French autograph. GASSH.

we can for the glory of the S.H. of J. and we have the consolation to see that our labors are not ineffective.

At the moment our house is all in vogue and we have as many children as we can take, and the happiness of making them children of the Church, for religion in Grand Coteau is popular. To God be the glory.

Mother Duchesne asks for 5,000 francs, and in her last letter, mother recommended that I give it to her. Since I don't have all of that amount, I told her to ask you for what is owed us in France. For I think you have given up on the idea of sending us someone, even a second teacher for the music would be very useful, since we have more children for music than we can teach. You also know, dear mother, that the house is without an assistant since the death of dear Mother Dorival. Her loss is irreparable for me. I feel my incapacity every day. There is no one here to help me. Please tell my situation to our mother. I do not have her address, and here I am, deprived of being able to write to her. I think you have all seen Father Jeanjean, the most distinguished of our mission, and the most helpful friend and the most consistent of our colony here. If he visited you, you are surely up to date on all our transactions, success, etc.

We have received the package of veils with some letters, but not one from you or your house. Sacrifice. *Fiat. Fiat.* You probably know that Mothers Dutour, Bazire, Toysonnier, and Prosper are here. The last one made her vows last October. Everyone here remembers their dear mothers in France. Mother Coppens, after taking the steamboat from St Louis to go to St Michel, was obliged to return to St Louis after one day of travel. She was very suffering. It seems that no house is good for her with regard to her health, etc.

Many warm and affectionate greetings, and filial, to my dear, dear Mothers Eugenie and de Marbeuf, Port., etc. Please give us news of them, receiving ours with the affection of our cordial indissoluble union *in Corde Jesu* for time and eternity. Amen.

Your devoted and very affectionate daughter Xavier R. du S. C.

[*On the outside*:]

Via New York

Mother Ducis
Rue de Varrennes [*sic*] No. 41
In Paris

[Postmarks]:
PAID 25

Opelousas, Louisiana
Overseas country via Le Havre
Le Havre 5 April (74)

Xavier Murphy to Bishop Rosati[293]

S.S.C.J.M.   Grand Coteau February 10, 1833

How could I dearest Bishop & great father let pass this opportunity without affording myself the gratification of saluting you most cordially and expressing to you the delight with which my heart glowed on hearing of the success that attends your steps in whatever path you direct them. The handsomest Church in the Union approaching its perfect completion, a Seminary, a Loyola College, an Hospital, several Institutions for the education of females, all all comprised in the Diocese and under the fostering care of the Venerable Prelate the good father Rosati. With justice may the anti-Catholic gazettes cry out "Look sharp to the Missouri State; not one Protestant Institution to be found there but myriads of Catholic ones" bur the fact is so very uncommon that I trust it will pass without amendment.

---

293 English autograph. Rosati collection.

Our Venerable foundress will give you all our particulars here. She appears entirely satisfied with the work of her hands and heart at G. Coteau. Divine Providence aids our feeble efforts & crowns our labors with success for A.M.D.G.

But father we want a college here. See what can be done. You are so successful in your <u>plans</u> & <u>undertakings</u> that if you interfered in our behalf I am sure all would be effected. Remember you hold the right of primogeniture in our regard, so that we have an undisputed claim on your exertions and what good for Religion in this state, and above all what a dire blow for Presbyterian intolerance which has nothing to impede its progress in our quarter.

Allow me dear father & bishop to offer you all the respectful attachment of your daughters of the S.H. at G. Coteau to bestow upon us your paternal benediction and give us a share in your fervent prayers.

With devoted Veneration & affection
Your daughter in C.J.
Xavier
R. du S.C.

[*No address. On the side in another hand in French:*]
1833 February 10 Mother Xavier G. Coteau
Received March 12

Xavier Murphy to Madeleine Sophie Barat[294]

      Recommended to St. A de P
S.S.C.J.M.   Grand Coteau February 24, 1833

God alone knows, dear and beloved mother general, how your letter of July 15 did me good, even though it remained in route for

---

294 French autograph. GASSH.

six months. The delay was caused by the European post because the stamp from New York is January 14. Now I have so many things to tell you about business that I see that it will be in eternity that I will have the joy of speaking to you from the heart about God and the state of my poor soul that <u>feels</u> so well everything that our divine spouse has done in my regard, above all to have introduced me into our Society and to have you for a mother.

I am at ease having your permission for the church. While waiting, I have made a plan that would require 30,000 francs. When the bishop [Leo de Neckere] came, I showed it to him and his decision was that it would be more advantageous for the good of the Society and more agreeable to the public to continue the Academy, and if I had the funds, to convert a part of the old house for a chapel. But for the moment I can do nothing, having last year completed an infirmary, a linen room, and the complete renovation of the old house, because I try to do the improvements here in proportion to our finances. Consequently, we are debt-free, so here we are, presented like Religious of the Sacred Heart. The bishop found us doing so well that he asked us to make a little house for him. It is almost finished in the center of our garden, and we will have the happiness of possessing the bishop for several months each year. His last visit did much good to the community and the children, to whom he gave some instructions on religion and the sciences. Moreover, I sent him to preach against the Methodists. He is so timid that he did not want to go, but I announced it in the paper and he was obliged to go in spite of himself. The result was that he charmed and convinced several. He is entirely devoted to our Society and he says that without it he would not remain in the diocese. He says that a Religious of the Sacred Heart who fulfills the Rule (which I think he knows by heart) should take the first place in heaven.

With regard to Mother Lavy, I communicated your orders. She is submitting. She is doing better since the last visit of the bishop, who believes that in respect to her, there is a physical problem.

He wants her to stay here because of her usefulness for the music and that this house suits her better than any other. I hope that we will not need to change, though it would be good to have another music teacher. The revenue this year will be 6,000 francs. We have an American but she is not strong enough. Ah! Dear mother, you do not want more than we do to have Jesuits, but right now they are too indolent. They do not have the spirit of Saint Ignatius. It is now three years that I have been asking directly and indirectly. The place is here and so is the response, because the citizens want an establishment <u>exactly like ours</u>. The bishop sighs only for this and these gentlemen do not do parish work.[295] Recently one of our fathers from Saint Louis came to see us. I sent him to preach in a place where they had never heard a Catholic priest, and the result was that a subscription was begun to have a church and a priest.

As for Mother A. Toysonnier, you asked for a year of probation. It is just finished, for it was at this time that she and all came here from the house at LaFourche. Dear mother, this is what I take in about her, that she is, as you remarked, given to judging others. With regard to me, she seems to be attached to me. She has a great depth of sensitivity and talks about her thoughts too much. All these faults at her age (40) are nearly insurmountable. But she has in her favor a great attachment and devotion to the Society, much talent for household management and even for economics. So I think, dear mother, that it will be better if she is completely linked with us. This present delay was a painful stroke for her because she was expecting your permission. So see if you can arrange it for her before the big feast of the Sacred Heart, so that she will be able to make her vows on that feast, with the sister of 40 whom you have permitted. Send a letter to her personally in mine, because a letter from the mother general cuts to <u>the heart</u> and does wonders in this country. I myself, when I read yours, feel completely interior, at least a great desire to become so. Speaking of this, we have the

---

295 *Ne paroissent pas.* Meaning unclear.

happiness of possessing one of your conferences on the interior life, done for the time of Lent. We read it often here and have sent a copy to all our houses. Oh! Pray and have others pray that the spirit of the Society will remain with us in its original purity, etc.

Undoubtedly you already know of the death of dear Mother Dorival. It was an irreparable loss here. Her death was worthy of a spouse of the Heart of Jesus. I am without an assistant and the burden is too much for poor me. While awaiting your orders, I pray the good master to direct us for his greater glory and for the good of this little house. Mother Dutour has gotten it into her head that you will permit the re-establishment of LaFourche, and to that end directs her prayers, her thoughts, and even partly her activities. She has communicated her ideas to some of our sisters. This makes me worry. She refuses to sign her renouncement to the donation made in her favor to transfer the place to the bishop according to your orders. If death comes knocking for the man who gave the land, the building will be in the hands of his heirs, and all our money as well as that of the bishop will be in the hands of seculars. The travel of the religious and their effects from LaFourche cost this house <u>here</u> 1500 francs. Add still a debt (that I paid) of 4500 francs for that mother, and after all that, this dear mother hopes that you will permit the opening of the establishment. I have sent the accounts of the last semester to Mother Ducis. I had to purchase a Negro for 3,000 francs.[296] We have now four adults and three children, which gives us, <u>according to this country, property of 12,500 francs</u>. I promised Mother Duchesne 5,000 francs. I told her to take what is due me in Paris, fearing not to have enough.

Thus you will see that with all these expenses, it would not be prudent to undertake anything this year, but on that point be sure

---

[296] David Eaglin, brother of Jenny, from Joseph Gardiner on January 19. Jenny, married to Frank Hawkins, had arrived in 1829. David married Julitte (Julie) the day of his arrival, January 21. It therefore seems that, like the acquisition of Jenny, wife of Frank, in 1829, this too was in order to unite a family.

that I will not do anything without having the funds in advance. Our children.....[*text illegible*]

Because cholera is in the area since the month of November. It has ravaged New Orleans just as it did Paris. Indeed, that city is a second edition as to vice, etc. I hope that by now you have seen Father Jeanjean. The worthy missionary will bring you up to date about all our houses. On leaving, he said he believes he will look for you in the most hidden corner. He now sees you as the queen of [*text illegible*, possibly *calm*]. He would have found it beyond his efforts. I presume that the council has been postponed. In the month of May, Mother Duchesne asked us for the vote for assistant of this country. I sent it in the envelope of Mother Ducis, to your address. This request has stirred up the curiosity of women because they are the same everywhere. The bishop during his stay here gave the black veil to Mother Prosper. She is a good religious. Now she is training to become useful for classes, since she had no education in the sciences. The latest news I had of Mother Coppens is that she left St Louis to come here or St Michel. I know nothing, and a few leagues from St Louis, she felt ill and had to return. I think she will not stay in this country.[297] Mother Bazire is very helpful here. She gives lessons in drawing. She is also very good for handwriting. She is training for classes, etc. Mother Bazire gave lessons on the sciences, etc. She has a good character for community. If she had continued as superior at LaFourche, she would have been completely spoiled, having little time in the midst of so many business affairs to practice interior life. I see with pleasure that the present situation makes her taste and appreciate the happiness of solitude and tranquility.

---

297 She returned to France in 1836.

[*On the outside*:]
Mother
Mother Barat

Eh! Dear and beloved mother, I am forced to leave you. Send your blessing to your daughters here, and a veil to me, please, with your response. I greet all my mothers and sisters in the Heart of Jesus.

I ask their prayers and also for this country. For you, dear mother, complete the work you have done. Consolidate the glory of the Heart of Jesus in the New World, because you are great in the kingdom of heaven. Amen says your affectionate and completely devoted daughter

In the Heart of Jesus. Xavier *R. du S.C.*

Thousands and thousands of greetings to my dear star. I wrote to him by way of Father Jeanjean.
Everything against nature. Consequently, he deprives me of the pleasure of a letter. X.

1834

Xavier Murphy to Madeleine Sophie Barat[298]

For our mother general   to St. A. de P. recommended
S.S.C.J.M.   Grand Coteau, January 19, 1834

How many times, dear and beloved mother, my heart feels the need to speak with you since your happy arrival in the motherhouse, but from day to day I delay that consolation while awaiting the arrival of Father Jeanjean in Louisiana. Finally, he is now in New Orleans, and I have just received your precious circular with the letter of the Sovereign Pontiff. What sweet consolation, what

---

298 French autograph. GASSH.

subject of gratitude have we not all experienced in reading these precious measures of the tenderness of the Heart of Jesus toward our dear Society. Every day I find myself filled with gratitude toward Jesus for having chosen me in his mercy as spouse of his Heart and <u>your daughter</u>, and in spite of all my weaknesses, my innumerable infidelities and my great faults, it seems to me that his delight is to forget all of them, and to give me more and more the marks of his benevolence. Oh! Yes, dear mother, venerated mother, the Heart of Jesus has done great things for you and for us your daughters. May he be eternally praised from age to age. Amen.

As soon as we knew the prayers that you had designated, we began them and we will continue them until we have learned the outcome of the council, which we hope to receive soon and <u>by post</u>. Undoubtedly you found in the hands of Mother Ducis upon your arrival our votes that we sent in May 1832. You are not unaware that since the death of Mother Dorival we have been without an assistant, and how much I feel the need for one, but I am convinced that the Heart of Jesus will inspire you to provide for the general need of your colony in America. And I say with the Apostle that this hope sustains me, for the moment, in joy.

You already know the terrible blow with which God has struck us in the premature death of our holy Bishop [de Neckere].[299] You know, dear mother, how much he esteemed our Society and how he was devoted to it. This was the most painful event that I have experienced since I have been in the Society. He was like a brother to me, making me part of all his projects for the glory of God, and as we were saying about the Holy Father, he had to witness to his sorrow in seeing the pitiable state of religion in his diocese. He often said to me that the Sacred Heart was the only balm to heal the wound in his heart. Because he would say that without our houses, religion would completely disappear. Nevertheless,

---

299 Bishop De Neckere had died in New Orleans September 4, 1833, of yellow fever at the age of 33.

dear mother, do not think that we do great things, with the lack of appropriate priests to help us.

In the East everything is different. They have apostolic and learned priests and especially those who have the language of the country. Would it not be possible for us to have a house there? For Louisiana will never furnish the right kind of vocations for us. Baltimore is the Rome of America. I think Mother Duchesne mentioned the council of 10 bishops held recently in that city. Their deliberations were approved by Rome. We will know who will be our future bishop. There is talk of a Jesuit. I have received frequent letters from the present administrator of this diocese.[300] He seems completely devoted to our Society. He is a Frenchman of merit. You know how much the Heart of Jesus has favored us this year by preserving us from cholera, which has been all around us. The Immaculate Conception obtained this grace for us. Since the return from vacation, we have 80 children. That is all we can accommodate now, in view of all the fatal occurrences through cholera, sending children home, etc., etc. I have not used the permission you gave me to build. Our present situation is splendid enough.

Now I turn to our resources. See the little note joined here for Mother Ducis. I would not have the means to send something to Mother Duchesne this year. In the one just finished, I gave her 5400 francs. I am sorry to have to tell you that Mother Lavy is still in the same state and even worse. I am afraid that soon her health will render her useless for the Society. She does not want to go to Mother Eugenie, for whom she has the same prejudice as for me. (Between us, I do not think she was well placed with the young novices and aspirants; she wants to go with Mother Duchesne). Please, dear mother, give me your answer as promptly as possible. Her departure from here would do a great deal of harm for the music. The lessons bring in 7,000 francs a year and the

---

300 Auguste Jeanjean was named bishop, but refused to accept it. Antoine Blanc accepted and served as administrator until consecrated bishop November 22, 1835.

parents want very much for their children to learn this accomplishment. I have a request to make to you for an aspirant who was the first novice received in S^ت Louis, sent here 6 years ago, who knew nothing on her arrival and who by her application and devotion became capable of doing the second English class. If you give the permission to make final vows for the lovely day of the Sacred Heart, her time will be complete. She is old enough and, I can add, has nearly all the qualities for her to be one of us.[301] I have not received your permission for poor Adele [Toysonnier]. I ask it again, please. I have already told you about her, that she continues to be full of devotion and is very useful here. She is in charge of the laundry of our children, which gives us 8,000 francs per year right now. Finally, if her head were as good as her heart, she would be an excellent teacher. She is 40 years old. About two years ago, Mother Duchesne sent me a young woman of 17 years, a choir aspirant, who was found by a priest and presented to him as an orphan. Good Mother D saw that since she was given by a priest, she should be a choir religious, and sent her to us as such, not knowing how to read and not able to be employed with the children.[302] I suggested to her to be a sister. She was filled with joy and now is very useful to us. I told Mother Duchesne about this and she answered that <u>I had acted beyond my authority; she had been received as choir religious by our superior general.</u> Tell me what you think.

Mother Bazire is becoming more useful every day. She is my right hand for help with the children. She is making progress in virtue as well as in her studies, and speaks English fairly well. Her willingness and character are excellent, and later you will have in

---

301 Eleanor Gray entered the Society in Florissant and made first vows at Grand Coteau in 1829. She was professed, not at the feast of the Sacred Heart, but on September 26, 1834.

302 This is possibly Marcellite Coté, RSCJ, born in St. Charles, Mo in 1812, entered at Florissant 1829, and made first vows in St. Louis in 1831. She then went to Grand Coteau, where she was professed in 1839. She later lived at Mater in New Orleans and died at St. Michael in 1898.

her a person to put at the head, etc., etc. Recently Mother Eugenie has asked me to send her Mother Bazire for a while. I answered that I cannot give her up. We are only 18 here. There is a Creole aspirant here, a novice from St Michael for her health, who has illness of the chest, and is otherwise useful here. It seems good to me, dear mother, that there not be any change of personnel like that of Mother Bazire without your approval. Dear Mother Dutour by her *je ne sais quoi* is incapable of helping me organize either the boarding school or the community, nor Mother Lavy because of her head at this moment. Mother Bazire is the only one who can be counted on. Mother Prud'homme does 4 classes, and to be able to do that, she must study constantly. There is a religious who is regular and very tenacious. I see "the bond of perfection," of mutual charity, thanks to the Heart of Jesus, more edifying among the religious from LaFourche, though I do not know why each of them has something against Mother Bazire.

Among our students there are several for baptism this year. Since the religion of Grand Coteau is in style now, I hope a few will be for us. The ones I send to St Michael are good religious. In that regard, I will say nothing about that house, assuming that Mother Eugenie will keep you updated about everything that happens there. That good mother has been very tried by the death of 6 and the departure of 2 in the year just ending. Mother Van Damme was an irreparable loss in the country.[303] May God's will be done.

Finally, I must leave you and my dictionary, too, because I must hold in one hand my heart, and in the other my pen, and in spite of it, these three things are not enough to share with you my sentiments, my thoughts, and my wishes. So read in the heart of our spouse, him only. There you will find my thoughts, my labors, and my devotion for you and yours. Finally, for the glory of the heart of Jesus. Oh! My dear and tender mother general, believe me to

---

303 She died May 30, 1833 at St. Michael.

be your completely devoted and completely attached daughter, a happy title, *in C.J.* Xavier

P.S. Sister Marguerite is well. Her death will be brought about by the love of her spouse. She is a perfect and devoted religious.

Xavier Murphy to Father Charles de la Croix[304]

S.S.C.J.M.   Grand Coteau, February 9, 1834

Last evening I received my very Dr. and ever valued Father Lacroix's letter at the moment that all here were indulging the fond hope of seeing you amongst us. For Mère Eugenie had announced your intention of accompanying the *père* Elet—well then what have I to say of our disappointment. You who well know my heart can the better judge of its feelings. But the idea that this almost abandoned state should lose in you one of its most efficient missioners is more than I can digest, and actually all my courage and <u>*devoument*</u> appear to vanish. So that I have scarcely heart to inquire what could or can induce you to leave us, and to quit America without seeing G. Coteau. Since the fatal month of September I have never addressed you, fearing to increase your sorrows by recounting mine, for when the dire blow was struck, you were one of the first I considered.

The rugged road of my earthly pilgrimage is not, I perceive, to be travelled in company with the very few that would beguile its difficulties. *Fiat voluntas.* The nomination of *Mère* Eugenie [as assistant general] I deem as a most auspicious omen for the

---

[304] English autograph. GASSH. Charles de la Croix (1792-1869) was one of the Belgians who came to America with Bishop Dubourg in 1817. He left the St. Louis area for St. Michael in 1823 and was the impetus for the founding of the convent there. He returned to Europe in 1839. He is the recipient of 17 letters from Philippine Duchesne, who continued correspondence with him even after his return to Europe.

future advantage of our Society in this country. I long to see her. Perhaps <u>fate</u> may also deprive me of this consolation. Nothing but God alone can be calculated on, for creatures too often change.

I cannot finish without offering you all the sincere attachment and gratitude of all the community. Few amongst them that have not had the advantage of your acquaintance and of appreciating your intrinsic worth. You may count on our prayers whilst I engage you not to forget the promise you made me, of remembering me on the Holy Mount. All goes on here smoothly, a full house and obliged for want of room to refuse several boarders. I am sorry not to be able to give you before departure a circumstantial account of the Rapidian Church but if we have the consolation of creating it, I will write you all the particulars. In the mean while I recommend this affair to your prayers, should we be able to establish a Priest, etc. in that parish, it would be a great triumph for our religion. The greater part of our boarders have the permission to embrace as they call it the Religion of G.C.—*enfin* A.M.D.G.

I hope this letter will overtake you and express to you all the sentiments with which at this moment of final adieu, my heart is replete for indeed I am deeply affected at your departure and as ever remain full of esteem and devoted attachment for you

In C.J.
Xavier
R. du S.C.

P.S. two S.B. have arrived this week but no *père* Elet.

[*On the envelope*:]
Postmark: Feb 12; *city illegible*
1834
Rev. Chs. De La Croix
St Michels
Brangier office

Anna Xavier Murphy, RSCJ (1793-1836)

Sister Xavier, Sister of Charity, to Bishop Rosati from Grand Coteau[305]

Sunday Morning April 20th Grand Coteau 1834

My Dear Father

I write to you from the white cottage situated west of the convent; we arrived Tuesday 15th at twelve o'clock, much fatigued. During the whole of our journey I have suffered more or less as the weather changed, every breeze from water or land seemed to threaten to extinguish my feeble lamp of life, tho since we are here I have gained strength and feel now as if I had yet some part of my task to finish on earth.

The Ladies received me with much affection and lavish on me their united attentions; their institution here very far exceeds anything I could have expected to find in this country. They have 85 pensioners all in good health, in a word it is a little heaven on earth, the garden and surrounding country charms the eye, the warbling of the little birds enchant the ear, while the innocent gaiety of interesting youth, the solid and cheerful piety of these admirable Ladies, rejoice the heart yet cannot content it, for I prefer, yes, and greatly prefer my old Hospital filled with human miseries and my little orphan boys to every thing on this earth. My heart is strong, and for those beloved objects, still retains all its energy. Ah could I but see them half as comfortably situated as I find the rich people's children of this country, I think I should neither hunger or thirst any more this side of Eternity.

Madam Smith is well. I see Rev. Mr. Cilina [?][306] every day. He seems disappointed that I do not recover faster. He intends leaving here next week; in that case I shall see you soon. Please tell my Dear Sisters I will send them an account of my travels as exactly as

---

305 English autograph. Rosati collection. Identity otherwise unknown. See Xavier's reference to her in the next letter.
306 Perhaps Francis Cellini, but though he was at Grand Coteau earlier, it is doubtful that he was there then.

my health would allow me to keep it. It will amuse them, besides, they will see <u>how wise</u> I have become.

Mother Xavier invited me to visit the pensioners but poor children, they did not know what to make of me. They found me "<u>too tall</u>, so Deathly looking, and black cap too!" One said, "If I had met her in the woods I would really have been frightened." This was my first visit. Mother Superior took me a second time. I remained more than half an hour. I compared their situation with that of our orphans. Their young hearts were touched, and they are now making for their benefit a collection. Several have written to their parents to have something, but I fear I shall not be here long enough for them to receive their answer.

Well my Dear Father, since I commenced this one of the Ladies came to make me ride out. Have the goodness to say to Mother Duchesne how very kindly I am treated here among her spiritual daughters. They make many inquiries concerning her health, etc. You my Father are very often named. They calculate on seeing you this summer.

I pray you to remember me affectionatedly [sic] to all my Dear Sisters not forgetting the three in or at Carondelet. Poor little Dominica! How I wish to know if *Soeur* E. is home; must have patience.

Now my Dear Father I will conclude as my hand is not very steady, tho certainly I am gaining more health.

Very respectfully & affectionatedly [sic]
Sr. Xavier

Xavier Murphy to Bishop Rosati[307]

S.C.J.M.   Grand Coteau, April 29, 1834

I was indeed Beloved bishop rejoiced at receiving a few lines from you as also to hear of your fine health, splendid church, and the magical rapidity of Catholicity in your peculiarly favored diocese. Now cannot but exclaim with the apostle: "Blessed be the Lord the God of all consolation,"[308] etc. You have further conferred a singular gratification on the community here and on your humble servant particularly by procuring us the satisfaction of possessing Mother Sup. What a holy soul and what a treasure for the Institute to which she is attracted. She says that her health improves here. If so, you have only to remember that G. Coteau always exists and that should change of air be again deemed necessary we shall be too happy at her presence. All the local intelligence plans, contracts, etc. I shall leave for the recital of our visitors who assure me that I shall see y. Lordship ere long, and what a delicious anticipation in the midst of all my pain. For further, the daughters of Sion[309] had not more cause to mourn than we now have over the ruin of Religion, and was I not supported by a supernatural force, all my courage and plans would vanish. Pray for us also and accept of the devoted veneration and attachment of your daughters of the S. H. at G. Coteau.

Xavier

---

307 English autograph. Rosati collection.
308 2 Cor 1:3, paraphrased.
309 Baruch 4:14.

Xavier Murphy to Madeleine Sophie Barat[310]

SS.C.J.M.   Octave of the Assumption, Grand Coteau
August 22, 1834

Just now, dear and beloved mother, I have received your letters from Bordeaux dated in March. I will take the opportunity to enclose this page in the letter of Mother Dutour. You are asking for an explanation about the laundry. We are obliged to do the laundry of the children who come from a distance. The washing is done by our enslaved, who cost us a great deal, and the ironing for the community. Not having to buy the wood, which we take from our lands, leaves us about 6,000 francs per year. We will not find people here who can do the laundry and we charge less for this than the other boarding schools. Our sisters are devoted to this, persuaded that this gives us a way to help the houses up there [Missouri] and to take a few poor children, but with good parents. At present, we have nine who are with the boarders. In addition, for three years, we have spent $2,000 to hire a local to do the laundry. It is not enough, and at the moment, we will need another, which will come to at least 3,000 francs. Now you will see, dear mother, if I can continue on the same footing. I see well that I do not express myself well with regard to the money due to Bishop Neckere, because I never borrowed money from him <u>nor from anyone</u>. Thanks to God, I have never needed to. Here is the thing. At the moment of the suppression of LaFourche, that house owed its priest 4555 francs.[311] I made it my obligation to pay this priest the sum when he should ask for it. The priest died, leaving the bishop as his heir. The bishop wrote to me three weeks after his death: "I have your note. What should I do with it?" I answered

---
310 French autograph. GASSH.
311 The five RSCJ left LaFourche March 26, 1832. According to Baudier, the pastors at that time were J.T. Drapeur, CM, September 1831 to January 1832; then briefly Pierre Ladaviere, SJ, who had been pastor in 1831; then H. B. de St. Aubin, 1832 to early 1838. Baudier does not mention the death of a priest there.

that at the moment I did not have the money. The bishop died and his administrator wrote to me: "I have your note. Keep the amount until I see you." And I have never seen this man. ~~when he will ask for it.~~ I think there was an understanding between the priest to whom I took on the obligation and Mother Eugenie, because it was only at her visit here that she learned that the bishop had asked me for that money. That is the only temporal affair that I have had with priests, because for me it is an inviolable law that they are never involved in my affairs nor those of the house, and it is to that that I attribute all the tranquility that I enjoy.

In my letter of the 19th [of January] you see my present determination with regard to Mother Lavy. Your little word assured me that for now it is the will of God. With regard to Mother Toysonnier, you will see in the same letter the information you asked of me. I thank you for the permission you gave about that aspirant. I would like her to make her vows during our vacation, but at the moment we do not have priests suitable for this great ceremony. You will find in Mother Eugenie's papers the page on her information. Finally, I thank you even more for having named Mother Bazire as my assistant. I hope that when Mother Eugenie returns, she will return that person to this house that feels her absence, but A.M.D.G.

Believe me, dear mother, your devote daughter *in C.J.*

Xavier

I greet with affection Mother de Limminghe. Her place near you, dear mother, makes her very dear to my heart. X

Xavier Murphy to Bishop Rosati[312]

S.C.J.M.   Grand Coteau, October 27, 1834

If, my Lord and Very R. father, it is customary on great events to offer congratulatory wishes, feelings, etc., methinks I may now offer you these of your daughters of G. Coteau on the completion & consecration of the splendid trophy erected under your Lordship's auspices for the pride & glory of our holy Religion. Oh! What a consoling—what a delicious sight—the transaction of the memorable 26th must have offered to your feelings. "In the simplicity of my heart have I joyfully offered all these things & I have seen with great joy thy people which are here present, etc."[313] How often in spirit did I mingle with the admiring crowd—indeed I could think & speak of nothing else. I even fancied that your Lordship's <u>portrait</u> smiled more than usual. Happy Feast. All smiles with complacency for you but forlorn loss. Nothing save a despoiled Diocese, a few worn out clergy, with an uninstructed flock are now thy portion & inheritance. The fat of the land & rich pasturages can only remain for our future condemnation.

Father Rosti, after an absence of four months, has returned, his health not much improved, from his Eastern trip. During our vacation Father Blanc came to give us our annual retreat. It was the first time I had the pleasure of seeing this gentleman. At his return to the city, Father Jeanjean has fled. Father B. christened three of our children & made the first communion of a young person formerly baptized here but not then permitted by her parents to perform that great action. In general, the Religion of G. Coteau, as they term ours, is preferred for our youth in spite of the hostile

---

312 English autograph. Rosati collection.
313 1 Chron 29:17. The new stone cathedral of St. Louis was dedicated on October 26, 1834, the previous wooden structure having been destroyed by fire three years earlier. Xavier must have known of the dedication day in advance and she writes on the next day.

animosity of the Presbyterians against us. They declare that this Institution is the destruction of the youth of the country and that it is dangerous to see such influence and money between the hands of women. In short, that it is the ruin of the parish. Their sect which is now numerous in this quarter have proposed forming an Institution similar to ours in another part of the parish. The subscription has commenced and they look for religious from New York who are to live <u>like the sisterhood of G.C.</u> After all this projected farce I have recently contracted for the completion of our Academy for what do you think—for $14,000—don't you think I have courage. I hold the plan be fully executed. It may well be called a splendid building. After this we shall commence a Church. That we are in great need of. This was the work I wished to undertake but at the solicitations of parents I ceded for the Academy, not having room for more than about eighty which number is full. Have the goodness, father, to offer our affectionate salutations to the dear Sisters of Charity. The improvement in Mother X. health rejoices all here. When you visit the S. Heart say that all here are well. Surprised at their silence in our regard. We also wish to be presented to Mrs. Chs. Smith. Finally, request the Benedictions of our worthy father
> who I am sure prays for one full of veneration and
> Attachment in C.J. Xavier R. du S.C.

[*In the margin of the first page, in French in another hand:*]
1834 Oct. 24 Mother Xavier, Grand Coteau
Received the 15 December
Answered the 17, sent the report of the dedication of the church

Xavier Murphy to Eugenie Audé[314]

S.C.J.M.   Grand Coteau November 4, 1834

Finally, dear and beloved Mother Eugenie, from the various reports now made concerning your return, but particularly from that stated in the circular of our mother general, I see that I may in all safety address this letter to your own dear self, persuaded that it will find you in Paris. Before this reaches you, you will have a note I enclosed [in] your packet addressed to Mother de Marbeuf. Methinks I see you both smiling at the present I asked from this good mother for our future church.

    I forgot to tell you to bring a few crosses. I have not one now for disposal. The purport of this letter is to ask some explanations on the subject of the recent circular which has but reached me and that I desire to observe as faithfully as possible. N. 18: By this it is forbidden that the children quit the salon whilst with their parents. Now does this prohibition extend to G.C. where the parents come, some once, twice, or at most 5 or 6 times in the course of the whole year? And when at the distance, the nearest, say Opelousas, which is 15 mile, others 40 even 100 and remain all day bringing provisions as you remember, to dine in our woods. Our children never go but with father, mother, or aunt. Explain this with *notre mère* and I shall make no change on this article until you either come or write the decision.

    N. 15. Not to admit to Baptism except those whose parents promise to allow their children to practice Catholicity. On this score I never permit a child to be christened unless at the request of their parents or guardians, but they in general understand to make them Christians. So far, all those who have had the happiness of receiving this sacrament here profess our faith only but to make the agreement previously with the parents that the child

---

314 English autograph. GASSH.

be a ~~Chatolic~~ Catholic would have a bad effect on the American character. Explain this fully for me.

There are several now whose parents demand to be baptized but nothing shall be done until you arrive with my decision.

The next point is advice to superior. The conferences must be given exactly according to the Constitutions, that is, every 15 days. Now this I have not done on account of the difficulty of expressing myself in French. I give them previous to all our great feasts, when there is any particular observations, etc. to be made, but to make them every 15 days is more than I can promise. It is for this that I have been so long calling for a suitable assistant. The instructions for the community are regularly made every Sunday by *Mère* Dutour, who is strong and every way calculated for explaining the Gospel, rules, ordinances, etc. Having no priest to preach or instruct us makes me more exact that this defect be obviated, and she can do it in a masterly manner. *Voila* the points I wish you to discuss ~~with~~ (for me), with *notre mère* for I wish for uniformity and regularity considering them as the soul of our existence in this country. A.M.D.G.

Now for a little local intelligence. The weather has been for the last 4 weeks favorable for our brick work, which advances but not as quick as we desire. I fear that Mother Prosper will become quite infirm. Did you observe something queer in her eyes? I am not quite sure of her vocation. Of course, you have not thought of asking the cross for her. Be particular in selecting our future vocations, not to choose those who have been in any other religious order before joining ours. I remark that they are always more difficult & prone to have ideas etc. after all, *notre mère* wrote me on the chapter of Toysonnier. I do not well know how to act. She is still as I represented her to you. Sr. Marguerite is in her dotage, quite useless but always united with God. Mother Lavy has improved since I told her our intention to send her back to France. She has never made a scene but she expects to be sent to St Louis as soon as our religious arrive. This we must effect. In a recent letter *notre mère* said that if I pleased, I may change *Mère* Dutour for Mother Coppens but this person could never live in our solitude. She is too accustomed to bustle, arrangement, etc. She would die of the spleen here. At this moment, *Mère* Dutour is most useful. She takes 3 classes a day, has the work, Instruction & surveillance for you may suppose with our infirm that we are overpowered with labor, but when done for our Divine Spouse, He helps on the very name of Jesus when pronounced with (…) animates & accomplishes all.

I heard recently from St Louis. All are now well. The pensioners re-entered. This is the day also for the opening of the classes at St Michel, where it appears all goes *à merveille selon Mère* Bazire. *Dieu soit loué*. She writes me that they found our poor Philippine much changed for the worse. Three accesses of fever weakened her considerably. Since she returned, the fever has not appeared. I ordered them to get the (…) ready in case she should be again attacked by fever.[315] The chaplain they report as a man of God.

A great heat in this place. Apropos, it is this day 10 year since Father Rosti came to us, and what a blessing. His example suffices instead of preaching. He is generally esteemed for his retired habits, etc. On his return from the East I said, "Father R., you did not inquire if I heard from *Mère* Eugenie." "*Mère* E. I never for one instant thought about her." Upon my inquiring if he had received the answer I wrote to his letter, "and who told you to write me. I am sure I did not want you." His health has improved & we have all (as to spirituals) as usual. I salute *notre mère*, *Mère* de Gramont, Marbeuf, Desmarquest. *Enfin,* all your precious company with affectionate veneration, a large portion of which keep for your dear self. Hasten back to yours inviolably in C.J.

Xavier R. du S.C.

---

315 Philippine Jourdain, RSCJ, born in St. Louis, September 7, 1812. She entered the Society at Grand Coteau in 1823 and made first vows at St. Michael in 1827. She died there on March 4, 1835, a few months after this letter. See also the reference to her in Xavier's second letter of this month to Eugenie.

[*On the envelope*:
Five illegible postage stamps, destination stamp]:
Pays d'outremer, par Le Havre

Via New York
Mother Eugenie Aude
Rue des Varennes No. 41
A Paris Marseille

Notre Maison de St Joseph a Marseille (... ... Le Havre)
Did I tell you all that your daughters here desire me to say for them. You are aware of their feelings, sentiments, etc. but I must not omit: hasten back—all unanimously join in demanding. You will find enclosed a snap I cut out of the "Shepherd gazette." See what the Presbyterians say of this house. They are using all their influence to put us down but "God is with us; of whom shall we fear." Courage & confidence, motto *de notre fondateur* Pere Varin.

The burning of the Ursuline house at Boston I already mentioned. You will see all the horrors of this vandalic act in the *Ami de la Religion*. I am almost disgusted with our establishing in New York where all this fanatic party spirit is at its height. God will arrange. 4 sisters of Charity have died in N. Orleans since July. 6 are coming from Baltimore to replace their departed sisters. Consumption was the disease. No epidemic in the city, healthy all the summer & fall. Do you return by our port or by the East. X

———

Xavier Murphy to Eugenie Audé[316]

S.S.C.J.M.   Grand Coteau Nov 25th 1834

---

316 English autograph. GASSH.

Yours, *chère et bien aimée Mère* Eugenie, of the 12 Sept. duly came to hand. We were delighted with your description of the 15 August & felt the attention of your addressing it <u>here</u> for our perusal. I lost no time in wafting it across our bayous to our dear friends at St Michel, and already have received thanks for preserving them, all the gratification of getting such precious marks of your maternal tenderness. *Mère* Bazire announces the arrival of all our so much desired papers, adding that all hands are employed to send here the copies, etc. she says they have. 105 children and that all goes on well. God be praised. This I attribute to the fervent petitions you present to our Divine Spouse, in whose presence you no doubt pass many delicious moments now that you are more mistress of your time. How often I envy you. At times methinks I see you absorbed at the foot of the sanctuary. There on a little tabouret *tête à tête* with *notre digne mère*, after in the amiable imposing circle that the recreation of the professed at Paris must afford. But why indulge in recollections that suggest so much self-gratification and that I am <u>far far</u> distant from seeing realized, even in miniature, in this quarter of our globe.

On the reception of the letter concerning the abuses etc. I wrote you requesting your arranging with *Notre Mère* on the articles in which I felt most peculiarly <u>concerned</u>. <u>Again</u> I return to No. <u>18</u> and desire to know what course to adopt. When the children remain with us during vacation and that their parents come in the course of the year, or at the end sometimes of two year to pass a day or two, in order to repose themselves (for they come at distances that require journeys of 6 days to reach us). In this case can we permit the children to remain in the prairie with their parents, who never take them as far as Opelousas when they find accommodation in the neighborhood.

Since Philippine's [Jourdain] departure[317] I am obliged to go to writing. Mother Prosper since her illness appears unable to make

---

317 For St. Michael, where she would die a few months later.

her class. I fear that she will remain infirm.[318] She says that her mother never recovered [from] a similar attack. I mention this circumstance to show the force of imagination. Sr. Marguerite is now forced to sit in an armchair and terminate her useful laborious life by knitting. The head of Mother Lavy is nearly the same, so you may infer that it is God alone who sustains the house. I think I must apply to *Mère* Bazire for one religious. She already told me that it was your desire but I answered that as her number of children exceeded ours and as I limited our number to 80, I hated to deprive St Michel of anyone. Yet I see I shall be forced to call on her for a mistress of 4th French class. I am also in great want for a mistress for a 4th English one. If you could procure me a religious from St Louis and have her come down in the spring, you would render us here a great service. As you saw all the aspirants on your way to Europe, you can the better decide the description of person that would suit here.

Not one line from *Mère* Duchesne, and judge of my surprise on Mr. Louaillier handing me a letter (addressed to him on the subject of his orphans that he confided to her). In this letter, *Mère* D announces that she was on the eve of quitting St Louis for another of our houses & that she deemed it her duty to inform Mr. L. thereon. This was all I heard on the chapter.[319]

Notre mère will be amused when you tell her the term that the Americans now adopt when they desire to know when such a child will quit. "Madam, at what epoch do you suppose Miss ___ will be able to graduate. Is she to be in your class this year." The fashionable idea now is that if a child pass a year in my class, she is finished. Importunably [*sic*] I have but 5 who say they are to graduate at the close of our year. They have been in the house

---

318 She too would die at St. Michael at the end of the following year, December 31, 1835.
319 At the direction of Madeleine Sophie Barat, Catherine Thiéfry and Philippine Duchesne replaced each other as superior in the two St. Louis houses. Philippine arrived from the City House to St. Ferdinand in Florissant on October 11, 1834.

four & five years and followed up all our plan. The grown girls who enter from other Institutions can only follow our 4th or 3rd class. Consequently, the mistresses are overcharged and if I take a few to place in mine, they would consider themselves also qualified to graduate at the close of the term. And with all this infatuation my class is only a 2nd & they study but common literature, not a book of Botany, Philosophy, or such nonsense. All of which the parents now desire to be discontinued, seeing the little essential good their children derived from such pretended knowledge.

The bricks are now only burning for the new building. The rainy summer we have had retards the work. This is disagreeable, having in advance the sum of $3549 and only one thousand of that advanced the day that I signed the contract. Tell *notre mère* that I hope to have funds to finish the academy & after put up an handsome church for A.M.D.G.

The cotton crops are short, but the sugar ones abundant. The autumn is beautifully fine. How our mothers would be surprised to see our garden & building all hanging with roses & a bouquet before the B. Virgin. I asked you in one of my letters to bring me one piece of *voile*. I now see that we shall want 2 pieces *pour nos Dames* and one piece *pour nos soeurs*. Don't forget the crosses and above all get a veil *de notre mère pour* X. We also require a Revelle. All these I will pay you for. I have the consolation that all our debts are liquidated so that we can go on smoothly. Next month I will send the receipt of this year. You ask me to recount something amusing but our solitude here affords little variety except to frighten all the Presbyterian & Methodist host. All of whom are lined against the Institution but cannot prevent the parents from placing their children with us.

My heart bleeds when I see our poverty as to Catholic priests. Not one in this Diocese capable of preaching English, all the parishes abandoned after an ample field for these preachers to proselyte [*sic*] & gain the ignorant inhabitants. There has been a report that the Archbishop is dead since the consecration of his

Coadjutor, which took place last September.[320] Should this report be true, our Society have a warm friend in the Archbishop actual (Eccleston) of Baltimore[321] & who frequently expressed a wish to have one of our houses in the Metropolitan city. His friend Bishop Purcell of Cincinnati has also expressed himself to this effect. He has in the space of six months erected a fine church solely for the Germans, who are numerous in that place. A seminary has also been completed, called St. F. Xavier. It appears by all this that the Prelate is an active & zealous one. Religion flourishes in every part of the N. States, Lou excepted. Even the Sisters of Charity seem to suffer more here than elsewhere. Four have died since July. Of Father Jeanjean there is no mention, no person is aware of his retreat. Father Blanc acts as usual. *Père* Ladaviere has returned from Kentucky, what for I am ignorant. The President of St Louis writes me that their superior general absolutely forbid their locating in Lou. Poor Louisiana—

The consecration of the Cathedral of St Louis was a splendid ceremony. The day or two after, the Bishop of Indiana was consecrated also,[322] and the dedication of the church continued eight days. Mons. Rosati must have been in all his glory. All this is indeed consoling. The S. Heart will also extend its thanks. Until we have a house in the East, we shall ever be poor on the score of subjects. Lou will at all times furnish us with pensioners and primary resources but will never supply the Society with a sufficiency of proper subjects. Yet, as we stand, we are too few to separate and you say that the prospect of bringing religious is not encouraging, so few are to spare. However, we must determine on

---

320 The report was true. Leo Raymond De Neckere, Bishop (not archbishop) of New Orleans, died September 4, 1833. His named successor was Auguste Jeanjean, who refused the nomination and never took office. Antoine Blanc was then named but was not consecrated bishop until June 19, 1835. It is odd that more than a year after the death of Bishop De Neckere, Xavier seems unaware of the facts. New Orleans did not become an archdiocese until 1850, and Bishop Blanc was its first archbishop.
321 Samuel Eccleston had become Archbishop of Baltimore on October 19, 1834.
322 Bishop Simon Bruté de Rémur (1779-1839), first bishop of Vincennes, Indiana.

some way to procure subjects, and the prejudice which the Eastern states have against this will ever be a preventative to young persons joining us as we are situated. I dwell on this subject in order that you may make all the reflections and arrangements whilst with *notre mère*. Since the horrible catastrophe of the burning of that splendid Ursuline house at Boston, I feel a something against N. York. There is a great similarity of manner, prejudices etc. between these two cities that merits our consideration & ought to be fully examined by our Divan [?] which no doubt the Heart of Jesus will inspire and direct for A.M.D.G.

Mother Lavy has just been informed of the death of her father. Philippine, they write me, still has daily fever, which I hoped to remove by change of air. Of course, her end fast approaches, and what a soul to fly to its God.[323] All here were charmed with the circular *de notre mère* and requested that I would assure her of their firm determination to observe faithfully all the recommendations that her <u>maternal tender solicitude</u> for our perfection suggested. Offer for me and mine to this dear good mother all that respectful and venerated affection can dictate. This language can better be guessed than well expressed. <u>You</u> at least possess a heart full, capable of defining what I could wish to be said. Do it then *selon votre façon*. My mothers Degramont, Charbonnel, Desmarquest, de Marbeuf, etc.; my fathers Varin, Barat, Perreau, <u>all all</u> are now full arrayed in order before me. You can define for what purpose. I salute them accordingly. In one of my former, I mentioned the return of Father Rosti, whose health permits his offering the Holy Sacrifice every day where you have your moments and the present assurances of the invincible attachment of yours in C.J.

Xavier R. du S.C.

---

323 Philippine Jourdain, RSCJ, died March 4, 1835. See further notes on her in the letter to Eugenie three weeks before this one, November 4.

Xavier Murphy to Father Antoine Blanc[324]

S.S.C.J.M.   Grand Coteau Dec. 19, 1834

Enfin dear and good Father *me voilà* I find myself in my little room at Peaceful G.C. after a most agreeable trip – for as spouses of the Heart of Jesus we found friends ready made in every quarter. I brought with me Mother Penel[325] and a young sister taken from amongst our orphans. They appear satisfied and will I trust prove useful religious. I was much gratified during my stay at St Michel. It appears Mother Bazire suits *à merveille* the community, pensioners, public etc. etc. All perfectly satisfied, but my <u>highest contentment</u> was derived from the acquaintance and information of all the good operated there by their Godlike director. Providence has indeed been bountiful in thus giving them a man after, I do believe, His own heart.

Whilst there I had the pleasure and mortification of receiving yours of the 8th for I did so desire to see you. On my return found yours of the 3rd and tho' last not least have just got yours of the 17th. Now with the case in prime condition. The books were most acceptable, as for the *relique* let *père* Ladavière arrange as he pleases. I shall not claim it but certainly will accept it if presented. As we are going to commence a new year I must try to become more perfect disengaged and so forth. I feel with the apostle the desire but then again *la nature* counteracts all my projects. I wish I was emancipated from my earthly prison yet alas!

Respecting the person below I have heard nothing recently. I always avoid inquiring after him fearing the unpleasant consequences on pronouncing his name. Should he trace anything to

---

324 English autograph. New Orleans Archdiocesan archives.
325 Louise Marie Penel, RSCJ, was born in Rouen in 1810, entered at St. Michael in 1832 and made her vows in 1834. Ill with consumption, she was sent north to Florissant to be with Mother Duchesne. She died there in 1837. See PDCGO letter 510.

your visit here and that what we desire be effected I shall have no regret on the subject.

Estelle Nugent left us this week with Dr. [?]. There was no question on her departure of settling out, but I had arranged one for Mr. Beuvaise up to the close of the 2nd year and informed him of the credit you allowed me for the sum in question. On my passing through Opelousas I saw with pleasure Father Rossi again on terms with my friend there. He passed an evening with us. He appears always busy and contemplates some distant mission in our forests this winter.

I was glad to hear from you something of the Church in Alexandria. The Presbyterians have become so numerous and so fashionable in that quarter that my heart bleeds with fear and disappointment, yet if God be with us who can prevail against us.[326] It appears these preachers have used all their influence to dissuade the parents from sending their children to us on the pretext of our Religion. The American gentlemen observe "that there is no risque respecting the religious of Mother X. for she teaches but pure Philosophy." Poor infatuated people, little do they know from what source we derive our science and that the Heart of Jesus is a rich and inexhaustible mine to draw from, and that the promise made must be fulfilled – "When I shall be raised on high then I will draw all after me."[327] All continues here pretty much as you left us, our children good, the community aspiring to be so, the brick only burning. Mr. Rosti's health improves.

I feel most anxious to hear from you the particulars and the result respecting our dear persecuted sisters. This I am sure you will not omit communicating. Pray offer Sr. Regina my affectionate regards and the sincere sympathy I feel in common with all the sisterhood. To the good Ursulines I also beg a particular word of attachment etc. etc. Apropos I see by a recent paper that Dr.

---

326 Rom 8:31. Father Blanc was at this time apostolic administrator of the New Orleans diocese but not yet consecrated.
327 John 12:32.

England has brought over to his diocese Ursulines from my native city.[328] The superior is or was once the most beloved object of my heart and the same person who wrote the chapter on Instruction which you so much admired in your little cottage. The first impulse I felt on seeing her name was to write her but God whispered "That what I had left ought to be forgotten" and as I had forgot my people and the house of my father[329] all ought to remain in oblivion – well then how I do that with you. Perhaps you may not be displeased that my perfection would also induce me to be more laconic. If so I must obey.

The season of good wishes fast approaches, mine in your behalf you can easily define.

Your position and that of our poor Diocese are constantly before me. May the ensuing year provide us a balm salutary to all our wants and desires – If the Prophet in former days obtained what he demanded because he was a man of desires, why now a days can we not also do violence to heaven & have our efforts crowned with success.

Have you heard particularly from our isolated friend. I saw in one of the papers that he was on the Indian mission.

Allow me, Very dear father to present you all my flock old and young – remember that you are our shepherd and that we graze in a wild and unfrequented prairie far far away from all spiritual assistance save that of the prayers of those interested – when on the Holy Mount place us before you –

Your attached daughter *in C.J.*
Xavier

---

328 John England 1786-1842) was born in Cork, Ireland, where he was consecrated first bishop of Charleston, S.C., in 1820, and served tirelessly in that office until his death.
329 Ps 45:10.

1835

Xavier Murphy to Madeleine Sophie Barat[330]

S.S.C.J.M. Grand Coteau, January 27, 1835

How happy I am, dear and beloved mother general, to know that you approve of all my activities at present. I am sure that it is the Heart of Jesus that has directed me. You have filled us with so much consolation this past year by sending us the precious results of our last council. All is put into practice in your house of G.C. and your daughters seem to love you and venerate you more than ever. For me, when I read these precious papers my heart so expanded that I could say with the Prophet: "I have meditated on your law and I have found it of nearly infinite expanse."[331] How good and kind you are to have your intelligent secretary write to me in my birth language and thus to provide for me an easy way to express to you, my venerable mother, and to the whole body of our Society, all the movements of our "camp" in the New World. Do as much as you can to carry on the connections by letters among us. It is a very powerful link to attach the religious here to our dear Society, for a letter from France for them is everything. I have just made a little trip to St Michel because of our poverty of religious here. I found that everything was going well there. 120 children and Mother Bazire pleases everyone.

Is it true, dear mother, that you will be sending me no one? Mother Eugenie told me not. But I know your heart too well to believe it. We hope that this good mother is now making her preparations to return, that she has rejoined you at Marseilles. What a

---

330 French autograph. GASSH.
331 A loose quotation of Ps 118:97.

privileged soul. Imagine how her arrival is awaited here by your daughters![332]

You will find attached here a little note. I think that it will be enough, even though Mother Charbonnel wants more. Oh well, tell her that she will be <u>satisfied</u> for the <u>future</u>, but at this moment we are occupied with organizing here according to the *coutumier*, etc. etc. Good Mother Dutour is putting to profit her talent for *explication*, instruction. That is her strength. Judge what a consolation for me.

I hope, dear reverend mother, that this note will greet you upon your return from the Midi in perfect health, filled with consolation and wanting more and more to spread the knowledge of J. Christ. It seems to me that it must be rather easy for you to put yourself into prayer, for like St Paul, you can say: "I have worked well..."[333] Permit me to present to you all your daughters here who have shown much good will for acceptance of everything in the Decrees.

A special remembrance to Mother de Limminghe by recommending me especially to her prayers. Here I am at your feet, dear and reverend mother general, asking your blessings and assuring you of my filial attachment and my entire devotion in C.J. Your

Xavier
R. du S.C.

[*Separate note*:]
Here is the total of the receipts of this year: 64,688 francs.
This note offers you the receipts of this house for the year 1834, being so considerable that all our debts are paid and there is due to us 22,300 francs sure tuition, and we have on deposit for the building 17,740-50 francs to have the means as time goes by.

---

332 Eugenie Audé did not return to America, but remained in Europe. She died in Rome in 1842.
333 2 Tim 4:7.

[*On the envelope:*]
Mother
Mother Barat S. General
of the Religious of the S. Heart
In Paris

Alice Regina Cloney[334] to Bishop Rosati[335]

Grand Coteau February 24th, 1835

Right Reverend and our dear Father,

I have often thought how happy and satisfied I would feel if I had an opportunity of addressing your Lordship, and expressing the grateful effusions of my heart, for the interest you have always evinced in my behalf, but more particularly for your having been instrumental to my entering the dear society of which I have now become a permanent member, by the solemn profession I have just pronounced. The conviction that it is God himself who has called me I may say in so visible a manner, and the peace and contentment this thought gives me is better conceived than expressed, my present happiness, that I must attribute to your charity. Oh! Yes, it was you, that opened to me the sanctuary of the adorable heart of Jesus, peaceful asylum, where in the daily discharge of my duties, I feel the promise of the hundred fold in this life, so hearing my happiness, you may at the same time be persuaded that you have been the *primary* cause. Do also obtain for me from the heart of Jesus, that I may faithfully correspond to such a grace and privilege,

---

334 Agnes Regina Cloney, RSCJ, born in Baltimore in 1804, entered the Sisters of Loretto at age 16 and was at LaFourche when the Society of the Sacred Heart took it over in 1828. She transferred her vows in 1830 and was at Grand Coteau from 1832, holding many important positions, including doing the accounts for Xavier. She died of a mysterious chest abscess on October 11, 1835, age 31.
335 English autograph. Rosati collection.

and by devoting myself generously and constantly prove worthy of so sublime a vocation.

I remember I had the pleasure of seeing you, after you had conferred me this favour, and also an opportunity of returning my thanks, but must now make a candid avowal of my pride and self-love. I was ashamed to appear before you with the white veil. This neglect often cost me no little pain. Providence has since destined me to Grand Coteau, and by placing me under the auspices of dear Mother Xavier, has complied with all my desires. She is so holy and prudent. All her movements are directed by the spirit of God. If I am not mistaken, you once promised to send me to Grand Coteau, but owing to circumstances, it could not then be effected. The great regularity and charity which reigns in this community furnishes me with every means of becoming a perfect religious. Our institution is in a flourishing state. Several of the young ladies embrace the Catholic faith, with the entire permission of their parents. Rev. Father Elet made them several instructions, and I am certain will produce a good effect. It was in his presence and encouraged by his unctious eloquence that I sealed my last and solemn engagements. He will present this letter to your Lordship which I beg you to accept as a token of my eternal and grateful attachment.

We had recently the consolation of hearing by your interesting epistle a description of the ceremony and consecration of the splendid cathedral of St Louis. It must indeed have been an imposing and magnificent sight. The details afforded us a delightful recreation. Every one appeared happy to hear of the great success of your apostolical labours and the propagation of our holy religion particularly at St Louis. *Ma Mère* had it immediately transcribed and sent as you requested to the Ursuline ladies.

I trust you have not entirely given up the idea of visiting Louisiana. I still indulge the fond hope that some favourable gale will waft you one day to our sweet solitude. Every member expresses the greatest desire of seeing you, especially our worthy Mother Xavier, who begs to be remembered in your holy prayers, and please also to bestow upon every one of us your paternal benediction. Receive in this, dear Father, the warmest sentiments of gratitude and all that a sincere heart dictates for you at this favoured moment, with the assurance of the profound veneration and devotedness of your daughter in J.C.

A Cloney
Religious of the S.C.

Xavier Murphy to Bishop Rosati[336]

S.C.J.M.   Grand Coteau March 14, 1835

I have, my very dear Lord and father, to acknowledge the receipt of your amiable letter and the paper containing the description of the imposing consecration of the glorious and proud achievement of your labors and persevering zeal. In unison with your desire after having the copy taken, I sent the original to the Ursuline community.

The perusal of the ceremony – your Lordship's letter and the relation of the astonishing miracles recently operated in the Christian states filled all your daughters here with consolatory admiration. To hear of prodigies effected that would in better days call forth the tribute of belief against incredulity and excite the gratitude of the faithful at being numbered as members of that Church to which also belongs the exclusive privileges of supernatural effects and causes. "The arm of the Lord is not shortened" and in compassion to our weaknesses has permitted those events to enliven our faith and encourage our hope. May all be perfected in Christ.

Père Elet passed a few days with us and gave a lecture to our boarders who seldom or never have the advantage of instruction

---

336 English autograph. Rosati collection.

from a clergyman. The father was pleased with their attention and desire to hear him and paid them a compliment most delicious to my heart. He will give you all the particulars of your favorite house and the ameliorations now in train, which if perfectly completed will render G.C. quite finished. The weather has been against us. A severe winter felt here to the 7th of March. The cattle expiring by hundreds. No meat to be found. Provisions of all kinds rare and exorbitantly dear. Such is our present situation.

But I must not fail imparting to your Lordship intelligence which as it regards the glory of God, will be a balm to your heart. That we have at last succeeded in having all arrangements for the speedy erection of a Church in Alexandria, the contract passed for $3500. The present subscription only amounts to $2200, but the inhabitants frequently assured me, could they see the work commenced, the money would be found. They propose blessing it on the 3rd of next December, feast of St. Francis Xavier to whom it is to be dedicated. A.M.D.G. another quarter now reclaims our attention. New Iberia (Parish St Mary) I have promised the people there a Church & at this moment they could raise $500 had they anyone to encourage or come forward to decide. All begin to languish and get fatigued at the delay of choosing (or rather giving) a bishop. Why do they not once for all show us the anointed of the people. Procrastination is at times a disadvantage. In ours I fear the consequences.

But why trespass on your precious time by relating the miseries of this our <u>despoiled Sion</u>. You once found us a remedy efficient indeed: God in his adorable designs judged proper to take from among us all his mighty men. The will of God then must be our sanctification. We lost one of our sisters last month. You did know her. She was one of the last colony from France & came to G.C. when our house at the Assumption was suppressed. Her death was that of a saint.[337]

---

337 Adele Toysonnier, RSCJ, died at Grand Coteau on February 6, 1835.

At Sᵗ Michaels they have just lost M. P. Jourdain,[338] one of those privileged souls who I am sure appeared before her Spouse & God in her baptismal garments. Pray for them, dear and good father, and don't forget your poor Xavier. If I have received many graces, I have also much to answer for those deducted by my great infidelities. So do when on the Holy Mount, think of me & mine and of my young charge. Shall I ever have the gratification of presenting them to your Lordship? The railroad is projected. So a few hours will suffice to transport you amongst us.

Your attached daughter in C.J.
Xavier

[*On the outside*:]
The Right Reverend Dr. Rosati
Rev. Father Elet   St Louis

This will have the honor of saluting your Lordship about the great approaching feast. Well then, in spirit I shall see you surrounded by all that can improve or gratify the human heart. May you long constitute the pride and delight of a grateful and attached flock and above all, when the time of your godlike career terminates, enjoy all the triumph of a glorious resurrection.

Amen

Xavier Murphy to Bishop Rosati[339]

S.C.J.M.   Grand Coteau May 26, 1835

I am really concerned, Dearly Beloved father and bishop, to hear of your illness, and also of the recent accident occasioned by

---

338 On March 4.
339 English autograph. Rosati collection.

fire that occurred nearly within your precincts. The state of debility you then labored under must have added much to the shock but thanks to all-directing Providence, the monument of your zeal, the pride and boast of the Western states, has been preserved for the future consolation of the adoring and enraptured Christians.

I wish I could offer your Lordship something worth acceptance. At this moment can only dispose of $400, so trifling a sum for my heart and your imperative [...]. As I fear enclosing the money shall place on the other side of this letter an order for Mr. Vergh... who will hand you the above sum, which I will have reimbursed to his agent in New Orleans. Should this plan not meet with your approbation, why then devise any other you please and I shall be ready for its execution.

I have now quite a history to discuss with you, dear father. Do you remember when you visited G. Coteau to have seen an old countryman of yours called Josey, who was so charmed with you that he declared you his heir (they say he has $5,000 all at interest). From the time you saw him until about 6 months since, he resided in a miserable hovel near the Church, refusing himself the common necessaries of life and disciplining himself so as to call forth general pity. At the request of some acquaintance, he determined giving up his house & going to reside with him at some place in this Parish. He now seldom assists at Church and to come to the essential point of my narration, I fear that the result of all his eccentricities will be the exclusion of your Lordship from all right to this donation. I have frequently spoken to Father Rosti on the subject but could get no satisfactory answer.

This morning prayed him to send me the old fellow the next time he came to church. I want to tell him how pushed you are for money. He has $1500 at interest with a merchant of Opelousas. If he could take up the note, and that he refused to give the sum to your Lordship. I will offer him the interest of this state and shift ways & means to pay the old miser. Just say if you approve of this plan. I have been thinking that could you send here some clever person to chat with this original or propose his ending his days at the seminary, all may be amicably adjusted and the property be secured for the good of Religion. Otherwise, at his death it will become a prey to all the unprincipled persons by whom he is surrounded. As soon as he calls on me I will put you *au fait* at our conversation, & I shall terminate by assuring your Lordship that all here deeply participate in the regret occasioned by your indisposition; that we all with one accord petition the Giver of all good gifts to accelerate your perfect recovery, dissipate all your pernicious embarrassments, and preserve you to see your children's children. May peace reign all over the Western valley. Does Mrs. Smith mean to profit of the offer the Doctor has made for her land? If she does, she may count on *cash*. This may be of service to you.

Your Lordship's devotedly attached daughter in C.J.

Xavier

Xavier Murphy to Eugenie Audé[340]

S.C.J.M.　　St A. de P.　　　　Grand Coteau, June 9, 1835

Yours of March, dear and beloved mother, has just this moment saluted me. It is the first intimation I have received of the serious illness of our dear mother general, whose sojourn in the South has always been accompanied with dire consequences as regarding her precious existence. But our Divine Spouse has heard the supplications you all offered, and you console me by adding that our <u>all in this planet</u> was seated in an armchair dictating orders that shall be executed in all their force. Too happy at receiving them from such a source not to greet them with veneration & difference.

The suppression of the dining in the woods is a balm to my feelings, for I ever considered it a <u>vulgarity</u> as well as <u>abuse</u>. The

---

340 English autograph. GASSH.

Americans for whom the exception is made do not require it. They never profit of the custom and forbid me from allowing their children to go with the French on such occasions. Not having yet a house to entertain them, that is, *auberge*, Mrs. Mudd, who is entirely alone with her daughter, accommodates the American fathers or mothers who never permit a third person to accompany them. I allow the child to pass the night with her parents. *Voici* my plan to effect the abolition of the wood parties. Your letter has only arrived as the visits are confined to every month. The greater part are now suspended until vacation. Then I will address a letter to the Creoles informing them of my determination; such as find the rules too strict can keep their children, as Bishop Rosati honors me with his correspondence, I can easily have his ordinance. I am surprised that he never communicated it to me. I hear rarely from Sr Michel yet believe that all agree or will with the exception of a little enthusiasm on the part of *mere* Bazire for the *cure* [pastor].

Apropos do you remember a letter addressed you last July by Aloysia [Hardey]. This letter you shewed some person who communicated its contents to Mr. Bonn who was much mortified at your comments etc. etc. Should you come by St Louis Father Elet will put you in possession of the whole so you will know how to act on your arrival at Sr Michel, perhaps before we meet. I wanted badly to write you as you never addressed me since last November. Together with the hope of your return in spring, prudence prevented my risquing a letter fearing it may have the same fate as that of Aloysia. You are basking in the presence of *notre mère genl.* whilst I poor Xavier am fighting alone the battles of the God of Israel. This country is in the greatest commotion. Bishops, laity all assailed by sectarian parties. They have used every engine that malice and jealousy could suggest to insure G.C. the rapid improvement of which excites their envy. I will not annoy you or *nos mères* by recounting all the scandalous absurd stories in vogue. Shall only for your amusement recount a few of the most amusing. They accuse me of being the queen of Love, that I have more power to enact laws and have them observed than Genl Jackson, that I am perverting the present generation by European fashions, that I have infatuated the American gentlemen so as to be able to propagate my Religion. *Enfin* that this convent ought to be <u>burned down</u> as that of Boston for the public safety. They have even gone so far as to assert that I had fled from the Institution. Several respectable parents have come to assure themselves of my being here and to entreat that such foolish reports would have no effect on my mind. I reassured them they had nothing to dread, that I looked on myself as representing our Society on Love and that with my diadem, holding up my cross, they may be sure of my holding firm to my post and of my not relinquishing my royalty.

We have 90 pensioners. The new kitchen with its appendages finished. The foundation of the Academy laid, the brickmaking all going on prosperously, money coming in abundantly, so as to be always more than prepared for the payments, and the conviction I feel that the Heart of Jesus will be more and more glorified in the new building, since the Devil is using all efforts to contradict the undertaking, suffices to give me courage, indeed supernatural, for I have scarce a puff of life in my body. But my mind is full of peace and confidence, and I feel how delicious to suffer for the name of Jesus.

The church of St F. Xavier in Rapides is nearly finished, the first in that section, another to be created in Nll. Iberia, all to satisfy the children raised with us.

Your note for Sr. Adele [Toysonnier] came too late before this. You are acquainted with her death, which was a most edifying one. All the community give me consolation. You forbid me in a former letter to mention our poverty as to subjects. Yet consider how pushed we are with such a number of children. I have used every means to induce a music master to locate here – not yet succeeded. I shall also be forced to make some sacrifice to get an *auberge* established. The country is fast improving. New settlers – rails – roads projected. The College of Opelousas at last dedicated on the plan of that of St James on the coast. They have a considerable sum to commence.

Father Jeanjean has arrived and is now replacing Father Moni who was ordered to travel for his health. I have got his letter or letters by or from Father J. No bishop nominated nor to be until winter. The Diocese poorly off for clergymen. Those in our vicinity I never see or desire. Could not the Holy venerated archbishop of Paris do something for this despoiled portion of the Church. The Presbyterians are taking firm root here and the ignorance of Catholic population with their depravity of manners gives scope to their zeal and biblical knowledge. The Americans are some of them of opinions that the Religion of G. Coteau, as they term it, and that of the Creoles cannot be the same. This you can easily access, for should this letter find you at head-quarters see with *mère genl.* what is to be done with Mother Short whose time for Profession approaches and I shall never consent to her mak...[torn page].[341]

Stanislaus [Aguillard] is much changed, both as to health and piety. She is a devoted subject and may when her term expires be admitted to Profession. Don't omit the papers necessary for the form of demand, also a good supply of veils. I will pay you all the advances you may have occasion to make for us. I will try and have a little purse to meet yr. expenses. Also the rest of the precious Instructions on the summary. What a treasure we have discovered. Sr. Marguerite now occupies her chair and prays for the Society.

The young novice, [Mary] Knight, that I brought from St Michael last winter, is an excellent subject, but Mother Penel[342] the reverse. I fear she cannot remain in the Society. I await your return to decide. Her will appears good but she has no head or consistency. Mother Lavy goes on pretty well. The change of superiors in St Louis cooled her desire to leave here. But on your return

---

341 Margaret Mary Short, RSCJ (1807-1870) entered the Society in 1826 and was professed in St. Louis in 1842.
342 Louise Marie Penel, RSCJ, was ill with consumption. She went north to Florissant soon after and died there in 1837.

I trust she will have to go. It was fortunate she did not quit since such a number of boarders have entered here.

[*On the envelope*:]
Happy convalescence. *Mère* de Gramont ought never permit her visiting the south. ~~When~~ at Grenoble what a malady *notre mère* endured. When at the foot of the dormitory think of me and mine. Offer us to the adorable Heart of our spouse as His victims immolated for A.M.D.G. I wish these four letters were imprinted in my heart, which now says hasten to the field of battle.

Chère et bien aimée Mère Eugenie, let me fold you to a heart devotedly attached to you in C.J.

Xavier R du S.C.

[Address:]
To Mother
Mother Eugenie Audé

Should this salute you in Paris greet all my friends there. Yours here offer you their attachment and desire to see you with filial impatience. Offer our respectful homage to our *mère genl.* with our congratulations both to her & Society for her.

Xavier Murphy to Bishop Rosati[343]

S.C.J.M.

Grand Coteau Nov 14, 1835

I am, very dear father and Beloved bishop, led to hope that these lines will salute you in New Orleans and consequently infer that your Lordship cannot, will not resist the impulse you will

---

343 English autograph. Rosati collection.

doubtlessly feel to visit your favorite prairie and its expectant flock. No, your heart is too good to refuse this gratification.

I have just received yours, which is dated the 27th Sept. yet am inclined to suspect you wrote in Oct. as you mention the anniversary of the dedication of what we may well term our pride and glory. The visit of Mrs. Smith etc., etc. The decision you so kindly give was what I had anticipated and the means to be taken such as have hitherto invariably been followed up in the Institution, so that I have nothing more to add or diminish on this chapter and suppose I may continue giving new members to the <u>Religion</u> of <u>Grand Coteau</u>.

The consoling affairs of Natchez I had already heard. Our intercourse with that section has of late become consequential. Several young persons have been sent over for their education. The report is that a lady of some standing (Protestant) on her return from here declared herself Catholic. The alarm bell was rung with sectarian force in the little town of Washington and lo, the result of the sonorous peal was –sad to relate—the natural death of the female academy in that town.

A.M.D.G.

Our boarders were delighted to hear that the orphans will be so comfortably adjusted this winter. You are indeed, father, a most privileged son of Providence. Only take a glance of what He has done for Religion and society at large through your judicious agency, but you must now come and exert your magical arts in behalf of Grand Coteau. I allude to our embryo church, for the plan and particulars of which I refer you to our dear friend Father Jeanjean. Discuss the matter *ensemble*. Your results cannot be but advantageous. The precise end of adjusting the affair would be your both coming up as a Christmas gift. You cannot, you will not refuse. In the event of your not coming to the consecration, do not omit when writing to Father J. to speak on this subject. I prefer his giving your Lordship an idea on our plans, etc. He is so concise and clearheaded.

Tout va bien ici as far as regards the pensioners, parents, guardians; the building does not advance nor can I say when it will be completed. The funds are waiting in advance. The places demanded from all quarters. 100 boarders are more than we can accommodate. This number we now have. The subjects (that is, if left to ourselves) could not suffice but an all-amiable, all-presiding Providence sweetly pervades throughout the whole and supernaturally effects its causes. "To Him alone be honor and glory."

I recommend to your memento our dear Sr. Cloney[344] who like with autumnal fruit was gathered into the store house of our Divine Spouse.

With sentiments of confidence,
Veneration and attachment your daughter
In C.J. Xavier R. du S.C.

Xavier Murphy to Madeleine Sophie Barat[345]

To St A. de P.

S.C.J.M.   Grand Coteau, November 30, 1835

Yes, dear and beloved venerated mother general, the Heart of Jesus is good, for at the moment when I have the most need of consolation, the little lines that you addressed to me have been a balm for me and all your daughters here, for although spared the anguish of your painful illness, which we learned only during your convalescence, nevertheless, the fear of being so close to losing you has left a *je ne sais quoi* that still endures.

By the circular written in October you have learned that we lost the best teacher, the religious who promised the most with regard to all the religious virtues [Agnes Regina Cloney]. The Master

---

344 Agnes Regina Cloney died October 11, 1835, at Grand Coteau, age 31.
345 French autograph. GASSH.

has harvested her like autumn fruit. In olden times, the people of God were too numerous to accomplish his purpose,[346] and we have never had a boarding school so numerous: 100 children and the whole community consists of 16 persons. Because of difficult weather, our building is not yet finished, which greatly constrains us. It obliges us to refuse children and put in the bank the money destined for payments because of the delay of the building. Our church is again delayed, which really hinders us. Different from the rest of the world, it is not money that we lack, for we have an abundance from last month, of 10,000 francs.

For you, dear mother, I sent this year 2,100 francs to the house in St Charles, and since Bishop Rosati was so constrained after this glorious enterprise he did for our religion, I gave him 2,000 francs. So it is a debt for the house, of which I was not sure. I made an agreement with God, that if I gave that for his church, he would give to the man who owes us the means to pay us, which happened even with interest. You charged me to pray that nothing would happen that would stop the reinforcement that you promised us. Our situation demands it, to render justice to everyone here, (who) are very devoted. Regularity reigns in the house; at least that is the opinion of those who give the annual retreat. To God alone be the glory. He said once upon a time: "Think of me and I will think of you." For me, I am agent for life[347] for after my class, I have to do the accounts and write letters to the parents and guardians of our children who are surely coming, and all the letters of exchange are done on businesses from New Orleans and all that in English. That gives me enough to do. If it were not for the promise to my star, to do everything against nature, never would I be engaged in this kind of work, for since I took the books ten years ago, I did not know how to do the accounts, but I asked God and he showed me

---

346 Probably a biblical allusion; see Josh 17:14; Ezra 10:13.
347 *Un commis du berceau*, committed from the cradle.

consequently.[348] It is he who acts, and you only, venerated mother, could worthily thank him.

A propos, how happy you must be in your new house. Reading the details of your installation, I said to myself, perhaps my mother will call me to her presence to die there. For a long time, I have neither asked nor refused anything. A propos of Mother Rose Prud'hon, I remember having asked you in a letter in 1833 not to accord her any favor for her time. For the rest, you will see in a note attached here in English, which I ask Mother Eugenie or your secretary to translate for you, but after the conduct of that sister in this house, I think it is better to let her renew her vows like the others.[349]

According to letters coming from Missouri, it appears that good Mother Duchesne is coming to the end of her labors. She can say: "I have struggled well, I have finished my course."[350] I do not understand the situation of the house in St Louis. Here is the expression of Mother Thiéfry: "Our humiliations are more than we can support." She adds, "Our boarders are diminishing every day," nevertheless, this good Mother has refused me an American religious for a fourth English class.

Is it true that our Mother Eugenie is not coming for several years? In this case, I think the Heart of Jesus will direct you to send someone of <u>mature age</u> to St Michael, where they say that everything is going well, but the people there are really <u>young</u> to completely run such a considerable house.

The mail tells me of the visit of two bishops in the first days of December, Rosati and Purcell from Cincinnati, who came down to New Orleans for the consecration of our new bishop.[351] They absolutely want to visit Grand Coteau, they say. I think that for

---

348 During the years 1825 to 1836, precisely the years when Xavier was superior at Grand Coteau, the treasury journal is written in English, whereas before and after, it is in French.
349 Whatever the difficulty, she died one month later at St. Michael.
350 2 Tim 4:7.
351 Bishop Antoine Blanc was installed June 19, 1835.

Bishop Purcell, it is to speak about having one of our houses in his city. In my letters I have always delayed until the return of Mother Eugenie to our vicinity. I think the Holy Spirit will direct me to give him a response in that moment. I do not have one.

Father Jeanjean, true friend of our Society, has come to spend two months here. He gave us our annual retreat. He spoke so much about Rome, about you and the concurrence of happy events that you have experienced there, especially the extraordinary favors of the Holy Father in your regard, like true children of such a mother. We seemed to see you filled with celestial consolations.

Perhaps it would be good to say that Mother Dutour likes it here very much. She is very useful and very attached to me, after all the difficulties that person has experienced and suffered with such patience and submission. Everything would be renewed if her position were changed. She loves you tenderly and is full of attachment for the Society. Name her as my secretary. She is very good at keeping the archives, copying your directives, and especially for giving the explanations of our rules, customs, and instructions. *Apropos*, we are missing the rest of the instructions of Father Grasi [?]. ha! He is a father according to my heart and my soul that is often pushed as far as it can go, for lack of encouragement, and in the last years, I feel very close to Father Lallement, with my constant friend, the *Imitation*. For the rest, dear worthy mother, I think it will be in heaven that we will speak, or that I will give you an opening of heart. Let us go there in the Heart of Jesus, our center of light and awareness. We will see everything that this heavenly spouse has done in us for A.M.D.G.

I had prepared a letter to Mother Eugenie to accompany this one, but thinking that I will have something important to add in two weeks, and that this letter would say it, I will end it now. Nevertheless, I want the religious not to leave before the letter I am preparing for Mother Eugenie arrives.

All the little families here offer you their affectionate devotion, asking you again to bless them. As for me, I do not doubt that you hold me constantly in your maternal heart and from there, present me to the Heart of Jesus in order to be in everything the worthy daughter of a worthy mother. Here I am at your feet to say goodbye, beloved mother general. I am all yours *in C.J.M.*

Xavier
R. du S.C.

Here is a little supplement. I forgot to tell you, dear and reverend mother, of the conquest that the Heart of Jesus has made this year in our little house. An American Protestant woman, age 22, came for a year, knowing nothing much except an implacable hatred against our holy religion. She often said to her companions, "How I hate this name Catholic." Nevertheless, her modesty and recollection in church were striking. Finally, she opened her heart to me, telling me of her desire to be baptized. After she got the consent of her family, the ceremony was in public on Pentecost in our little chapel. The chaplain was godfather and your very humble servant was godmother. She took the name of Maria Xavier. On the happy day of our feast, she made her First Communion, with angelic devotion. In the evening, she put her hand on the Holy Gospel, knocked with great strength and spoke with such a loud voice and so emphatically, that the children remarked on it. "Yes," she said with emphasis: "This evening, I slapped the Demon in the face." She is at home now, with the hope of making her mother et al. Catholic. Recently, I received a letter in the post from her mother, thanking me for the progress, etc., of her daughter. She proposes to send her little sister in the spring. So, dear mother, you will have the sweet consolation of harvesting several souls to present to the Heart of Jesus.

Since I began this letter, 3 more children have been announced, but I am afraid to take more. We are too weak. 25 are even too much for 2 people.

I have no news of the father, your nephew [Dusaussoy], though I wrote to him 3 times. It seems that the atmosphere in this country makes him forget the manners of his country. We are 5 here. Old Marguerite is the only French person. Her health is good; she is a model of obedience, regularity, devotion, and attachment to the Society and its superiors. She speaks often of her dear mother and gives the others such desire to see you that they would be happy to leave at once to have this consolation. But this supreme happiness is reserved for another life.   Xavier

1836

Xavier Murphy to Bishop Rosati[352]

S.C.J.M.

St Michael April 9, 1836

It is here Beloved father and worthy Prelate, that I have the consolation of answering to your esteemed of February. Our dear Bishop [Blanc], not being able to cross the bayous to see his prairie flock, ordered me to meet him here, where I arrived in Holy week and had the gratification of kissing his Lordship's ring on the 5th. This you know is a privilege that the Irish heart exults in. I have just taken my farewell with him and expect to leave here in a few hours but could not resist tracing you a few lines which I fear from a tremor in my hand will be illegible.[353]

Since you left G. Coteau all continues as usual. The boarders derived essential good from your lectures. The tall Methodist was so captivated and convinced that with the full approbation of her father she joined <u>our church</u>, was christened on Palm Sunday A. Xavier and made her 1st Communion Easter day. Three other Baptisms have been the result and several have petitioned for permission. So you see, your exertions amongst us have not been useless. For my part, tho' convinced of the truths of our Religion

---

352 English autograph. Rosati collection.
353 On the contrary, the manuscript handwriting is clear.

– yet methinks I never felt their full force and *attrait* until I heard you. I also desire much help in the discharge of my duties, on reflection on your advices, etc. When fatigued or in bad spirits I enter the parlor, <u>look</u> at your portrait, and feel all that calm & courage you do peculiarly inspire. I gave the bishop $50 for Mother Xavier,[354] sent the orphan boys by the boarders of the S.C. Grand Coteau. I also beg you will remember me to her with cordial sentiments. I have given the name of Philomena to some infants at Baptism. At a future period I hope to be able to say more to Y^t Lordship
whose devoted and attached daughter I am *in C.J*
Xavier

Xavier Murphy to Bishop Rosati[355]

S.C.J.M.   Grand Coteau April 30th, 1836

This will be handed, my Beloved father and Bishop, by D^r. Littell who accompanied by his amiable wife, M^{rs}. August Souaillier and daughter, unite in a party to visit their precious deposits in y^r. City. They will wait on your Lordship, whose attention I solicit in their regard. From them you will hear all our local movements, situation of building, etc. etc.

Now for a little history, father, *entre nous*: since my last, which I wrote on leaving St Michael's after making my adieus with my dear Bishop to whom I consigned the letter for your Lordship. As I expected, the S. boat called to take me, when judge of my surprise to see Father Jeanjean accompanied by another gentleman whom I after discovered to be Bishop Portier. The latter remained at St Michaels, whilst Father J. with the captain conducted me to the boat. It was late at night. In the morning, I learned with pain

---

354 Sister of Charity, one-time visitor to Grand Coteau. See her letter of April 20, 1834.
355 English autograph. Rosati collection.

from Father J. that he had <u>escaped</u> from the city, having left a letter to explain himself with the Bishop, that he would leave me at Plaquemine and continue his route to Point Coupee. From his air and feelings, to which I could not administer any soothing palliative, aware of the anguish & confusion his step had occasioned the poor Bishop, yet I feared his going with strangers who would not be acquainted with his situation. I proposed his continuing on to G. Coteau, to which he assented. From Plaquemine I wrote the Bishop informing him of the determination of our fugitive, who on our arrival got sick, lost sleep, quiet, etc. By the first mail came a letter from the Bishop to my address enclosing one for Father J., which I presented and on my knees demanded he would return the next day by the S. Boat. After perusing the Bishop's letter, he consented, left here the following morning, stopped on his way at St Michael, from where he set off accompanied by Mr. Boné. Since he got to the city, I have had no official intelligence, but understood that our poor Bishop had determined to embark at his own Port. How cruelly disappointed and embarrassed he was, you can easily conceive, and the situation of our friend was truly affecting the conflict between his feelings and duty, [and] almost annihilated him. If he have for the present moment consented, still for the future I dread the consequences. God direct and uphold him. Do, father, write and encourage him. You have great power over this most useful man to our poor diocese.[356]

Father Rosti leaves us in a few days, although on parting from the Bishop he assured me that Father Timon in your presence had consented to Father R. remaining at G. Coteau until the close of this year.[357] I brought him a letter from his Lordship adding the report he had made me on his chapter of remaining, but he insists

---

356 This dramatic story probably refers to Father Jeanjean's refusal to accept the position of bishop, to which he was named in 1835. He nevertheless held the position of vicar general until his death in 1841.
357 Father John Rosti, CM, was a member of the Lazarists (Vincentians). Father Timon was his superior.

on departure after finishing the church where the pews this Easter sold as high as $50 apiece. At all events, God cannot leave us. In him I put all my confidence. I will try & cling to him more than ever and ruminate <u>over</u> & <u>over</u> the counsels I had the consolation to receive from your paternal lips. *Apropos*, I profited of the departure of our Bishop to write our *mère générale* on the topics I conversed over with you at the cottage, at the same time, noting the decisions I had the consolation of hearing from y^r. venerated person.

I regret to state y^r. Lordship that the situation of our house at S^t. Michael's wears the most alarming aspect. It is even thought we shall be forced to abandon the place. A law-suit is in operation respecting the ground disputed by the church wardens, and last week the fence was pulled down by about 50 men assembled for the purpose. *Entre nous* father there is too much zeal in that quarter, and the church & convent are too much amalgamated for the general good. Pray that all may terminate for A.M.D.G. Here all goes on smoothly. We have the consolation of seeing and hearing daily some <u>good</u>, the result of your solid Instructions. The Methodist who made her 1st Communion at Easter is embalming. Father J. could not resist his admiration of her angelic appearance. Since her Baptism two more have taken place and several are in contemplation—*Dieu soit loué*.

I have also the consolation of seeing the devotion & confidence in S^t. Philomena taking root. I have given her name to two infants for whom I had to stand godmother, and seven grown persons demand her intercession & picture. We have also additional graces of a special nature by the medals. All their favors induces one to hope that the time to have mercy on <u>this our Israel</u> is nearly come.[358] Oh! May we not by our infidelities ward off the goodness of our mediator.

---

358 Ps 102:14.

I saw by the *Shepherd*[359] that the day of your arrival in the midst of your happy flock was a day of peculiar graces & favors. What is the 25 A day of eternal remembrances both for High Priest and people. Oh! Dear father, what have you not been able to accomplish for the glory of God & the permanent good of our Religion since that epoch. Go on & prosper until seeing the progeny of y^r. childrens-children fixed & established rulers of the people.[360] You take your exit welcomed by Well done, good & faithful.[361]

Such is the prayer of y^r. attached Daughter Xavier

Xavier Murphy to Bishop Rosati[362]

S.C.J.M.

Grand Coteau May 25, 1836

You will, Beloved father & Bishop, easily conceive with what feelings I see this opportunity present. God alone for the new desolate daughters of G. Coteau. Will you say mass for all my charge on the secret feast of S^t. Philomena? You see I anticipate for the 13th August. Father Rosti will give all our local news. So full a house that I am forced to refuse <u>even</u> the children that are brought and to write to others requesting they will not come, etc. etc. I see by the parting letters of our Bishop [Blanc] that he had to relinquish the consolation of seeing you. Has he sent you my letter? Father Jeanjean appears inundated with occupation. No appearance of the plan of the Church. Impossible to get it from N. Orleans. The 200,000 brick are nearly ready to burn. The season is so favorable that I have contracted for the same quantum for the corresponding

---

359 The *Shepherd of the Valley* was a Catholic newspaper published in Saint Louis 1832-1836 and 1850-1854.
360 Ps 128:6.
361 Matt 25:21, 23.
362 English autograph. Rosati collection. Xavier's last preserved letter.

wing. No assistance from France not even the reason why aid is not sent. Delicious news from our houses at Rome. His Holiness full of goodness in their regard. A.M.D.G.

I shall expect a letter by Dr. Littele, *apropos* the life of D^r. Leonard Smith of New Iberia has been preserved by the medium of the miraculous medal. It appears that God requires of me to give up all consolation, for I have now only time to assure your

Lordship of our devoted attachment *in C.J.*
Xavier R. du S.C

Hélène Dutour to Bishop Rosati on the death of Xavier Murphy[363]

S.C.J.M.   Grand Coteau September 11, 1836

Monseigneur

I have already told you of the immense loss that we have just had, but I did not have time to give you the details that your esteem for our reverend mother no doubt makes you desire. On the 22nd of the past month, dear Mother Xavier was attacked by a bilious fever with very alarming symptoms. From the first day, she made the sacrifice of her life, and as if she had foreseen her approaching end, she had done all her accounts and put everything in order for the great prize day that would be on the 30th. She had the happiness to receive the sacraments and all the help of the Church, to suffer all the way to the end with admirable patience and peace, without ever refusing anything or showing any repugnance. When we came to visit, she was only concerned about us. She said not a word about her illness nor did she seem concerned about it, but she prayed nearly all the time. Nothing gave her more pleasure than to hear

---

363 French autograph. Rosati collection.

talk about Our Lord or the Holy Virgin. Her last words were the holy names of Jesus and Mary that she had ceaselessly on her lips.

She died peacefully on the 6th of September after 15 days of vivid suffering. The perfect resignation and all the virtues of which she has left us an example make us hope that she now sees God, but if she still owes anything to the justice of God, we owe it to her goodness to us to help her. To fulfill so dear a duty, we have written to Father Jeanjean to send you as soon as possible $100 to celebrate one hundred Masses for our reverend mother. I am sure, bishop, that I cannot ask it of anyone who will do it with more interest and promptitude than you will, for I know the esteem you had for our reverend mother. Can you believe it, that she did not have the consolation of seeing the plan of the church that she wanted to do, nor read the letter that tells us of the arrival soon of some of our mothers from France.[364]

We are still without a priest since May; but Our Lord remains with us in the Blessed Sacrament. The thought that nothing happens except for the glory of God and by his order sustains us, with the hope of prompt help, for we have received in writing from France that Bishop Blanc intends to leave the first of October, and our sisters will come with him.

It is now, bishop, that we have greater need than ever that you pray for Grand Coteau and that you call down upon us all the blessings of heaven.

Please receive, bishop, the respects of my sisters and of her who is in the Sacred Heart with the most profound veneration for your Excellency

Your very humble
Servant and daughter
H Dutour r of the S.H.

---

[364] Three RSCJ arrived in 1836 bound for Louisiana: Monique Lion and Maria Cutts for Grand Coteau, and Annette Praz for St. Michael.

Present grave marker in convent cemetery, Grand Coteau

[*Written on the outside of the death notice sent to Mother Duchesne (see original in biography)*]

I do not have the time, reverend mother, to treat in greater detail as I would like the virtues and sufferings of our holy and excellent mother, wishing to write to our mother general for tomorrow, but I will not fail to do so as soon as possible. Sr. Marguerite is dying of the same illness, and Sr. H. Mayet is also very ill.[365]
    H. Dutour, r of the S.H.

In another hand:
Circular of Mother Xavier

[*Address*:]
Mother Duchesne
Florissant, Mo

---

365 Helene Josephine Mayet (Mayette) died February 3, 1837. Marguerite Manteau died only in 1845.

Our beloved Mother Xavier fell ill on the 22nd of last month of a bilious fever that resisted all remedies. She gave us the example of heroic patience, of perfect conformity to the will of God, and of perfect obedience even to death, allowing the application or giving of the most repugnant and the most painful remedies, without hesitating or showing any repugnance.

APPENDICES

Appendix 1: Anna Murphy's Irish Background

If the identification of Anna Murphy as the niece of the bishop of Cork is correct,[366] she was a member of the Murphy family that prospered in the leather tanning industry and as traders and merchants. Their influence spread as far away as the Americas and the Far East, which may have influenced Anna's interest in the missions in North America.[367] More is known specifically about Bishop John Murphy, eldest of five brothers. He was ordained in 1796 and was bishop of Cork from 1815 to his death in 1847.[368]

Anna Murphy was educated by the Ursulines at their institution in Cork, founded in 1771, when the Penal Laws were less strictly enforced, and many congregations were eager to establish convents in Ireland. At this time, there was a tradition of Irish women entering convents in France. Father Francis Moylan, future bishop, escorted to Cork four novices and a professed sister from the Ursuline Convent on the Rue St-Jacques, Paris, with a professed sister of twenty-five years from the Convent in Dieppe. By 1805, the community had been blessed with strong, fervent vocations, so much so that "there were not enough copies of the Rules and Constitutions to go around.... So the Superiors decided on having the Rule of St. Augustine and the Constitutions translated."[369]

According to extant school records, Anna was a pupil at this time, enrolled in the terms beginning in October 1803 and March

---

366 PD-MSB September 25, 1823. See B–D Corr. II-II, pp. 136-37: "Her bishop in Ireland" thinks she could be a superior.
367 See http://murphyclans.com/murphy-heritage-locations.
368 See http://corkandross.org/priests/most-rev-john-murphy/.
369 Clarke, Sr. Ursula, OSU. *The Ursulines of Cork*. Blackrock, Cork: Ursuline Convent, 1996, pp. 3-5; 19-20; 48.

1807.[370] Her uncle, Bishop Murphy, was deeply involved in the early history of the convent in Cork.[371]

> Information from
> Society of the Sacred Heart, National Archives, U.S.A.
> Entrance Report.
>
> Murphy, Anne Xavier
> (To US 1822). Vows   Profession   Death: Supérieure
>   11/6/21 5/14/22   9/17/36
>   Paris   Grand Coteau
>
> Birth Date 7-26-1793 ; Entrance Year   ; age
>   5/5/1820 Paris'   27
>
> Murphy Family Tree.   Entrée. Paris
> 1794-1849 [error?] died 1836   16 · 10 · 1819
> Anna Maria youngest of eleven
> Francis, Martin, Kate, Jeremiah James, John (Archdeacon), Henry, Edward, Nicholas, James, William, Anne Maria.

Card in archives of the Irish-Scottish Province, Society of the Sacred Heart. Even though the note says this information comes from the USA National Archives, some of the information is not found there.

---

370 E-mail to M. Blish from Sr. Karen, OSU, Cork, 5/13/07.
371 Clarke, 99; cf. pp. 57–101 passim.

Anna Xavier Murphy, RSCJ (1793-1836)

See Correspondence: St. Madeleine-Sophie Barat / St. Philippine Duchesne (Parish See Tome 1 & Tome II) Before the time of our LA or Catalogue. Information in Circular St. Philippine's Life.

Name	MURPHY	Christian Name	ANNA XAVIER
Nationality	IRISH	Date	Place
Father's Name	James Murphy	Birth	26-7-1793 — Cork
Mother's Maiden Name	Mary Galwey	Baptism	
No. of Brothers older or younger	4 brothers older	Entrance	May 1820 — Postulant in Paris, habit from St M S/phie
No. of Sisters older or younger	1 sister older	1st Vows	6 November 1821 — Head of the Sacred Heart 1822 — 5-5-1820
Name and Address of Parent or Next of Kin		Renewal	Because of her age and maturity
		Profession	14th May 1822 — the various stages had been short and for her — Grand Coteau
	(1772-1847)	Exclaustration	
Near relative of Bishop of Cork, Monsgr Murphy (1772-1847?)		Secularisation	17th September
		Death Aged 43	8-9-1836 — Grand Coteau
Primary Education at		From	Until

Secondary Education at		From	Until
Ursulines, Cork (p.247 Life of Ph. m.s.B 1917)			
See Society of the Sacred Heart in North America - Callan P. 125-129			
Tertiary Education		From	Until	Degree or Diploma

Other Training "She is well informed." "Speaks excellent"	From	Until	Degree or Diploma
English and can teach it. (S.M. Sophie)			

Languages V9. 9. F.	Speak	Write	Read	Understand	Language	Speak	Read	Write	Understand
We are teaching her French. (S. M. Sophie)									

Work Experience before entering: Duties and Responsibilities.

Duties and Responsibilities. Grand Coteau	Local House	Organisation	From	To
Arrived in America 1st April 1822 (page 247)		Left for America November	1821	
According to a letter to Fr. Barat		Arrived at New Orleans		1822
of Philippine Duchesne, abridged edition	1825	Superior at Grand Coteau	1829	
by Louise Callan RSCJ 1963				
page 248.		Died 1st September		1836
Was sent to Opelousas with the Decrees				
in her trunk (and did not reach St. Philippine)				
Page 250. On July 20th 1822				
she made final vows in Opelousas.				
Page 399 Died after a violent fever,				
just 43 years old (Philippine wrote				
in her Journal) at Grand Coteau	October 1836	? Aged 43		

Appendix 2: Ship's Log

Report of Passengers on board the Ship *Hector* of Philadelphia W. W. Sheed Master from Bordeaux bound for New Orleans.

LeBlanc de Villeneuve	New Orleans	65	gentleman
C____ Chapelle	ditto	45	merchant
Madam Chapelle	ditto	40	
. ____ Chapelle	ditto	6	
Charles			servant [enslaved?]
P. H. Tuyes	Bordeaux	23	merchant
Louis Gillet	New Orleans	33	merchant
Norbert Broutin	New Orleans	30	trader
Madam Broutin	New Orleans	26	
Hyacinth			servant [enslaved?]
Mr. Evault	New Orleans	48	dealer
Agathe Fauchon		45	
Alfred Evault		5	
E. Evault		6	
Agathe Evault		2	
Madam Xavier Murphy		30	Ursuline Nun
Madam Lucile Mathevon		30	Ursuline Nun
New Orleans Feb. 11, 1822			
			[signed] W. W. Sheed

Anna Xavier Murphy, RSCJ (1793-1836)

Annotations

Since there is no entry for Nagliss in the log, one assumes that he was owner of the ship or commissioned the ship, since all the merchandise on the ship was his – see beginning of Lucile Mathevon's journal.

There is no separate listing or log of the cargo as there is for other ships arriving in the same month and year.

Annotations to the Ship's Log, gleaned from *New Orleans City Directory* 1823, Sacramentary Records 1823–26, and the *Dictionary of Louisiana Biography* [DLB]; all found in the Williams Research Center of the Historic New Orleans Collection.

Several names on the Ship's Log may be identified in the City Directory as follows:

Broutin, N.	cordial distiller	233	Royal
Chapelle, C.	merchant	55	Ursuline
Gillet, Louis	brass founder and related enterprises	27	St. Philip
Tuyes, Pierre	merchant	56	Bienville

One may be a descendant of the following found in the DLB: Broutin, Ignace François. In New Orleans by 1720. First important architect/engineer in New Orleans. Died 1751.

The first name on the Log, identified as 65 years old, would be the following in the DLB:

LeBlanc de Villeneuve, [Joseph] Born 1760. Son of Paul-Louis LeBlanc de Villeneuve. Soldier, Indian agent, playwright. The earliest extant Louisiana play is his *La Fête de Petit Blé ou l'Héroïne de Poucha-Houma* (a five-act tragedy in alexandrines).

Appendix 3: Building Details

The care with which Xavier Murphy handled business transactions is clear from business documents preserved in USCA: IV E 2 Box 13, Packet II.

Contracts:
—Final notarized document stating that William Moore has received the final payments of the full $9,200 for erecting the first building, January 7, 1831, although final payments were guaranteed only as of October 1833.

—Notarized document with detailed plans for extension and payment schedule, totaling $13,500, with provision for interest to be paid if Xavier Murphy requires a delay for the final payment after the building is completed. Signed May 30, 1834.

—Second notarized document on the same date, with detailed plans for the kitchen building, to be completed in November 1834 for $1,428.

—Also for the pond, August 8, 1835, to be built near the cemetery.

—Agreement (no date) for 200,000 bricks, with payment of $200 for every month of delay; also agreed that the store of bricks will be fenced and covered with good cypress.

—List of bricks needed for convent chapel 744,513 @ $7 per 1,000 for a total of $5,211.50. Dated 7/7/18[36?]

In March 1837, Julie Bazire was named superior at Grand Coteau. Her letter to Bishop Blanc of July 24 continues the story of Xavier's building plans.

[at end of letter: Grand Coteau, July 24, 1837][372]

Monseigneur

I have often, for some time, told you of the pain and bitterness of my soul; it is right that today I tell you with the same straightforwardness and frankness the joy of my heart. Yes, Monseigneur, it is today that I bless God with all the strength and breadth of my soul, all that he has permitted; and all the while showing him my weakness, I pray that I may never be without the cross; the plots and the malice of men end by being sweet when one sees such a happy result. My joy has doubled in learning that you gave your approval to an establishment that ought to make ours flourish. The more I reflect on it, the more I admire lovable providence that conducts all with sweetness and strength.

We have offered to these gentlemen the bricks for the construction of their first building; in this I am only following the intention of our good Mother Xavier who, without counting too closely, had had made more than five hundred thousand bricks, not content to have had made the three hundred thousand required to build our chapel. It is that which put the house in debt, but the wrong is done and by the permission of God for a greater good. I know, bishop, that I am blamed and even by persons in whom I have confidence but I am not hurt by this as long as it is not from our reverend mother [general] to whom I have written and detailed the reasons which made me act. If I am given some years in this house, I hope to reestablish the financial base and

---

372 French autograph, Archives of the Archdiocese of New Orleans.

take care of the deficit of about $11,000. After that we will rejoice and then I will willingly give up my position.

The little solitude of Grand Coteau thus will have a future as a charming place and twice the home for the Lord by the abundance of spiritual help. But do not fear, bishop, that this house will in any way be withdrawn from your shepherd's staff. No, bishop, our rules will be observed and you will always be our superior in everything. Thus we beg you please to appoint our extraordinary confessor.

But not to fatigue you with too long a letter, I will put off settling our business until your visit, which we await. The little cottage is doubly at your disposition for you and those whom you wish to send there; we take great pleasure in receiving with our best efforts those whom you send here. The community are well and ask me to offer you their respects. Receive a new assurance of the sincere respect of one who is in C. J.

Monseigneur, your humble

Julie Bazire

P.S. I am confident that you will have in a short while the money we owe you for the travel of our religious. It should be remitted to Father Veragin [Verhaegen] in Saint Louis, who will send it to you by his correspondent.

Though never before in debt with her building expansions, at the end she did acquire a large debt for a great number of extra bricks. Those bricks, offered gratis, became the incentive for the Jesuits' decision to locate at Grand Coteau. The first bricks of the Jesuit building were laid on July 31, 1837.

Appendix 4

Notes on Reverend Mother Xavier Murphy, given by Miss Rebecca Terrel, alumna of Grand Coteau[373]

I hurry to respond to the request made to me by the Religious of Grand Coteau by sending some notes concerning our much loved superior and class mistress, Mother Xavier Murphy. Her conduct with regard to Protestants was the most attentive, the most suave, and the most considerate that one could desire. Her maxim was that of St. Francis de Sales: flies are not attracted by vinegar but by honey. An elderly Methodist woman so loved and venerated Mother Xavier that she was intrepid to pull her away from the errors of Romanism, as she called our holy religion. Mother Xavier received her each week over several months with the greatest kindness, listening and refuting her arguments.

The Protestant students attended morning and evening prayer and Holy Mass, as well as religious instruction where, without questioning them, they were required only to keep silence and good conduct in order not to disturb the others. Children from the north and the center of Louisiana were students at Grand Coteau, and a good number of those were Protestants; with few exceptions they all embraced the true faith. From the Rapides area of Louisiana we were 48, of whom only two or three were Catholics.

The little church of Alexandria, in Rapides parish, received its name from Mother Murphy who had it named after Saint Francis Xavier. It was built by her care and at the expense of alumnae of Grand Coteau; Mother Murphy provided all that was necessary, and these same objects are still kept as relics in the little wooden chapel. Our holy archbishop, Msgr. Blanc said, "My children of Grand Coteau give me great consolation."

---

[373] French copy; location of original uncertain. Rebecca Terrel was born in 1817 and entered the Academy 7/14/1829. Her sister Henrietta, born 1815, entered the same day. They were from Rapides Parish.

In my travels, whenever I enter with a family, I recognize them, because the influence of Mother Murphy shows itself in their dignified and reserved conduct, in the cleanliness and arrangement of the house, but especially in the way in which the children are maintained.

She received visits from lawyers and other high dignitaries, but the humble craftsman and the poor worker had easy access to her. With the first, she was the educated, intelligent, agreeable woman; with the second, she was more affable, more tender, leading them to speak about themselves, their business, their families; she made herself everything to everyone in order to gain all the world to God.[374]

She had a great knowledge of the human heart and her penetrating regard could read the most intimate area of your soul. I never knew her to be deceived. The sure way to merit her favor was to be truthful; unhappy the child who was lacking on this: a fault openly admitted was never punished. "I was born in Ireland with an American heart," she said, "and when I die you will find the word *America* engraved on my backbone."

Our mother easily consented to those Protestant students who asked to be baptized and confirmed. "We will make them Christians," she said, "so that later, when they are able, they will be nourished with the Bread of Life." Many have persevered in the true faith. I remembered this when one after the other brought all their family into the fold. Their Protestant husbands and children were baptized together, under the care of the wife and mother.

Until the death of Mother Murphy, her students felt her happy influence, whatever their position, even in families the most adamant against Catholicism. All venerated her name and regarded her as a protection for their home.

As to her last moments, we students knew very little. I remember only to have heard it said that she had asked what day it was

---

374 1 Cor 9:22.

and when she heard the answer she said, "I will leave this evening." And thus it happened (she died September 7, 1836[375,] five minutes before midnight, the beginning of the feast of the Nativity [of Our Lady], according to the notes of Reverend Mother Hardey, taken from the journal of the house of Grand Coteau).

Profound, calm and solemn was our sorrow when the death knell [tolling of the bell] told us that it was all over. Each one repeated, "Lord, have mercy on our Mother, take her to heaven with you."

We were so convinced that Mother Murphy was necessary in this area that Mrs. Littell, wife of her doctor, having a sick child, offered it in sacrifice to God to spare the life of our Mother. The whole parish prayed, with offerings and promises made to God; but the good fight had been fought,[376] the fruit was ripe, the harvest abundant, and our good Savior gave our Mother the reward promised to those who serve him.

I am now elderly, I have known the world well, but never have I known, nor do I hope to see another Mother Murphy. Such a combination of gifts, of talents, of virtues is found in very few whom God wishes to use to do great things for his glory. Her judgment was sound, just and straight: those in difficult positions came to consult her. She often was able by her wise counsels to restore union and peace in families by settling the difficulties that had divided them. The young found in her a support for their weakness; older people put all their confidence in her.

If I had to do her panegyric, I would give up on writing, because no pen would know how to do her justice.

---

375 Both the death notice and the letter of Hélène Dutour to Bishop Rosati, September 11, 1836, give the day of death as September 6.
376 2 Tim 4:7.

Appendix 5

Last Will and Testament of Anna Xavier Murphy, September 26, 1835[377]

I Anne Fransis Xavier Murphy. Religious of the Sacred Heart Being in perfect health but desiring to precaution against the surprise of death declare what follows to be my sole testament and last will.

1st I protest that I desire to live and die a docile and obedient child of the Roman Catholic and Apostolical Church and I declare to believe most particularly in the Communion of Saints. Consequently I recommend myself to the prayers of all the faithful particularly to those of my friends. But oh! My God here permit me to thank you for having bestowed on me unworthy the inestimable favor of my Vocation to a Religious life, for having broken all my ties to my family and my country and so mercifully conducted me <u>even</u> into the sanctuary of your Adorable Heart. Oh! Precious grace. Oh! Sublime Vocation_oh! Dear Venerated Society from which I have received so fostering a protection so many distinguished favors! Pardon sweet Jesus oh! Pardon all the errors I have committed through weakness or ignorance in the discharge of the various duties annexed to my charge and station. I particularly ask pardon of this community for all the disedification I have given - as also for my countless negligences in their regard and here express my gratitude for the charity with which they have supported my failings as well as for the attachment they have ever evinced in my regard_____

2nd I name and constitute as my universal and sole heiress Madame Catherine Thiéfry at present superior of the house of the Sacred Heart in the city of S.t Louis, State of Missouri. And in case said person dies before me and that I have no other will made – I name and constitute as my universal and sole heiress Madame

---

377 Autograph with seal; USCA IV.E.2 box 13.

Julia Bazire – at present superior of the house of the Sacred Heart of St. Michael parish of St. James in this state_____

3rd I name as testamentary executive of my last will Madame Carmelite Landry a religious of this house praying her to fulfill immediately my intentions – I revoke and annull all prior testaments_ Made, double, and signed at Grand Coteau Parish of S^t. Landry. State of Louisiana This day ~~of our Lord~~ the twenty-sixth of September A.D. one thousand eight _ eight[378] hundred and thirty-five _ all written by my hand and sealed by my seal

Anne Fransis Xavier Murphy
Religious of the Sacred Heart
(seal) and Superior of the house of
Grand Coteau

---

378 The number is mistakenly repeated at the turn of the page.

I Anne Francois Xavier Murphy. Religious of the Sacred-Heart. Being in perfect health but desiring to precaution against the surprise of death declare what follows to be my sole testament and last will

1º I protest that I desire to live and die a docile and obedient child of the Roman Catholic and Apostolic Church and I declare to believe most particularly in the Communion of Saints consequently I recommend myself to the prayers of all the faithful, particularly to those of my friends — But oh! my God here permit me to thank you for having bestowed on me one of the the inestimable favor of my vocation to a Religious life. for having broken all my ties to my family and my country and so mercifully conducted me even into the Sanctuary of your adorable Heart. Oh! precious grace — oh! sublime Vocation — oh! Dear Venerated Society — from which I have received so fostering a protection so many distinguished favors—! Pardon sweet Jesus oh! Pardon all the errors I have committed through weakness or ignorance in the discharge of the various duties annexed to my charge and station. I particularly ask pardon of this community for all the disedification I have given — as also for my countless negligences in their regard — and here express my gratitude for the charity with which they have supported my failings as well as for the attachment they have ever evinced in my regard.———

2º I name and constitute as my universal and sole heiress Madame Catherine Thiefry at present Superior of the house of the Sacred Heart in the city of St Louis, State of Missouri. and in case said person dies before me and that I have no other will made — I name and constitute as my universal and sole heiress Madame Julie Bazire at present superior of the house of the Sacred Heart of St Michael parish of St James in this state———

3º I name as testamentary executrix of my last will Madame Carmelite Landry a religious of this house praying her to fulfill immediately my intentions. I revoke and annulle all prior testaments. Made, double, and signed at Grand Coteau Parish of St Landry State of Louisiana this day of our Lord the twenty sixth of September. A.D. one thousand eight —

Xavier Murphy's last will and testament, September 26, 1835

eight hundred and thirty five - all written by my hand and sealed by my seal

Annee Francis Xavier Murphy
Religious of the Sacred Heart
and Superior of the house of
Grand Coteau

Reverse side of Xavier Murphy's last will and testament.

INDEX OF BIOGRAPHICAL NOTES

Aguillard, Adelaide Stanislas, RSCJ 136
Audé, Eugenie, RSCJ 17
Barat, Madeleine Sophie, RSCJ 8
Bazire, Julie, RSCJ 48
Bruhier, Neline, RSCJ 87
Cloney, Regina, RSCJ 272
Coté, Marcellite, RSCJ 247
Croix, Charles de la 249
De Neckere, Leo, C.M., Bishop 172
Detchemendy, Therese, RSCJ 47
Dorival, Louise, RSCJ 22
Dubourg, Louis William, Bishop 15
Duchesne, Rose Philippine, RSCJ 8
Dusaussoy, Louis 118
Dutour, Helene, RSCJ 47
Eaglin, David 242
Eaglin, Jenny 36
Gray, Eleanor(e) Josephine, RSCJ 145
Hamilton, Mathilde Xavier, RSCJ 27
Hardey, Mary Ann Aloysia, RSCJ 27
Hawkins, Frank 36
Jeanjean, Auguste 60
Jourdain, Philippine, RSCJ 260
Knight, Mary, RSCJ 60
Labruyère, Judith Ignace, RSCJ 27
Landry, Carmelite, RSCJ 17
Lavy-Brun, Felicity, RSCJ 51
Layton, Mary, RSCJ 17
MacCarthy, Nicholas, S.J. 10

Manteau, Marguerite, RSCJ 164
Marbeuf, Catherine de, RSCJ 29
Martial, Bertrand 84
Mathevon, Lucile, RSCJ 11
Melite and Martin 35
Meneyroux, Josephine 15
Nebbitt (Nesbit), Liza (Eliza) 27
Penel, Louise Marie, RSCJ 267
Rosati, John, C.M., bishop 32
Rossi, Flavius H. 19
Rosti, John, C.M. 151
Shannon, Mary 215
Short, Margaret Mary (Madeleine), RSCJ 215
St-Cyr, Emilie, RSCJ 136
Stegar, Anna, RSCJ 279
Summers, Mary Ann, RSCJ 28
Tison, Marguerite Aloysia, RSCJ 27
Van Damme, Xavier, RSCJ 134
Van de Velde, Jean Olivier, SJ 271
Varin, Joseph, SJ 10

www.ingramcontent.com/pod-product-compliance
Lightning Source LLC
Chambersburg PA
CBHW071804080526
44589CB00012B/686